D...

12

10

On Birth & Madness

ON BIRTH & MADNESS

Eric Rhode

Duckworth

First published in 1987 by
Gerald Duckworth & Co. Ltd.
The Old Piano Factory
43 Gloucester Crescent, London NW1

ISBN 0 7156 2170 X

British Library Cataloguing in Publication Data

Rhode, Eric
On birth and madness.
1. Pregnancy—Psychological aspects
2. Childbirth—Pathological aspects
3. Parenthood—Psychological aspects
I. Title
618.2′001′9 RG560

ISBN 0-7156-2170-X

Photoset in North Wales by
Derek Doyle & Associates, Mold, Clwyd
and printed in Great Britain by
Biddles Ltd, Guildford and King's Lynn

Contents

Introduction

STRAY SEEDS OF SUGGESTION

A woman attends a funeral. The coffin is lowered into the grave. A man approaches her and says, 'He was not your father.'

I heard of this incident some time ago at a case conference. The woman had suffered a breakdown in childbirth – it was not known what part the incident had played in her breakdown. It lodged itself in my mind and it entered into the genesis of this book. It was, as Henry James puts it, 'a stray seed of suggestion'.

I kept thinking of the funeral. It insisted (in thought at least) on taking place in mist or rain. The stranger seemed to condense out of vapour. There was a quality of hallucination about him, as though the woman had felt compelled to summon him up. Why should he have made that remark? And how, or why, did she take it seriously – if she did take it seriously?

She comes over as blank. We do not know whether she thought of him as a portent – or as a mischief-maker. We do not know whether her feelings about the dead man were intense enough to make the issue of his having been her father important. I conjecture that her blankness – her passivity in regard to the stranger's having approached her at such an intimate moment – is typical of a certain kind of relationship: the woman feels the other person (the stranger) to be controlled by a part of herself – a part that she thinks to have projected into the other person. The stranger is her mouthpiece.

One way of looking at the incident is to see the woman as using it to act out a tendency (which exists in most of us) to betray the ones we love. The ones we love expect us to pay the price of love, as when in their dying they oblige us to mourn them. She probably wishes to deny that the dead man is her father – to release herself from pain.

Goldilocks

Estrangements in definition lie at the heart of psychoanalysis.

Estrangements relate to questions of loyalty and treachery. Who is my father, my mother, my brother, my sister? In a sense, the answer is simple – in regard to our mother at least. There is documentation; and the documentation is unlikely to have been faked.

The answer is not so simple so far as the *meaning* of the relationships is concerned. A child can be brought up by a loving family. It has no reason for complaint. Yet it feels itself to be an orphan.

Its predicament is reflected in fairy tales. A prince wakes one morning and discovers that he has become the son of a swineherd. A shepherd's daughter awakes – and learns that she has become a princess. Many of us respond to the birth of a younger brother or sister by some such change in identity: we become dissociated.

Consider Goldilocks. She breaks into a house belonging to a family of bears; or so she wishes to think. She is so estranged from members of her family (because her mother has given birth to a little baby, the youngest bear) that she thinks they belong to a different species. She is a stranger in her own home. She thinks of her parents as aliens. Nothing fits. Much gets broken. She is unable to see the traces of the youngest bear as confirming the existence of a newborn brother.

Freud wrote of a type of reverie, the family romance, often unconscious, that comes to the fore when a child feels slighted or frustrated by its parents – in ways that the parents are sometimes unable to recognise or modify. Family romances arise when some Oedipal wish of the child fails to be gratified. Post-Freudians have thought that Oedipal distress derives some of its intensity from another, probably earlier situation, whose pain is more immediate: the fact that our mother can give birth to other babies. These babies are felt in some way to unseat us.

Whether our mother gives birth to another child is marginal to the pain of the situation. A child will feel the pain – even though it has no brothers or sisters. The pain is intrinsic to the primitive, possessive manifestations of love that most of us have to work through. A baby that can love without desiring to control the object of its love is an exceptional being.

Primitive love has to find some outlet: it has to dramatise itself. It is in the nature of jealousy that a jealous person without a rival will invent one. A jealous person has no need of siblings; and indeed may deny that siblings exist as other than pulses in the imagination.

A child can deny pangs of jealousy by thinking to appropriate its parents' creativity. It plays dream games – travesties of its parents' generative powers – in which it becomes the offspring of different parents. It can transform its mother and father, as figures in its mind, to a point where they become unfamiliar. Sometimes the child will allow its parents sexuality, but only of the meanest kind. It can think to escape from degradation by becoming a member (in thought at least) of elitist groups or noble families. Freud believed that the shift into idealised kinship derived from a one-time idealisation of the now degraded parents. You think yourself a member of some royal family – because you once revered your mother as a queen.

We look for excuses. We argue with ourselves: if only we had parents of the same calibre as our idealised parents, we would not be so contemptuous of our actual parents. We lie to ourselves. The desire to be treacherous has no *necessary* relationship to the quality of those we wish to betray. It is unlikely that anyone has been outwardly compelled to become a traitor – we do not become traitors because we are under pressure. (Think of those who, under pressure, do not become traitors.) In moments of treachery, we deceive ourselves, and others, when we say that we intend to betray someone or something because the someone or something is inadequate. A good person will be loyal to the nurturing figures in its mind, whatever their quality in fact. A wicked person will always find an excuse to act disloyally – and will relish trading in people as though they were used cars. Both types of personality, the loyal and the treacherous, exist side by side in most of us. Our capacity for treachery is as bound to our jealousy as Iago is bound to Othello.

Oedipus

The woman at the funeral finds her reflection in a Greek play, often read as psychoanalytic holy writ, Sophocles' *Oedipus the King*.

The infant Oedipus, abandoned by his actual parents, is adopted by Polybus and Merope. He grows up. He loves the couple; he thinks of them as good; consciously at least, he believes them to be his natural parents. One day, during adolescence, he attends a banquet. A man, drunk, claiming to be a friend, comes up to him and precipitantly asserts, 'Polybus is *not* your father.'

Oedipus responds as blankly to this man as did the woman to the stranger at the funeral. He does not ask for evidence. In panic – and in flight from the uses of intelligence – he turns to the oracle: and the oracle compounds the worst elements of the stranger at the funeral or the drunken acquaintance at the banquet.

We cannot be sure whether the oracle is portent or mischief-maker: whatever the case, the oracle does not allow us space to think dispassionately about its pronouncements. It predicts that Oedipus will kill his father and marry his mother. Oedipus quits the court – to shake off these constraints and to spare his beloved parents. He enters upon a long journey.

In my view, he travels through landscapes of the inner world and comes face-to-face with fantasticated phantoms who represent the parents of his wishes – although the story in fact would have us believe that Laius and Jocasta are his natural parents. Laius and Jocasta are bound up with his anguished experiences in childbirth. They *are* the anguished experiences. Birth and madness, the annihilation of self we most fear, are here at one.

Far from entering into a family romance, Oedipus discovers himself caught up in a family catastrophe. He might be a somnambulist. He is robbed of his capacity for deliberation. That he fails to see the old man that he meets at the crossroad (and murders) as his father is not improbable: that he fails to sense that the bereft queen (whom he marries) might be his mother strains credulity. All marriages are made in heaven, and many lovers have a sense of having met before. Seldom so extremely, and so denied, as here. The play is sublime because in its improbability it is (as we shall see later) so true.

The murder of a father seems to bring about a collapse in the capacity for judgment. It brings about a rushing together of mother and son in a spaceless conjunction (as of atoms filling a void), a rushing together which destroys structure and individual identity. And yet this is not entirely the case. The collapse in judgment had occurred some time before the meeting at the crossroads. It had occurred at the moment when Oedipus swallowed without question the claim made by his drunken acquaintance. 'Polybus is *not* your father...'

Hamlet

Another work of fiction, often associated with *Oedipus the King* in the psychoanalytic literature, throws a different light on the relationship of the stranger and the woman at the funeral. The prince in *Hamlet* is full of doubts about the value of the information he receives from the Ghost. He is like the woman at the funeral – but with one difference. The dead man in the coffin, the woman's possible father, in his case also becomes the stranger. Dead father and stranger are fused, in the shape of the Ghost who comes from a far country, possibly to tell lies to the prince.

Hamlet believes that 'the devil hath power t'assume a pleasing shape.'[1] He cannot be sure whether all things that have a pleasing shape indicate the devil – or whether all things that attract him must necessarily destroy him. His way of teasing out the truthfulness of the Ghost is, from any forensic viewpoint, eccentric. He is left with no method but the 'method' of madness.

The Ghost, like the stranger at the woman's funeral, disturbingly comes too close to unconscious wishes. Because of this, he is able to muddy our ability to learn. We find ourselves unable to exercise our native scepticism: we lose the power to ask the right questions.

Indicators

I think of the experience of two patients. A woman recalls how, during the Second World War, the government changed the direction of signposts in country lanes – with a view to foxing possible invaders. Changing directions did not allow for the probability that the enemy, if it had invaded, would have been equipped with maps.

[1] *Hamlet* 2.2.603-4

The woman did not know her enemies from her friends. She presumed that anyone who submitted her to pain, of any sort, must be an enemy – and anyone who eased her pain must be a friend. Masturbatory alliances were for her prototypic of goodness. She did not realise the difference between an object that nourishes and an object that depletes. Emotionally, she knew nothing about maps. She knew about lying, or changing the direction of signposts: she had that sort of topographical idea. Changing signpost directions was associated to a childhood memory of once having eaten rotten cabbages from a dustbin – just to see what it was like.

The second patient began a Friday session resonantly. 'When I am absent, bad things occur.' He sounded like the kind of small child who insists that it must be at the centre of the universe. His absence brings about the bad things. We want to demur: his absence might not be all that bad.

Linking absence with bad things sounds sincere. Its underlying meaning was made plain in the patient's next remark. He referred to a young girl who was being tortured by a cure known as 'sleep deprivation'. An unkind picture of parental intimacy? Not quite. He did not really believe in the existence of parents, let alone of their having an intimacy. He used the concept of father freely: but emotionally he had as little understanding of fathers as the previous patient had had of maps. He was unable to allow a father to exist as a presence in his mind. In fact, he was worried by someone other than a father. A hostility of a seemingly Oedipal kind covered over a crisis of a different order. He was gradually, and fearfully, becoming aware of another couple: not father and mother, but unborn sibling and pregnant mother. And the sibling was about to be born.

He now sadly said, 'My indicators are not working.' Car indicators, he meant. The nature of the setting allowed us to consider the indicators from another point of view – and roughly in the same way as I had formerly seen the signposts in English country lanes: as demarcating factors in judgment. If his indicators were working properly, he could use his attention constructively. He was able to discriminate good from bad, true parents from false authorities – he was able to deal with the stranger at the funeral. Without indicators, he was in danger, largely from an unconscious belief in his own infallibility. He would find himself driving his mental car with a delusional confidence in its safety, unaware of the fact that its indicators were not working.

Hans

Freud wrote of a boy, aged three-and-a-half, named Hans, who was dashed by the news that his mother had given birth (at home) to a younger sister. Hans began to construct a mythology out of overheard sounds and half-seen events. His reasoning, and his attempts to check out the evidence, were magical and mostly wrong. He became depressed. He felt himself to have been abandoned. He became, in a sense, ill.

But he experienced illness in a way that led to his development. He recovered – and his curiosity was heightened. He entered into a series of imaginative games that were like arabesques on the great mysteries of procreation and birth. He had felt betrayed by his mother. But by not betraying her in turn, and by suffering loneliness, he came to a desire for certainty in knowledge. (The meaning of such a desire is perplexing: especially when it is taken to Cartesian lengths and thought of as a desire for indubitability.) For Hans, the need for certainty contained another theme. He hungered for truth. He had loved his mother and had not betrayed his love for her when she had put him under stress. He had not turned away from her. He had seen her as embodying the truth in some way. In his games and questionings he had shown himself more and more fascinated by her interiority, and by some notion of unknowability as related to her interior. He had become aware of limitations in knowing. Aristotle proposes that the meaning of the question, 'How are babies made?' might be central to any understanding of how the universe is formed, or indeed of how anything is put together. In his own way, Hans rediscovers Aristotle's theory.

Father into foetus

If we think once more of the woman at the funeral, we may find that our image of the coffin descending into the earth has begun to transform into some picture of the woman, as a child, brooding over Mother Earth and the pregnant life within. The dead father in the coffin transfigures into a foetus *in utero*, about to be born.

I raise this archaic possibility for one reason. A child may find the experience of its father's death to be excruciatingly painful. But mourning a death need not necessarily undermine self-idealisation. Hamlet has worthy feelings about his dead father – until he is told that the ghost of his dead father haunts the battlements. His feelings then change. The thought of his father's death has taken a nasty turn. The death now sounds suspiciously like a birth. Being told that your mother has been invaded by a little stranger stirs an ignominious sense of distress. We have been given no chance to mourn decently; jealousy intrudes; and jealousy seems to foul everything.

A woman who doubts whether a buried man is her father is, by the same token, liable to doubt whether the newborn baby in her mother's arms – and, in time, the newborn baby in her own arms, when she too becomes a mother – is in any way related to her. In puerperal breakdown, mothers often find themselves in a state of dissociation from their babies. They are estranged from something extremely precious. (By its nature, what we value exacts a price in love. Sometimes the price is thought to be too heavy and what we value is abandoned.)

Our understanding of the stranger at the funeral – his quality of otherness, his seeming to appear out of nowhere – may derive from some displacement in thought concerning an incipient baby inside a potential mother. We tend to condemn the unborn foetus as an unloved alien because, under the harsh contracts of birth and death – at least as the older child understands them – someone must suffer the experience of being excluded. We realise with sinking heart that once the foetus has become the object of our mother's love, we shall become the alien and estranged member of the family.

Conception by ear

Taking a cue from Freud, Ernest Jones wrote an essay on the relationship between the Oedipus and Hamlet stories. In another paper, Jones considered the unconscious meaning of the scene in *Hamlet* in which one brother murders another by administering poison through an ear. It is no coincidence, surely, that someone who reasonably should have been so interested in poisoning by ear should have attempted elsewhere to investigate the meaning of the often unconscious belief that sexual conception can take place through the ear. I want to look at the kinship of these auricular themes, but somewhat to move away from Jones's treatment of them.[2]

Jones's argument depends on certain passages in the Bible. The opening chapter of the Gospel according to St Luke contains two events that parallel each other in structure. The archangel Gabriel informs an elderly couple – the wife is barren – that they will parent a child. The archangel's words, being *logoi spermatikoi,* promptly impregnate the wife. The husband is struck dumb. (It is as though his powers of speech had impregnated her – and in entering her, had been lost to him.) The husband is able to speak once more when he agrees that his son should be named John. It would have been culturally more appropriate if the son had been given his father's name.

In the sixth month of pregnancy the archangel once more appears – and this time to a Virgin who, in spite of her virginity, has been married for some time. The archangel announces that the Virgin is about to bear the Son of God – 'and of his kingdom there shall be no end.' The Virgin fairly asks how this conception can be brought about, since she has never known a man. The archangel reassures her: she will be impregnated, not by man, but by the Holy Ghost. 'For with God nothing shall be impossible.' Jones invites us to look at certain Renaissance paintings of the Annunciation, in which the archangel's inseminatory speech is represented by a line drawn from his mouth to one of the Virgin's ears.

[2] Jones proposes that theories about breath and voice as inseminatory powers are idealisations of our usually unconscious and comfortable belief that flatus is procreative. He misses the important cultural point that our capacity for abstraction appears to be bound up with our experience of breathing. From a physicalist's point of view, we pump into ourselves great gouts of nothingness. Our senses do not tell us why air should nourish. The breast that feeds us comes and goes. Breathing is an abstraction from the feeding process, and felt to be more fundamental, if only because we can last longer without food than without air. The sense we have of pumping lungs inside us, accommodating themselves to the breath-food, offers us a prototype for the introjected breast, the mother who lives within us as a presence in our inner world – and who does not come and go.

Theories about the soul as anima (or breath), theories about inspiration (with its roots lexical and otherwise in breathing), mark an increasing assurance in abstraction in human thought.

Birth and mystery

The biological discoveries of the last two hundred years seem to diminish the mystery formerly ascribed to pregnancy. Primitive theories about sexual generation – of which conception by ear is only one among many – are pre-scientific fancies that fail to do justice to the facts.

Biological facts are important and often awesome in their own right: but in terms of the life of the mind, of our feelings and our capacity to symbolise, they occupy only one layer of possible meaning. In feeling, in dreams, in unconscious reference, the uterus remains the paramount source of mystery. The epigraph to John Locke's *Essay concerning Human Understanding*, a quotation from Ecclesiastes, asserts that our ignorance concerning the history of the foetus provides a model for the limitations of knowledge – and for the means by which we come to knowledge. The child in many of us continues to assent to this view. It is a tributary to religious insight. Trust in knowledge through the senses as a condition for all knowledge collapses in the face of our mother's conceptions. In the face of birth, we all – if lucky – enter into states of doubt.

Primitive sexual theories can be deliberate misconceptions, slanders (in the first instance) on our parents' private lives. Just as often, though, as Hans seems to have understood, they are ways of testing out thoughts that embody truths about our feelings. Obviously babies are not conceived by ear. But words can blight or inseminate us. The transactions between thought and body, between psyche and soma, which puzzled and impressed Descartes (and have continued to puzzle and impress many people since), are central to any consideration of birth as a physical act – or as mental transformation.

'And the word was made flesh and dwelt among us...' To be present at a birth – any birth – is to witness more than a physical happening. The originality of the event – disrupting, incurring the wildest envy – is of a spiritual order. It signals the emergence of a personality, seemingly out of nowhere. At the same time, it is among the most physical of events possible. The body opens in a state of muscular and biochemical transport.

Henry James, dining out, listening in, thought of anecdotal inspiration as the 'stray seed of suggestion'. The Word made flesh takes the power of inspiration to its highest degree. Speech can give life – or it can kill. The woman at the funeral was probably undermined by the stray seeds of the stranger. The Ghost in *Hamlet* makes the prince pregnant with bad dreams.

Mothers in breakdown

For a period of over two years, I visited a Unit for mothers in breakdown at the time of childbirth. Mothers and babies lived together under close supervision. On one of my visits, the locum consultant told me the story of a mother he had met during service in Pakistan. The mother, clearly, had thought herself inseminated by ear.

Locum Consultant: I remember a woman in Pakistan, who had given birth to a great number of children, about nine I think. One day a fakir, or holy Muslim beggar, paid her a visit. (Fakirs are quite common in Pakistan. They go round begging alms and often pronounce some kind of prayer.)

The fakir asked her for alms. He then fixed her with a beady eye and said, 'You are going to get pregnant again. And you are going to have a lot of trouble in your pregnancy. If you don't believe me, I'll come back in nine months, and we'll see.' Well, she became pregnant once more. In the middle months of the pregnancy she became depressed. (She had tended towards depression in her previous pregnancies.) She became quite ill. She began to think that the thing in her abdomen was not exactly a baby. Finally, she was delivered of a healthy and robust baby boy. She told me vividly how robust the baby was, and how it would lie with its arms folded and look at her. (I don't think babies in fact fold their arms but that is how she described it.) She was terrified. She could not breast-feed her baby. Nor go near him. After a couple of months, she killed him. The husband was a butcher. There were lots of knives around. She killed him with a knife. And that was that.

Belatedly, the husband then decided that she needed some help. They lived in Peshawar city – they were moderately well off by local standards, lower-middle class. He took her to a famous shrine about twenty miles outside the city, towards the isle of Carca. They treated all kinds of diseases there – they specialised in cases of mental or spiritual possession. While she was at the shrine, she had a vision, in which she was told to go to the mission hospital in Peshawar – which is where our psychiatric department was. She later claimed that she had never heard of the hospital before. When she got home, she asked a neighbour, 'Where is this hospital?' The neighbour answered, 'I've just been there.' He brought her to us.

At this stage she was, I would say, psychotically depressed, severely depressed, quite agitated and filled with delusional thoughts about the baby. She felt – and I could never get this quite clear – that she had some sort of creature inside her. The fakir had put it inside her. I couldn't get further. My impression was that she thought the creature inside her was some spiritual being who was going to destroy her – and she had no choice but to kill it.

She continued to be our patient. We did not need to admit her. Often members of the team went and visited her at home. She was a chronic patient. Until the time I left, she continued to visit us regularily. We gave her anti-depressants. We worked with her and, to some extent, with her husband.

She soon lost any psychotic features. She was full of remorse. She was in part agitated, in part depressed. She tended to be histrionic. She always brought us gifts of eggs. In Pakistan, we often used to be paid in goods rather than in money. I do not think there was anything symbolic in her bringing us eggs.

She was harassed by her great number of children. In fact, they were nice children and lively. The older ones said that she was always getting into fits and rages. They accepted her for what she was. The new child was a burden to them. But, there again, women in Pakistan accept large families as part of their lot – it's a common cause of depression. The husband was exasperated and baffled by her. Fortunately, there were no legal complications. He quietly buried the baby and did not report the death to the police. In England, of course, we would have been obliged to report the death, but we didn't feel we had to there.

She was filled with remorse, but not overwhelmed by it. Pakistanis tend to think that things happen according to God's will. Perhaps this fatalism relieves guilt. In comparison, I think of an Irish woman who has killed two children and whom I am seeing now – not at the Unit, but at a local hospital. Her guilt and inclination to suicide is far more intense. She killed her children in a fit of profound depression. She felt her life was hopeless. She thought she was going to die and wanted to put them out of misery as well.

The husband, usually supportive, was at work that day. I had not seen her for months. She had been admitted to hospital about nine months previously, as mildly depressed. She had done well and stayed only a couple of weeks. She returned home – and gradually went downhill. Her husband said he did not know how she got into these states. Nobody had taken much notice of her.

What was so striking about the Pakistani mother was her belief that the child inside her was inhuman. There is a kind of magical feeling about this. I once worked with a very psychotic woman who was convinced that she had some strange kind of creature in her abdomen. She was not pregnant. But she had given birth to children before. She had the idea that the creature in her abdomen was causing her pain.

In Hinduism and (for all I know) in Islamic thought, fertility is related to religion: think of the fertility gods and goddesses. Certainly in Pakistan infertility can be treated by the local Mullahs and Hakims – although I do not know how they treat it. I remember once hearing, as a child in India, about a woman who got pregnant after she had washed a holy man's clothes. I remember my Dad told me that story. It is funny, I must have been about ten when I heard that story – and I have just remembered it now. The woman believed she got pregnant after washing a holy man's clothes...

I have one tentative thought about work in this Unit, derived in part from my work in Pakistan. I think it is a pity that there are so few men here. I have been wondering if it would not help if fathers were not more present in mother and baby units.

The wandering uterus

For over two thousand years doctors and learned men have accounted for insanities, anorexias and hysterias in women by the theory that an object inside the woman, the uterus, could become unanchored under certain circumstances and drift about the body interior. The uterus was thought to exercise an occult influence over any organ it came close to in its wanderings. By sympathetic pressure, it could make the organ diseased.

The idea of the occult, of something inside one body influencing in untraceable ways something at some distance and outside it, is closely related to speculations about the creative nature, and emanatory power, of women's insides. (Perplexities about the psychosomatic often originate in such matters.) The wandering uterus was thought to drive women out of their bodies and minds; it induced breakdowns in childbirth; it was satanic and duplicitous, the work of the arch-deceiver himself. The woman from Peshawar thought the fakir had placed a malign thing inside her. At one time or another, she might have imagined she bore a world redeemer, a demon, or a malicious and unbounded bodily organ. All these are prospects, or potentialities, that any decent mother might wish to deny.

If a womb is to wander, it must have some free space in which to do so. Anatomical investigations (as in autopsies) reveal that this space does not exist. Asserting the existence of spaces where spaces do not exist – confusing notions of inner space with actual space – is to make a deeply problematic claim. Learned men have maintained this doctrine over millennia. Why they should have done so is baffling. Was the doctrine related to medieval disputations concerning the nature of space? Was it motivated by the belief that all events must have a cause?

One day, two of my children enlightened me as to the meaning of the theory. We were talking about childbirth and about the nature of labour pains. One of my daughters, aged four-and-a-half, proudly announced that she had given her mother a lot of pain. Her mother answered that birth pains were caused not by the baby but by the contractions of the uterus. The girl asked what the uterus was, and I said that it was the baby house. My eldest son, almost eight years old, now took my breath away by asking, 'You mean, the uterus flies around?' Having recovered my breath, I said, 'Why should the uterus, by flying around, make the insides hurt?' He answered, 'Because it knocks into things.'

My son supposed (as many children do) that all pain is a form of hurt – and hurt must be inflicted by some kind of hurting agency. If a mother feels pain inside her, then some moving object – baby or uterus (or some unconscious representation of penis or breast, as incorporated from her own mother) – must be hitting her. In order to hit her, the object must have the power to be able to move. (By this account, those who feel a pang of love will presume that Cupid has fired a dart into them.)

Times of trouble

Birth and death are always times of trouble. I remember W.R. Bion making this rather grim assertion. His tone was apprehensive, and yet he was being ironic about those who expect an easy life. If you want things to be disciplined, avoid birth and death. Well-run institutions, especially, should shun them. In birth, in death, we come to unwelcome views. Pregnant women are found to contain unpredictable forces of good or ill, that radiate immense power. The forces are like the wandering uterus. They act on us as though we were organs about to be smitten by disease. They bring about drastic changes; in the short term, usually for the worse.

The belief that hormonal or chemical imbalances account for breakdown in childbirth – a theory that may have truth in it – does not cover the fact that the breakdown tends to be communal. Not only the mother emanates madness. At times of birth a whole family can go berserk. Similarily, when someone dies, relatives often seem to lose their screws. They steal trinkets, litigate over a will, turn to adultery. During pregnancy fathers and children (as well as mothers) buy impossible pets or grow giant marrows. Dylan Thomas, as father-to-be, took to drink. No longer the baby in the family, he put himself at the centre of the stage with a vengeance. Another poet, Coleridge, experienced the birth of his first son as though it were a visitation of the muse – not as catastrophe but as inspiration.

The American psychiatrist Gregory Zilboorg wrote a fascinating monograph on the relationship of witchcraft and the emergence of modern psychiatry. At other times, he wrote two papers on a cognate theme: breakdown in childbirth. The first paper was devoted to mothers, the second to fathers. Puerperal breakdown is not limited to women – or to men either. Zilboorg might have written about it as occurring in siblings, or even in the newborn itself. Some of the fathers lend themselves to spectacular episodes, as in the case of some of those who had attempted suicide and exhibited 'the throes of inverted violent impulses and of a painful concentration on their lower bowels.'[3]

Behaviour of this kind has long been half-acknowledged. Anthropological literature is packed with references to the

[3] Zilboorg (1931), p.941

strange customs fathers fall into at the time of childbirth: not all of them are scene-stealing. J.G. Frazer insists (in *The Golden Bough*) that phantom labour in men, the *couvade*, a painful concentration on the lower bowels, is not competitive. It is a way of warding off evil spirits during the time of the mother's labour. The spirits are supposed to attack the father instead – which supposes the spirits to be less wily than, in fact, they are.

Superstitions and miracles

Every family has its cherished superstitions concerning pregnancy and childbirth. Grannies and nannies are not the only repositories of whispered forebodings, although many of them are so accomplished at it that they deserve no rival. Advanced people want to see this rubbish labelled as rubbish; but the eruption of infantile fancies, not all of them malicious, cannot be easily disposed of. Breakdown in childbirth enacts what many pregnant women at most dare to think: the casting off of habitual expectations; the sense (often exhilarating) of journeying into the unknown; of new intimacies; or the shock of realising that pregnancy can arouse outspoken envy, often in attractive people.

Eating habits change. It has long been a male sneer that pregnant women give themselves over to 'pica', a magpie taste for exotic foods – which may include faeces or the chunk of a husband's shoulder. Dreams take on unusual dimensions. Mental space requires a different monitoring, as the contours and gravity of the body become unfamiliar. A woman late in pregnancy said that she felt like a conker coming apart at the seams. Psychiatrists talk about a mental unhinging round about the seventh month: is this true? We need more evidence, especially from the pregnant delegates themselves: diaries, narratives of the nine-months' journey, topographies of the spirit.

I became interested in these themes at the time of my wife's first pregnancy. Entering the pregnancy culture of mums and mums' advisors, we discovered that the culture was divided. On the one side stood those who practised the hygienic approach, seemingly sensible people, who played down anxieties and even denied their existence – as we learnt too well when we attended a course at the National Childbirth Trust. On the other side stood not so much people as the traces of people, influences, debris, the sort of thing that is seldom mentioned in the books on childbirth – the eccentric assertions, pseudo-medical pronouncements, old wives' tales and psychotic actions that make up much of the history of the subject. Some people on the sensible side of the pregnancy divide believed that birth belongs to the mother alone, as though it were an isolated or insulated business. And yet a mother in labour is almost always surrounded by people, sometimes hordes of people, in a place known as a theatre, in a rite-like atmosphere, medieval in spirit, celebrating ultimate things, death-in-birth, birth-in-death.

A mother in labour becomes an emblem for a whole condition. All birth experiences are unusual, irrational and communal, however normative the biological process might be. All mothers share one thing: not the same conveyor-belt process; rather, the chance to break away from the predictable. The term 'miraculous', nowadays seldom relevant, might have been coined for this situation.

Needing more information, I took myself off to the Unit, to meet mothers in breakdown. I assumed – and I know now rightly – that when things go wrong you can learn a good deal about what happens when things go right. Birth is a certain kind of crisis: in what way, I hope this book will reveal.

I wanted the mothers to tell me their own story, on tape, and to share with others their unusual histories. A wary venture. The Unit was often a tense place. But the mothers welcomed the chance to talk to someone. Many thought their suffering had been increased by their being left on their own. Or worse, left on their own with an incomprehensible and demanding infant. Some felt lonely because no one appeared to understand their condition. It was not clear whether or not this was always an accurate perception.

It seemed likely that in states of breakdown you project the figure of an uncomprehending or unsympathising personality into others. (Someone like Oedipus' Sphinx.) In such cases, death appears in the guise of an indifferent mother, a psychotic mother, indistinguishable from a faceless and cruel death. Nearly all of the thirty or so recordings that I made include the description of some meeting – with doctor, psychiatrist or friend – that is characterised by a state of incomprehension.

During the time of making the tapes, I began to look into the history of the subject, and with a consequence almost fatal to the project. I became immersed in histories of embryology, studies in birth superstition, early texts in midwifery. A network of seemingly lost ideas began to emerge and for a while I could not disengage from it. Before the eighteenth century, accounts of puerperal breakdown are scant and usually delegated to law books or writings on witchcraft. The early nineteenth-century psychiatrist Etienne-Dominique Esquirol gave me clues as to how to explore the subject. He indicates the importance to it of ancient Greek medical practice: a useful starting point. His case histories demonstrate how the mother in crisis often undergoes something like a disjunction in consciousness. It is with this idea – of disjunction – that I begin.

Chapter 1

OF SUCCESSIVE AND MUTATIVE EXPERIENCE

Among the many ways of looking at experience two of them – the successive and the mutative – are unusually interesting when compared. I owe my description of the successive to Aristotle. From it we can infer an influential if misleading picture of early development.

Succession

I imagine myself as blind, alone in this room, running my fingers along the top of a chair, along a desk, to a bookshelf. One thing follows another. I experience a succession, and the idea of succession, once experienced, takes on an unwarranted authority: if it happens so to me, it must be so out there. But succession, or proximity, is a magical relationship: meaningful in mind in ways that otherwise cannot be endorsed. The true forms in nature and art, often unconscious and usually difficult to elicit, owe little to succession. One room follows another; the succession has authority in memory – it tells us nothing about the possible architectural relationship of the rooms.

The snail-like way in which the blind man glues sensations together through touch has its reflection in the infant, newly born, whose lips and tongue latch onto its mother's nipple. The infant takes comfort from closeness. Physical and emotional intensity become inseparable. The successionist believes that the further away the infant feels its mother to be, the less warm are its feelings about her. Distance becomes a symbol for modifications in feeling. The feelings are then imposed on map places and map distances. The idea of space, suffused with feeling, remains undistinguished from the perception of actual places – nature as described by the Aristotelian physicist, undiscriminated from the emotional stagings of mind. The planets exhibit temperamental inclinations. Zones are warm or cold places where you want to go to or avoid. Geographers discover Sloughs of Despond. Locations come to allegorise feelings.

The infant acquires a certain knowledge. It registers differences between kinds of touch, taste, sights and smells, and arguably raises mythologies out of them. Reveries about the coherence of a mother, as a body and as a personality, may at some early stage in development find their outlet in cosmic mythologies, concerning contrasts in texture and temperature. 'How is the world put together?' asked the pre-Socratic philosophers. 'How is my mother put together?' asks the infant – and the infant who persists in the adult. How does the experience of the successive relate to the coming together of a maternal coherence?

The successive impels us. Misleading ourselves, we think to tap our way to conclusions. Resting flesh and bone against flesh and bone, the infant acknowledges hardness and softness. Proximities in sensation echo proximities in measure: the pulse of blood and the rhythm of breathing (both in ourselves in others), heart beats, tempos in sucking and digesting – one thing leads to another. With a slight leap in inference, the infant senses a life within the body as well as without. Familiar rustles and rumbles and odours from within add to feelings of security; much as we feel secure, at night and in bed, when we listen to the rattle of heating pipes in an old house.

Succession theories tend to be causal, in the sense of being sympathetically causal: they hint at the influence of some occult power, of some invisible binding energy, the unseen womb itself. Under the influence of the wandering unseen womb, a woman drifts away from male jurisdiction. She is no longer open to reason. Male doctors will summon up a concept of madness to 'explain' her behaviour.

Children at play in the sand pit invest the uses of sand with feeling. Hardness and softness, contrasts in touch, increase in meaning when connected with some source in emotionality. The infant has reveries about its mother. She is the moon that moves the tides, occult, exercising powers as invisible as the fragrance of her body. Parts of her body are hard or soft to touch;

sensations about her personality, also, can be hard and soft.

The infant thinks: my place is next to her. Relationships are proximities. Enquiring, the infant works through presences (or absences) of familiar surfaces. Changes – when acknowledged – are thought to take place within some continuous context; and continuity seems to require the need for fixed points. Aristotle, in his *Physics*, defines place as the innermost boundary of that which contains. Things fit together hand-in-glove. The sailor has his place within the boat. The boat has its place on the river; the river has its place on the earth; the earth has its place – where? – in the totality. Children write notable envelopes, on which they inscribe their addresses in ever-widening cosmic circles; starting from home, they soon reach the perimeter of the universe, and then boldly voyage on. At some point – or so the logic of continuity has it – the journey outward reaches nothingness (which we cannot imagine) or some immovable object, the *primum mobile*, the wall at the end of the universe, which spears cannot pierce.

At this point, the belief in the importance of proximity is checked. We think to make a leap. We find ourselves obliged to recognise the realm of mutative experience.

The universe moves, takes on patterns of change, like the patterns in the steps of a dance. Something – the First or Last Cause – exerts an attraction, and its power cannot be accounted for in terms of the successive. Music and love reflect the power of its attraction; the universe dances out of love for it. The movement of the planets celebrates a music so sublime that earthly music can only hope to echo it. Post-Pythagorean composers do not create music out of a void. They listen to the implicit music of the universe, whether in the sounds of nature or in silence.

The successionist conceives of the universe as a plenum. Nothing can be added to it, nothing can be subtracted. He seeks to deny the existence of gaps. Or, finding a gap, he sidesteps it by inventing a missing link. Gaps, like the idea of the vacuum, are profanities. Only witches and madwomen and mothers believe in them: gaps are the kind of place where someone new, unpredictable and horrible might emerge – such as a baby brother or sister. For the successionist, there is no void, no space unanimated by human qualities, no sheer nothingness. Gaps are places through which the enemy enters. Continuities, great chains of being, are means to keep out the unwanted. Officially, continuities join things together; they are constructive and therefore worthy; unofficially, they are esteemed because they exclude. They are like a passion for smooth uninterrupted skin: warts, moles, pustules, blackheads, unholy bumps, are dreadful indications that a rival is on its way.

The successionist believes in knowing your place. He expects teachers to emphasise the importance of proximity in differentiation. One number usually follows another. One idea leads to another, in a shoulder-rubbing egregious way. By stages so gradual that no human eye can see them, the seed grows into a plant. Comfortably cradled in the finite world, the essences of movement and change sway into meaning.

The successive is a source for poetry. A blind man nourishes himself by running a palm across the rough surface of a pine table. Step by step, we come to conceptions of loss as well as of accretion, of distance as well as of closeness. An Aristotelian end has the power to generate its beginning. The successionist comes to believe in the idea of imaginative conjecture – and comes to imagine the existence of that which is not. Accomplishments like this can begin in some awareness of proximity.

Mutation

But what of the mutative? I turn to Kafka's story, 'The Great Wall of China.'

A great wall has been built to protect our kingdom. It keeps out the enemy. On closer inspection we see that this is not exactly so. The wall has been built piecemeal, in sections. The sections are later to be joined. As we contemplate the wall, we notice that the gaps between the sections are greater than we had supposed. A weariness descends on us: and the gaps seem to increase. The built bits are less than we had thought.

Our security, ill-founded, had been gained from a belief that succession informs us about the structure of experience. One thing leads to another – deceptively, like the steps in an argument. Succession seems to guarantee the meaning of sensation. But the sole guarantor of succession turns out to be consciousness: and consciousness of itself cannot indicate truth.

We do not use our senses at night in the same way as we do by day. Our daytime ability to register the sensible passing of a passing world vanishes at night, as we lie in the dark. Senses dissipate and then re-focus – on images of bodies, on other images of uncertain status: hallucinations or visions, we do not know. Where do these night thoughts come from and what authority do they have? We no longer trust in succession.

In dreams, especially, night thoughts take on a syntax quite unlike the daytime one. Space and time are no longer necessary postulates of experience. Disjunctions and immense powers predominate: the imagination itself.

Faced by a language, any language – the syntax, let's say, of Kafka's wall – we can yield to the pleasures of translation, or immerse ourselves in an originality of structure. The continuities of daytime give us an alphabet. Some would argue that it is our one sure guide to sanity. Night gives us jumble and discard. Or a different language. One of the difficulties in unravelling night thoughts is that they come to us clothed in the idiom of the day. Dreams would be easier to understand if they were less photographic.

Mutation: naturalism and conventionalism

Often when reading Kafka, our first and wrong perception is that the author has given himself over to dramatising a psychopathology. Think of the drawn-out delight with which he disloses the inadequacy of the wall.

Through a microscope lens, the world appears to expand. Through an over-precise and obsessional use of eyes, it seems to fall apart. Knowing the right focus for lens, or knowing how we should look, obviously depends on how well we get a grip on our envy. Malignity masquerades as a disinterested scepticism. The gaps between the bits of wall increase: from our not having looked carefully enough at the wall before, or equally from some destructive element in ourselves, that can break apart even the stony crescents of China. In a dream, a face disintegrates: who is it brings about the disintegration? There is a kind of looking that by its looking makes the looked-at fall apart.

An imaginative interpretation of a psychopathological catastrophe, as Kafka shows, can lead directly into the clear air of visionary truth. A parable within the story changes our understanding of how we should look at the wall. By a twist in perspective, neurotic destructiveness becomes religious insight.

An emperor is dying. His last words are intended as a message for you, the lowliest of his subjects. The message is important – and the messenger will probably never reach you. The faster he runs, the greater seems the distance between him and you. As he runs, the courtyards of the palace multiply in number and in size dilate. It is unlikely that he will ever reach the palace precincts, let alone cross the mighty space of the empire. And yet it may happen one evening that the message will somehow reach you through the warm summer air, as you sit quietly on the verandah.

Two ways of reading the parable imply different orders of knowledge. One order is founded on biological naturalism. The other is a type of conventionalism – it presumes that conventions can depend on concepts that have no basis in naturalism. The first order of knowledge, naturalism, accounts for the nightmarish aspects of the parable – but it cannot illuminate its undoubted beauty. The parable conveys a metaphysical aspiration, and we need the second order of knowledge to explicate it.

A naturalistic reading begins in gut hunger. The infant, waiting for the nourishment of the message, projects its anxieties into the figure of the messenger. The messenger becomes imbued with the qualities of an infant self dying of thirst, crawling towards an oasis that forever turns out to be a mirage. Hunger mobilises some perennial sadistic presence in the self, a torturer who protracts, and plays on, the agony of waiting. And then the infant's mother arrives, at the moment when the infant has lost all hope.

The naturalistic reading of the parable, like all naturalism, depends on fixed points – biological needs and their symbolisation. It would see any claim to beauty in the parable as an idealisating of perverse impulses, that have been set in motion by a failure to tolerate the pangs of hunger. On the other hand, a conventionalist reading would claim that aesthetic understanding entails giving up any possession of the object. We abandon fixed points and enter into a condition in which the self and its object concomitantly disintegrate: the process known as mourning. Sight is lost and, hopefully, insight is gained. The senses die – and give birth to mind. We come face-to-face with ideas whose genesis owes nothing to the senses.

Socrates, in the parable of the Cave in Plato's *Republic*, thinks of the process as a conversion, a turning around of the self, a looking in some direction formerly unseen. The pilgrim must leave the deceptions of the shadow-play in the Cave, climb a steep slope and look into the glare of the Mediterranean Sun – a light that devours sight as sense so that insight can be born. The pilgrim was deceived by the shadow-play because he was unable to see that it existed within a convention. His neck clamped, impeded by posture and body, he was obliged to accept it as the total reality, a fixed point which he could not abandon without feeling totally abandoned. The fixed point blots out vision. In the same way, we cannot give up biological urges or hungers, or beliefs in the predicability of nature; and these act on us negatively, like fixed points.

If we turn in another direction, and concede the primacy of feeling, anything might happen. 'She suddenly realised that the number of people in the street seemed overwhelming, the houses strange and the sunshine artificial and unreal. She had to retreat into a quiet restaurant. But there she felt as if the ceiling were coming down, and the people in the place became vague and blurred.'[1]

Melanie Klein describes a woman in mourning. The maternal substrate to an experience, contemplated in unconscious reverie, disintegrates into swelling or shrinking bits. Persecution is endured. The believer in the truths of succession or proximity can make nothing of the vertiginous scene. Yet the world continues to make sense. If we turn in another direction, we discover ideas or intelligibilities, as we allow Plato's Sun to affect our eyes. Tears change perception – the world swells up as though magnified by them. Perhaps the concept of tears precedes physiological experience? Under the pressure of feeling, we begin to acquire Blakeian insight: eternity (and infinity) can be glimpsed in a grain of sand.

We are now in a position to look at the story of the dying emperor from a mutative viewpoint. The blind man sits on the verandah in the evening. He has no reason to expect anything. The message arrives without warning; its contents are not clear. The meaning of its being sent is obscurely related to the death of the person who sent it. At the moment when it reaches us (the moment when the infant, as it were, gives its first suck), the

[1] Klein (1940), *Collected Writings* 1, p.361

message seems to open up, in an expansive rush. It swells infinitely, and an empire spreads without bounds. It contains the heroic figure of the messenger, stubbornly jogging towards us and never seeming to cover any ground. It is like some ecstatic coupling which dissolves distinctions, a Liebestod, or form of death-in-love.

Infinity

In *The Individual and the Cosmos in Renaissance Thought*, Ernst Cassirer indicates that the evolution of the concept of infinity was primarily intended to satisfy a psychological need. Its use in mathematics and cosmology was almost an after-thought. Its use in science has no direct source in science as empirical enquiry. Cassirer refers to Giordano Bruno. Sanity requires some vision of boundless interiority. Our bodies crave for food: our psyches crave for an infinity of boundless worlds. Conceptions of the individual depend on conceptions of the cosmos – and the minds of certain Renaissance individuals sought for infinity.

> The idea of a plurality of worlds, even of an infinity of worlds, was not unknown to medieval speculation. It examined the theoretical possibility of this idea from all sides, but generally decided against it... (For Bruno) the concept of person requires a new concept of the world. In the entire representation of his cosmological views, one senses this subjective pathos. He always put a real emphasis not so much on the universe as on the Ego that must produce the vision of the universe within itself. The new view of the universe represents itself in the form of a new, urgent and swelling impulse. Man finds his true Ego by drawing the infinite universe into himself and, conversely, by extending himself into it.[2]

Concepts of place, of fixed points, of the habitual, disappear. We are cast into doubt. The moment when we receive this message on the verandah is the moment by the graveside. A stranger approaches the mourner and informs her that the dead man is not her father.

[2] Cassirer (1963), p.189

Natura naturans

A newborn sees its mother leave its room for the first time. It has no reason to believe she will return. Out of sight is not so much out of mind as out of existence. A mother goes into the darkness beyond the door and, entering the darkness, is annihilated. If an older child believes that its mother will come back, it derives its trust from custom and regularity. She has returned before. She will probably return again.

This is a successionist argument, impressively dramatic and misleading. A mother who moves out of the orbit of our perception does not necessarily leave the orbit of our minds. Mind is more than the sum of its perceptions. The fact that we have perceptions – an overwhelming fact – may give us a wrong impression about the nature of mind. I wish to propose that mind is only incidentally a system for registering perceptions. The capacity to experience the mutative – sudden losses, sudden discoveries – depends on mind having an immense range of imagined settings or scenes in which questions of justice and responsibility can be examined and lived through. In terms of the imagined setting, for instance, we might ask ourselves who is responsible for the annihilation of the disappearing mother? One answer might be – the person who sponsored the idea of annihilation: that is, ourselves.

Reluctantly I have come to the view that our heritage at infancy is some articulated yet unconscious Platonic idea, a necessary, mysterious substrate to our capacity for having experiences. The setting can be called an inner world, or it can be thought of more powerfully as *natura naturans*, a self-generating agency of an unimaginable creative intensity – so intense that we feel impelled to destroy it. On Kafka's verandah, we wait for metaphors – the impression on us of themes, images, scenes from daily life – to make manifest the unconscious presence within. In this sense, we are all novelists waiting for inspiration: cues in daily life to mobilise some fully-structured anticipation in the self that probably has always been there. I cannot demonstrate the truth of this belief. But my work as a therapist continuously pushes me towards it; and I am under the pressure of experience to try and understand it. But what of those who lose touch with it and believe that when their mother walks out of the room, she is annihilated?

Nothingness

A woman tells me that watching plays in a theatre leaves her in a state of disquiet. She has no idea where actors go to when they walk through doors and off the set. She prefers the movies. In the theatre, you have an intensely-realised area of light and exits that lead into nothingness. In the cinema, your attention is secured by images flowing across the unchanging dimension of a luminous flat screen.

Her mother dies. She becomes conscious, through a dream, of how she much she misses her mother. She dreams that she sees her baby daughter in a swimming pool. Her daughter tips forward in the water, in the manner of a duck bobbing its tail in the air as it searches underwater for food. Her daughter tips forward – and disappears beneath the surface. The dreamer dives into the water and descends to the bottom of the pool. She cannot find her baby. She sees no sign of it as ever having existed. She is filled with anguished perplexity: where has the baby gone to?

She has left her native element of air, of breath – the habitual source of life. She swims through a boundless oceanic element. She has lost the incalculably precious object that give her a fixed point of reference: call it a baby or a mother or a breast or her own heart.

In a stroke of imagination, she compares the baby to a feeding duck. An infant at the breast feeds on more than food. It has access to its mother's feelings and sources of creativity; it is allowed to look into the lake and to see that it contains more than the dark nothingness feared to exist beyond the door on stage. (The opening of the door is like opening the surface of the water.)

Anyone who has contemplated a mother and her baby at the breast will be aware of how the couple has withdrawn into itself; it has its privacy; at most, we are aware of a bobbing tail. People so bound up with each other will tend to experience separation as an annihilation of the self as well as a loss of the other. The baby had thought its heart, as well as the nipple, belonged to it. Its mother takes both away.

Where do these personalities go that leave us? The patient gave me an association for 'swimming to the bottom' and the vanishing of the baby. She thought of a conjuror who waves a handkerchief and a wand and brings a rabbit out of a hat. In effect, she converts an unexpected disappearance into an unexpected appearance. The baby is lost; a rabbit peeps out – at the expense of a serious loss in feeling.

The conjuror is like an elder sibling who teases his juniors by claiming to demonstrate how babies are brought into being. You wave your wand, and the baby is born. Men must endure their going hence and their coming hither; not so for the conjuror. The mysterious heart of things is reduced to legerdemain, metaphysical perplexity to an arid puzzle. The conjuror assumes the same role as did the stranger by the graveside. Mourning is a process that ebbs and flows. The patient continues to converse with figures in her mind. She tries to work out with them her loss. Not all the figures are as misleading as the conjuror. She tells me a few days later about the waiter in an Italian restaurant who delights customers by putting a match to the paper that wraps *Amoretti* biscuits. The ash from the paper has the unusual property of floating up to the ceiling.

The dreamer's mother – her *amoretta* – had been cremated; she had gone up in ash. Where does the loved one go to after death? We might ask the same question, even when we have a corpse before our eyes – baffled as we are by the limitations of our knowledge. (In a similar frame of mind we enquire, where did the loved one come from, before the moment of its birth?)

Ash rising to the ceiling – like the effect of a swimmer plummeting through water, troubles our sense of expectation. This is not life lived on solid ground by sensible people. Touching on the miraculous, it recalls age-old ruminations concerning the labyrinthine history of the soul – before it entered into an alliance with body.

All this induces despair. We need the steady diet of our senses. The patient kept coming back to the theme of loss. She talked about an old lady who had lost her memory. The old lady did not know where to put her rubbish. She had lost the concept of dustbin or lavatory. She would wrap up her faeces in little packets of newspaper and leave them by the draining board.

Thought originates in an interchange in our minds, between ourselves and the one who nurtures us. One of a mother's functions is to act as a receptacle for our memories. (And our mental rubbish. Provocatively, we might include memory among our mental rubbish.) In losing the one who nurtures us, we lose our memory. The function of memory is bound up with the exercise of judgment: a mother's capacity to discriminate good from bad on behalf of her baby – and to provide a drainage for the waste products of its mind (anxieties, gibberish, failures in conceptualisation, soiled and soiling interjections, murderous lunges in thought and action).

The patient felt I dumped the rubbish back into her when I went away on holiday. She had read somewhere about a doctor who, before going on holiday, had dumped all the drugs in his medicine cabinet into a basket and told his patients to take what they wanted. His reluctance to sort out the appropriate medicine for each patient resulted in his converting all medicines into poison.

The meaning of the food you eat depends on the way it is given to you. The woman at the funeral could not tell whether the stranger had told her the truth because at that moment he spoke to her she was out of touch with the capacity for discrimination; a sustaining presence had broken down, and she was faced by a gap. She allowed the stranger's thought to fill the gap.

The zone of creative unpredictability

My patient disliked the theatre because she feared the exits on stage opened up into nothingness. She denied a creative interiority to her mother; she just blanked it out. Within, or beyond, was darkness and oblivion. Animistic philosophy is full of conjectures about spears going through walls into a nothingness. We conjecture: the infant imagines the breast-dome to contain a uterine zone within of unbounded creativity, a cauldron of holy loves, in which a mother is involved with a father and unborn babies. To some extent, a mother's relationship with the presences within her mirrors her relationship to the child without – to some extent only. The uterine zone exists according to laws that are quite unlike the natural laws experienced by the child on the outside of the breast. From a sensible point of view, the interior will appear to be a vortex generating madness rather than what it is – *natura naturans*, Platonic idea, the source of awesome mystery, a mint for non-sensuous concepts.

We derive certain notions from it which we can understand but not imagine – Being, Becoming (i.e. the mutative), the infinite, the beautiful, the true. Envying mystery, we reduce it to mystification. Envying powers of transformation, we reduce them to sleights of hand. A trace of the original goodness may persist – as, I would suggest, in the following quotation from Henry More's *Antidote against Atheism*.

> As for example: bricks being carried about a room without a visible hand; multitudes of stones flung down at a certain time of the day from the roof of a house, to the amazement of the whole country; pots carried off from the fire and set on again, nobody meddling with them; the violent flapping of a chest-cloth, no hand touching it; the carrying up of linens, that have been a-bleaching, so high into the air, that table-cloths and sheets looked but like napkins, and this when there was no wind, but all calm and clear; glass-windows broken to shivers; boxes carefully locked unlocking themselves and flinging the flax out of them; women's pattens rising up from the floor and whirling against people; the breaking of a comb into two pieces; the rising up of a knife from the same place, being carried with its haft forward...[3]

One response to the quotation: it seeks to mystify: it is an anti-scientific attempt to pre-empt the universe of its natural mystery. A second response (sensitive to a poetic excitement in the writing) suggests that these images carry another meaning. They represent an infant's attempts to understand its mother's feelings about someone she loves. The infant allows its mother the liberating realisation that, in love, nothing is as its mother had believed it to be; stereotypes dissolve; the perceivable world re-forms, even violently, before her eyes.

If this were a dream, I might imagine some Puckish element in the dreamer were seeking to undermine the natural order of waking life – a Puck mobilised by the threat of scientific discovery (think of the terror incurred by the thought that a vacuum might be realisable). Henry More was as intrigued by the nature of the supernatural as he was by the the scope of scientific experiment. He was an intimate friend of Robert Boyle – and took care to observe that the author of *The Sceptical Chemist*, a great scientist, was a believer in reports about witches.

But the dream has another meaning – one owing little to Puck. It depends more on the emotionality of the details being taken as a whole than on the details themselves. Imagine them to be the

[3] More, bk. 3, ch. 3, section 7

thoughts of a Titania lying in the embrace of Oberon, a Titania given over deliberately to the disjunctions of the lyrical. Our forefathers had an idiom in which they could talk about epiphanies. In what sense are such discontinuities, such hints of the infinite, a kind of knowledge?

The natural world throngs with intimation. Bodily presences indicate a spirituality often categorised as past or future. Many sites in our cities codify memories of lost civilisations – less lost if only we could decipher them. Highland ruins are ghostly with the absent presence of exiled crofters. The dead are always with us – and so, if we are mindful of them, are the future living. Natural objects hint at passageways that take us through birth and death to some underworld, or overworld, that stands against sensuous experience. A stone or a tree intimate, to the literal-minded, a non-material kingdom.

The substantial world aches with meanings that reach us from some largely inaccessible realm within. We live in a land where all the languages are foreign. At the same time, we tend to presume that the text before us, the natural world, in spite of its fragmentary nature, is a touchstone for reality because our senses confirm its existence. For all that, we can never be sure that the text before us is not some gap also, existing within some context which our imagination cannot reach.

Creative rivalry

A gifted, omniscient man has the following dream.

He is cleaning his behind in a lavatory. To his back is a small window. The window looks out onto a narrow street. On the other side of the street is a window with a balcony. On the balcony is a young girl. An older woman stands behind her – perhaps a nurse. To his shame, the dreamer believes that the girl and the older woman have seen his naked behind. He relates the girl to a photograph of his mother – taken when she was aged about eight.

The dreamer inclines to be dogmatic. He tends to favour behaviouristic explanations of his actions. His opinions tend to be brittle. They break apart when looked at carefully and often reveal the dreamer to be imaginative and capable of warm feeling. The conflict of trite diagnostician and artist was apparent in his telling of the dream. He wished me to identify with his position in it and to share his shame and his excitement.

At the same time, through the atmosphere of his telling the dream, he allowed me to enjoy perspectives on it that were not consciously available to him.

His way of describing the young girl and the woman on the balcony had a strong feeling of Spain about it, his native country. They might have been an Infanta and a nurse in a Goya painting. He did not make this allusion: I did. Nor did he make the inference – I did – that the girl on the balcony was not really looking at his behind, as he had hoped and feared. I imagined his mother, whom he had kept pre-pubertal in the dream, as looking out over a white-walled, domed and roofed Mediterranean village, and beyond it to the hills, the sea and the unending sky. I sensed that this panorama contained hopes about the future. It anticipated the mother's love for a man she had not yet met: the dreamer's father.

In fact both the parents had met many years before, fallen in love, brought up a family and eventually died. They had long been dead. Facts of this kind did not impinge on the mother's way of looking out from the balcony. If the dream has a sense of time, it keeps it within the lavatory and the dreamer's need to wipe his behind. The look in the mother's eyes is timeless. She yearns for a love that will be fulfilled. She has a vision of beauty and the infinite. Her son is no more than an agitated point at one corner of her vista, a wasp-like behind busily being wiped.

I reported some of these conjectures to the dreamer. He roundly told me I had no right to make them. I was interpreting the dream according to my associations – and not according to his. I had to agree with him; I was breaching technique. Orthodox psychoanalysis would have me interpret the content of his statements precisely and without embellishment. On these literalist terms I might have been struck by how wiping the bottom appeared to bring the figures on the balcony into existence, like genii emerging from a rubbed bottle. A belief in masturbatory creationism was a belief (the dreamer knew) endorsed by other dreams.

An infant having defaecated and discovered its mother to be cleaning its bottom, may come to the cause-and-effect assumption that defaecating has the power to bring a beautiful woman close to its anus. One day the thought may occur to it that the look of happiness in its mother's eyes need not inevitably be associated with the honour it confers on her. At issue is the meaning of the look in its mother's eyes. The dreamer has no proprietory claims over the look in her eyes, nor over the meaning of the dream. We had thought the nipple in our mouths belonged to us. By a process of steadily-increasing (and dismaying) awareness we begin to learn that neither the nipple, nor our perceptions, nor our dreams, nor our associations to the dream, are under copyright.

I told the dreamer that I could not, nor wished to, impose my views on his dream. But I could feel free to conjecture about its heart of mystery, the meaning of the look in the girl's eyes, however much he might be intent to confine the dream. What was the young girl looking at? We cannot know for sure. At the same time, we might ask why should she be constrained censoriously to look at her son's bottom – or to imagine that this was all the future would hold out for her? The time-scheme of the dream, in which the mother is a child compared to the son, indicates the importance of futurity to its possible meanings.

The power to transform meanings

Dreams often contain an element which, if controlled or possessed by the dreamer, has a disastrous consequence on any impulse towards development. I had a wish to free the presence of the dreamer's mother from the tyranny that he would impose on her by forcing her to face his unappealing presentation. The dreamer would have nothing of this. He wanted a finite universe made up of fixed points – with himself at the centre. He wanted an Aristotelian universe based on the concept of place. His behind was a good example of such a place.

The glance in a young girl's eyes has many possible meanings. If his bottom-rubbing can be related to the successional account of experience – everything radiates out from his touch – then the look in his mother's eyes has its reflection, in its power to transform meanings, to the swelling ground traversed by Kafka's messenger, the water in the pool plummeted through by the swimmer, or Bruno's vision of the infinite.

The dreamer wanted to be at the centre. His behind was his primary organ of consciousness – a radio telescope that monitored a finite cosmos. Wiping bottoms was a creative act powerful enough to wipe out the procreativity of parents. His dogmatic adherence to materialist philosophy and behaviourist psychology was of a piece with this.

He was aware that his philosophy hampered the development of his considerable talents. He needed to move from self-centredness to a position in which he could allow his internal parents the freedom to generate potentiality. He scanned the intellectual horizon for an appropriate model. What does a father see when he looks at the beauty of his wife? He dreamt of himself, aged six, floating as Superman over a fine landscape. It did not seem quite right. He dreamt about boys, his brothers, climbing trees competitively, to get a better view of the ocean. It did not seem appropriate as a model for development either.

One day he reported a tension in his stomach. He put it down to a failure in digestion. An American authority had described the symptom thoroughly. The matter was cut and dried. We begin to look closely at the meaning of the tension. It was clear that it was bound up with some belief in being pregnant.

His mind moved on, and he began to talk about pre-menstrual tension in such a way as to indicate that he was talking about the tension a girl might feel before her first menses. The girl intimates a knowledge which depends – for its knowing – on a physiological change taking place. I had thought he had kept his mother (in the balcony dream) as an eight-year old in order to deny her adult sexuality. In part this may have been the case. It was also the case that she represented some part of himself that existed in a hopeful state of expectation – a self on the verge of a mutative change in understanding.

Asymmetry

A seed grows into a plant. We classify its growth in stages. One day we see the plant in an unexpected way: we are amazed by its beauty. Time might have stopped. We forget about classification. Our perception seems unique: we do not know whether it tells us anything about the object perceived or about ourselves. The history of the object throws no light on our present amazement.

Aristotle thought Aeschylus had been inspired when he decided that drama might consist of three (and not just two) characters. Who can watch the birth of a child and not agree?

The balcony dreamer failed to anticipate the emergence of a third centre of consciousness. Two buildings face each other. On the *outside* of one, on the balcony, the woman and her companion. On the *inside* of the other, the dreamer. Symmetry continues to be practised – in the dreamer's insistence that his mother's eyes must be fixed on his bottom, while his bottom (in happy exchange) monitors her eyes. Asymmetry breaks in – if we can free the girl's eyes from his tyranny. Asymmetry allows his mind to yield up information he had no conscious knowledge of.

Before the balcony dream, in the state of reverie preceding sleep, he had found himself (in his mind) roaming about his childhood home. He had not been back to his childhood home in many years. In his roaming, he discovered many details about the interior of rooms that he had thought forgotten. He was not sure he had ever seen these details.

The house existed as an independent entity in his mind. It yielded information, potentially of an unlimited kind, that he did not know that he (or it) had ever had. During childhood, he told me, he had felt free to dominate the women in the household. He would run his hands over their dresses, buttocks and breasts. The nature of his reverie implies that his wish to dominate the women in the household was not wholly realised. A residual mystery remains; an element he cannot dominate. He does not know why the house should go on giving up more and more information.

The look in the eyes of the mother in the balcony dream has a potentiality of meaning. We have some access to these meanings. We cannot possess them. They are sources of insight implanted in us by the mother who feeds us. In losing them, and in entering into a state of weaning, we become like Oedipus, blinded and led by his daughter. The dying emperor's message carries overtones concerning the infinite. It also brings our death one evening, as we sit on the verandah.

The blind man makes his way about his room. His lost eyes are like dark pools, in which a baby has vanished. A paroxysm in consciousness occurs – not easily separated from thoughts of dying.

We can roam through our thoughts and discover ideas in them that we did not know existed. Logically, there is no reason why we should not reverse the process and allow our thoughts to roam through us and in us discover the alien and the unexpected. We believe we have a mastery over our mirrors, our dreams and our works of art – in the sense that we believe we can impose our perspective over them. But what if they should insist on their asymmetry and look back at us from a different point of view?

Freud relates (in an essay on the uncanny) how once, in a railway sleeper compartment, he observed a door swing open and found himself facing a disagreeable old man. He was upset to realise that he was looking into a mirror. He had thought to pass judgment on a stranger – only to find the judgment redirected at himself. The great psychoanalyst meets his match in a shaving mirror.

We think to contemplate a work of art – as something intended to reflect our needs. But consider for a moment the needs with which a work of art contemplates us. We have no reason to believe that we can anticipate the needs of a work of art – in the same way, the balcony dreamer could not anticipate his mother's needs. A work of art might exist in dimensions quite different from ours. Indeed we may wish to believe that its superiority to us is genuine: something for us to look up to.

Stature in art often seems to derive from a critical, aloof quality in the work itself. The work declines to notice us – although we pause, deferentially, within its sight. We presume that since we are an audience that deigns to watch the actors, the actors (in gratitude) should devote some of their attention to us. But why? From our cramped position in the auditorium, we can see little of the stage. We know next to nothing about the motivation of the characters or the nature of the action. Important events take place on areas of the stage which we, as the spectator, cannot perceive.

A patient once began a session with the remark, 'If I do not speak, there is nothing in the room.'

God might have made something like this statement before he pronounced the *fiat lux*. The patient was not identified with a benign deity. She did not intend to switch on any light. She wanted to make silences unpregnant and pauses unmeaningful.

A room in which patient and therapist work is sluiced with an infinity of meanings. Meanings stream into the room, or they drain into a void. You and I being there, as physical presences, as minds (or absences where mind might be), channel this potentiality. Whatever we say or do, the potentiality continues to gleam undisturbed.

Chapter 2

THE CHILD WHO DIES WHEN WE ARE BORN

Tiresias:	This day must bring your birth: and bring you death.
Oedipus:	Man, must you still wrap up your words in riddles?
Tiresias:	Were you not famed for your skill in solving riddles?
Oedipus:	You taunt me with the gift that is my greatness?
Tiresias:	Your great misfortune and your ruin.[1]

A child has learned to walk. It explores. Its curiosity has acquired feet. Its mother becomes anxious about its new powers. She puts locks on cupboard doors and on the door of her bedroom. She warns the child not to put its fingers into the fire. Some things are prohibited because they are desirable; other things are desirable because they are prohibited. The child senses danger in thoughts of intruding into its parents' bedroom. A muscular and (often) sexualised pleasure in walking adds to its conviction. It may have trouble in sorting out the dangers of intrusive thoughts from fears of being hurt.

In *Oedipus the King*, people are over-apprehensive about powers of walking. When Oedipus' parents set out to murder him (by stranding him on a mountainside), they rivet his ankles together out of fear of his ambulatory powers. He is only three days old, and months away from even crawling. As a grown man, he is called Swollen-Foot (like Swollen-headed?). He is thought to be cursed because he moves from place to place. Corinthians wish him to stay in Thebes, Thebans wish him to stay in in Corinth. Motility is looked on with suspicion – for all the to-ing and fro-ing of messengers. 'Knowing your place' in this setting implies that you are seldom allowed any other place to know.

Good experiences can end on a poignant note. Perhaps we are

[1] *Oedipus*, p.38.

wrong to associate such endings to Oedipus' act of self-blinding: poignancy is not like burning your fingers. The equation of weaning and blinding only makes sense (unusually) if we envisage weaning as a mutilation, as when we think the object feeding us to be a bodily extension of ourselves.

Such a misconception hints at an important truth when its literalism is read as a metaphor. Spinoza reminds us that the core of goodness in the self is independent of self: it is an otherness. It is both the most private element in our being and (from another point of view) a reality in which the idea of self has little or no meaning. Such exchanges in perspective become hesitant in the face of a literalism which asks, plaintively: How can something that belongs to me belong to someone else?

The shock of putting your fingers in the fire will put you off fires for life. Learning of this kind supposes no convention. It is like looking into Plato's Sun. You have no need to dramatise a conversion which burns out retinas. Isaac Rosenberg thought that the only way he could survive as a poet in the First World War was by not leaving a corner of his consciousness covered up. He wrote to a friend that he would saturate himself in the extraordinary new conditions of life in the trenches. A counsel of madness sounds like the voice of sanity itself.

Among the ideas that Plato's pilgrim discovers when he looks into the sun is one that Plato does not mention: not sadism, but the kind of pain Rosenberg writes about. Such openness to pain precedes our birth or the coming into being of humanity. Its discovery as an undertow in the self is one of the sources of poetry.

The riddle

Oedipus must solve a riddle in order to defeat the Sphinx. Sophocles does not give us the content of the riddle. It is often assumed to take the form: 'What has four feet in the morning, two feet at noon and three feet in the evening?' Oedipus answers it correctly by saying, 'Man.' He means that man begins as a crawling baby, walks on both feet in youth and needs a stick in old age. More than one commentator has observed that Oedipus might have answered the riddle correctly by giving his own name, since his fate at the end of the play is to hobble to Colonus while leaning on a stick.

I would propose a different solution to the riddle. The four feet in the morning is a hieroglyph of a mother helping her infant to make its first steps; the two feet at noon of the infant exploring its new kingdom without parental restraint (and perhaps dangerously); the three feet in the evening of a child who has incorporated a teacher's ferule, or a capacity to understand indications (of a probably disagreeable kind). 'Don't play with your mother's brooches – or else!'

The question of being able to read signs or indications is a key to an understanding of the play. Oedipus is astute enough to solve the riddle. But it disables him in some way. Faced by his mother, he registers a blank. He cannot see that she is his mother. He misunderstands the meaning of his desires. A sign lights in him (falsely) saying 'wife', instead of 'mother', or 'the woman who tried to have me murdered'.

Oedipus might argue that a belief in the need for accurate signs minimises liberty of choice – but the existence of the sign is intrinsic to the desire's fulfilment. The meaning of a desire is part of the desire and not a part of the desired object. The way in which it is a part of the desire is puzzling. Is it like some genetic indicator in a chromosome?

To say that Oedipus is Oedipal and carries some nucleus of desires natural to family relationships begs the question. Given the fact that we all, more or less, lose consciousness of our earliest years, few of us find ourselves in the blank condition in which Oedipus later faces his father and mother.[2]

Charcot reports the case of a man who visited his native city, Paris, and did not recognise the streets and houses where he had

[2] The power of the prohibition depends on our acceding that, at some level, Oedipus knows that she is his mother. Otherwise he would not be horrified at learning what he has done. To be told that you have married someone who is your mother in name only would not have this effect. Revulsion entails the realisation of having violated some previously-established intimacy. In the case of Sophocles' telling of the tale, this is hard to argue, unless we presume some relationship in feeling, a history in intimacy – which can be betrayed, between mother and foetus.

Emotional allegiances are forged in the depths: the play's claim on our feelings depends on this postulate. To be told that in the same breath that you have betrayed your country and that your country is, say, Ruritania (a fact which you had not known) might well leave you unimpressed. Likewise if someone informs you that your wife is your mother. However, if someone informs you that your mother is not your natural mother and that legally you are now able to marry her, you might still have scruples about doing so.

once lived. He failed to see how these objects might be imbued with intimacy. He lacked the indicator which allows us to say, in states of reverie, 'This is your mother', or just as importantly, 'This is not your mother.' The same man looked into a mirror and did not recognise himself.

In *Beyond the Pleasure Principle*, Freud writes of a small boy who looked into a mirror to reassure himself that his mother still existed. The boy assumed that if his reflection could be made to come and go, then his mother, who had gone away, would be able to return. The quality of my reflection in a mirror is bound up with the kind of internal mother I have. Knowing who my mother is (and who she is not) is a condition for understanding appearances. She is a part of my history – a part of the structure out of which my history emerges.

Death in the womb

Imagine Oedipus as a child in a Greek village, whose parents farm him out at an early age to grandparents – who live at the other end of the village street. One day the boy wanders back to his birthplace. He cannot understand the landscape. He cannot read the signs; and he cannot read the signs because he has (in a sense) been murdered.

By a narrow chance, he was not killed. I imagine that he felt he had been killed – and had come alive once more. Does this sense of rebirth feed into any inclination he might have had for self-aggrandisement? Does it heighten a terror? We do not know. The experience is embedded in him and transforms him. Inevitably now, he must inflict disaster on his neighbours – or so he will be told by those about him.

Jocasta understands the meaning of these events fairly well when she informs the spectator that the past, as described by the messengers, could never have happened. In order for it to have happened, she states, her child would needed to have continued to live. And she knows for sure that her child died long ago. (She does not admit to having hired its killers.)

Oedipus will become an object of dread: the living and unkillable presence of a murdered infant. The outcome of his actions is the plague: and the plague is described as 'death in the womb'.[3] Oedipus turns into the plague; the plague condenses

[3] *Oedipus*, p.26.

into Oedipus. You cannot in this play say: better an intolerable yet eradicable past than an intolerable present. If you murder the intolerable past, it tends to re-appear as an all-powerful apparition known as the intolerable present. 'Death in the womb' echoes as an idea throughout the play, taking many forms.

Jocasta rationalises her desire to slaughter her newborn on the grounds that it has a potentiality, or original sin, that would, if released, destroy its father, the king, and the whole community. The truth is that for all our love of babies, most of us hate the ousting life that in time will take away the world from us. We wish to destroy, in the first instance, an idea: of something alien to ourselves, and perhaps opposed to our being, that is thought to dwell within our mother. The idea in itself is neutral. It becomes monstrous in our minds, plague-like, virulent, because we push the monstrous elements in our own character into it. The entity within becomes the mirror image we would disown – if you like, what Freud saw in the mirror in the railway sleeper compartment. The generalising magnificence of the play is that it encourages us to be in sympathy with the elder sibling, who would murder the foetus, and also with the foetus as well: the part of the foetus that wishes to come alive and not to be 'death in the womb'.

In attacking the foetus within, Oedipus frequently finds himself in the state of being the foetus afflicted. As an adolescent, he reached a position of some eminence at the court of Merope and Polybus. (Eminence is always an ominous condition in the plays of Sophocles.) He became the desired one, the baby-about-to-be, an object ripe to be aborted. The drunken, so-called friend at the banquet informs him that Polybus is *not* his father – and Oedipus is at once deflated. His inability to question his friend, or to surmise that his friend might be a liar is probably bound up with his being so blank in response when faced by his mother.

At this moment of fascinating doubt – a moment at which some conception of science might have sprung into being – Oedipus turns for knowledge to the oracle. Needless to say, the oracle gives him a bogus prediction; and, as so often with bogus predictions, it turns out to be of a maliciously disagreeable kind. In a sense, the oracle speaks the truth when it tells Oedipus that he will kill his father and marry his mother. We are all potentially capable of entertaining extreme and powerful feelings about those closest to us: and the truism hits at the heart of us all, for all its generality. It is like the prediction of an envious fortune-teller, who looks us in the eye and warns us that one day we will die.

The drunken so-called friend attacks Oedipus in the nicest and softest part of his personality. Oedipus is probably inclined to believe that he is not Polybus' son because he feels unworthy of so good a man. It is probably out of a wish to spare his good parents that he flees from Corinth to Thebes (and inadvertently enters into more regressed states of mind).

A place where three roads cross

An element of calm enters into the play as Oedipus travels from Corinth to Thebes. He is no longer the one under attack. He is about to be transformed. He is probably about to become an attacker. We become aware of a space in the play in which there is a freedom to choose, a world of possibilities rather than a world determined by predictions. A powerful image describes the new-found sense of dimension. Sophocles reports that Oedipus comes to a place where three roads cross. And this image of a place where three roads cross seems to detach itself from the narrative and to enter our minds at a different, more permanent level than the rest of the play. The mood is lyrical and radiant; it will not last. A querulous old man in a carriage, surrounded by guards, travels towards Oedipus. He orders the hero out of his way brusquely. Filled with fury, Oedipus kills him.

He is, of course, Laius, natural father to Oedipus. But he also has the force (for me) of a monstrous foetus inside its carriage-mother, who seems to control its mother's actions and to tell the older sibling to get out of its way. In the psychology of learning, Oedipus' 'brilliant' solving of the riddle parallels the annihilating of the Laius-foetus within its mother. What is supposed here is that we must vanquish an enemy in order to achieve an epistemological conquest. A brutal leap forward in development brings catastrophe in its wake.

If the Sphinx looks inhuman and odd (like a foetus monster?), she does so because her mind is possessed by the alien presence within her – much as (in a different way) the oracle was possessed. (The Sphinx's mother, Echidna, was known to have given birth to many monsters.) In certain cases, the elder sibling may view the foetus in its mother as a misconception. The foetus within has the power of a theory which must be proved false (or destroyed) in order for the elder sibling to acquire a capacity to make definitions.

Such a theory assumes that the defining self is an isolated figure, who lives in a limited Malthusian world, and who must cut out swathes in order to achieve definitions. It provides a model for definition quite unlike the model of definition as conception, a creative coupling operating in unbounded circumstances.

The solving of the riddle of the Sphinx is a parable about a certain kind of delineation in thought. It enshrines one belief about how we should master learning. It is far from being the whole story; yet it is often present. For a small child learning the alphabet, a page of writing can be as tormenting in its inscrutability as a text in hieroglyph might be for us. The page of writing, a racking puzzle, can have the meaning of a mother possessed by a malign foetus – who withdraws all love and reassurance from the young would-be reader in order to give them to the next baby.

At the height of the anguished dénouement – in a gentle, pastoral interlude – a shepherd informs us that Oedipus' mother was enthralled by 'a wicked spell' at the time of her son's birth. The shepherd's voice is different from the hieratic voices of priests, princes and messengers who otherwise dominate the action. He speaks out of a tradition as half-hidden, and yet continuous over the generations, as the traditions of fairy tale or child lore or granny superstitions about childbirth.

Jocasta has no ear for this kind of discourse. She says that her first husband, Laius, told her to kill the child – or it would kill him. Laius had this tip from the oracle, and like everyone else in the play, Laius is consumed by the oracle's pronouncements. The child threatens him: he has an investment in believing any pronouncement against him.

Under the pressure of pregnancy and birth, it helps to be circumspect about anyone laying claim to certain knowledge (as in the case of those who say they can tell you the sex of the child you are about to have). Part of the madness of birth is an increase in the claim to certain knowledge. We seek out the oracle in one way or another.

Arguably, the Greeks esteemed newborn life less than we do (or legally used to do, before the recent changes in the abortion laws). But the belief that Jocasta did not feel guilt because her culture sanctioned infanticide is not born out by the feelings in the play. She probably went through some kind of puerperal breakdown.

Laius is the agent who precipitates the violence, the voice in her head (as it were), who insists that the child must be killed. He is both the older sibling who destroys the foetus and (at another shift in the action) the foetus who must be destroyed. He is in a condition often generated by pregnancy – the elder sibling who imagines himself both inside and outside the mother. The baby inside is felt to manipulate, by remote control, those who are outside. It is thought to be occult in its great power. The outside child must kill it – and take its place – in order to survive.

Through the questionings that reconstruct his past, Oedipus goes through an ordeal that is like a killing of the self. Sophocles deftly dovetails the various discoveries, almost too deftly perhaps. The structure of the story is over-taut; and Oedipus thinks so too. He thinks the accusations come too pat. He presumes a frame-up organised by his brother-in-law. Sophocles does not entirely rule out this possibility. Creon is a sibling dispossessed. He had promised to abdicate and to hand over his sister as a bride to anyone who rid the land of the Sphinx. He cannot have been happy about Oedipus' achievement. He mirrors Oedipus' sibling ruthlessness in the same way as Laius does.

The brutality of Oedipus' downfall recalls his crushing of the Sphinx. The Sphinx collapses before Oedipus: Oedipus collapses before the suggestion of his so-called friend at the banquet; and again, Oedipus collapses before the oracle's pronouncements. History is a weapon to hit your opponents with. We do not learn why the Thebans tolerated the mass murder of their children by the Sphinx. I would suggest we compliantly give ourselves over to sacrifice because we desire the sacrifice of others. We collapse because we do not feel strong enough to fight the wish in ourselves that our mother's babies (and our own babies) should be murdered.

The play exemplifies the belief that a past repressed will return to us in an inimical form. Knowledge is seen not as potentiality but as fixed positions (or certainties) gained through imperial conquest. It can be used as incriminating evidence against anyone. The four children of Jocasta's second marriage are summarily dismissed as 'monstrous progeny' because of their parents' incest. They have no right to be themselves, or to have their own histories. A pedigree condemns them.

We sometimes feel that our siblings, born and unborn, suffocate us. They rob us of the very air we breathe. They rob us of our very embodiment. Oedipus is devastated by this climate. He has lived a life which sets store on status – and status as achieved through murder. He has no conception of life as an exercising of potentiality.

The foetus as threat

A mother of two children, who was well into the way of a third pregnancy, reminds me one day of an event – she is not sure whether it is a dream or a day-dream – that had occurred one morning almost six months before. It was the morning of the day in which she had lost a foetus by miscarriage.

She was lying on her bed in an exhausted state. The room grew darker. All sound became muffled. She was aware of a huge bird above her bed, with long brown feathers. It put her in mind of an angel. In its beak, the bird held an object (about four or five feet above her head). The object reminded her of a conservatory – it was no more than one foot by two feet in size. She thought, in passing, of a conservatory built by some friends near a swimming pool. The friends grew nothing in it.

I wondered whether the angelic quality of the bird's feathers was her way of alluding to her dead brother.

Yes, she thought it was. Her brother had died in horrific circumstances a short time before the miscarriage. He had died of malnutrition and neglect in a Middle Eastern country. He had now been idolised by some of his relatives, who talked about him as a kind of god. The dreamer thought of him as charismatic. She was the first child, he the second; there had been other children after them.

She had been aware for some time of how destructive had been her feelings towards her mother and the second child. She imagined a radiance between mother and child. Her brother's charisma had been a reflected glory: candle-light bathing a face.

Her mother's femininity had been transmitted to him: none of it had gone into her. She felt a drab. She was conscious of being a hypocrite when she congratulated friends on being pregnant.

She was unable to enjoy any of her own pregnancies. She thought she had in some way stolen her babies from her mother. She tried (in a play-acting, testing-out sort of way) to kill the foetus in her successful pregnancy, by starving herself. She was impressed by the belief that someone outside her was radiating malevolence. She talked of a detached house, in which bad things were happening.

It seemed important to the shock of the miscarriage that she did not know whether she was in a dream, or day-dream, or awake: or whether she, or the bird, was the figure felt to be inside something else. Her description of the bird conveyed extreme sadness.

Its monster quality, its resemblance to the Sphinx, put me in mind of an issue that many pregnant women worry about – whether or not their babies will be born malformed. The intensity of this preoccupation probably stems more from a wish to damage one's own mother's babies than from any realistic expectation. We project the monster in ourselves into our mother's foetus; and in turn become persecuted by the figure of a monster foetus inside our mother, intent on unseating us. I take the huge bird in the dream, or day-dream, to represent (confusedly) a mother and foetus who will deny motherhood and life to an older sibling. They retaliate against her hostility to them. The dreamer's unconscious thoughts had anticipated the miscarriage by a few hours.

She thought of the miscarriage as like Captain Oates's sacrifice. Oates walked out of the tent into the snow and died, so that Scott and his companions might have food for a few more days. She did not think Oates wished to project guilt into the others. The first child in most of us tends to be Malthusian in our belief that food supplies are limited and cannot be increased. If another child climbs aboard the raft, we shall be obliged to kill it – or fall into the water ourselves. A baby must die if we are to be born. Many of the proposals for legitimising infanticide – as a form of eugenics, or as a scapegoating of an evil presence, or as a way of coping with limited food supplies – appear to derive from this anxiety.

Separation and inscrutability

An infant at the breast often experiences nourishment as a communication of meaning. At the end of a feed, the nature of whatever meaning is being communicated changes. The first stage consists of a change in structure. Attributes become interchangeable, definitions unstable. The knowledge a mother and baby impart to each other turns metaphoric by inclination – and the parts of the metaphor are transposable.

A mother tells me the following dream. She sees her adolescent son through a window. As he passes the window, his mouth shapes a message to her. She thinks he is unable to speak because he has lost his voice. We might give the incident another explanation, if we transpose the lost voice from son to mother (as though transposing parts of a metaphor). The losing of a voice is the losing of a mother who leaves her child. The son's yearning for contact is increased by the losing of his mother's voice. The metaphor contains an isolatable phenomenon: a mouth that shapes a message. This is the mouth that sucks (at an absent nipple) and the mouth that communicates meaning. At moments of separation in analysis, people sometimes talk about difficulties in translation, as though the gap in meaning between languages were, at this second, like the widening expanse of sand as the tide recedes from the shore, mouth separating from nipple.

In a second stage of the ending, metaphor dies. The breast becomes inscrutable, and the infant suffers the thought: why must it leave me? The breast that departs becomes the land whose language we shall never understand, the examination paper (in hieroglyphics) which we shall never be able to decipher, the seemingly irrefutable scientific law that denies our intuitions about the nature of nature.

Oedipus asks, at the beginning of the play: what is the meaning of these garlands and wreathes? He can make no sense of the behaviour of his people as they pray to him. A priest informs him that death, in the form of a plague, has entered into everything, even into the womb. Oedipus is faced by portents that cannot be elucidated, unnatural conjunctions and botched metaphors – like the Sphinx herself (a dog-faced woman) or the hermaphrodite priest, Tiresias, who guards the oracle's shrine.

If the breast that leaves us becomes inscrutable, it does so (we may feel) because it is controlled by some cruel tyrant inside it, death in the womb – a living presence, the baby-to-be who will oust us. The alien land, whose language we do not understand, is ruled over by a tyrant, who delights in teasing us with riddles.

Reverie as a means of research

There are other ways of dealing with the rival we fear. Freud writes about them, almost in passing, when considering the case of the little boy he calls Hans. The theme of new birth, and the pain it causes, does not attract him. (I shall paraphrase the case to bring out these elements.) He is more interested in the nature of phobia – and of sexual curiosity. He relates Hans's sexual curiosity to the growth of a desire for knowledge.

'Where do babies comes from?' asks Hans. He is three and half years old. His mother is about to give birth to a second child. The time is April, 1903. He has always slept in his parents' bedroom. On the morning of the birth, he is moved into an adjacent room – where he can hear his mother in labour. He responds to her groans by saying, 'Why is she coughing?' He falls silent, having asked this question, and then (after some time) he asserts, 'The stork is coming for certain.'

Out of the infinite potentiality of his mother's body – the treasure house he had thought his – must emerge an unwanted presence who will claim her from him. His wishes have no power. His sister is born. He develops a sore throat. He becomes fevered. He is put to bed – and he is heard to moan, 'I don't want a baby sister.' His mother pours goodness into his sister's throat. Into his throat, though, someone else seems to pour soreness.

Absences are not voids. They can be malign – sore throats are the least of it. Absences are known to kill. People die because the one they loved has died. The universe in our mind throngs with absences. We can sink beneath the weight of our guilt (at being alive) and our sense of loss. And yet thoughts about death are different from thoughts about annihilation. We cannot conceive of death as an experience. But we can conceive of annihilation – as an experience to be entered into, and endured, as breakdown.

Freud informs us that Hans' sexual curiosity, 'roused the spirit of enquiry in him and enabled him to arrive at a genuine abstract knowledge'.[4] Freud thinks of Hans as interested in outward configuration. Sight and touch are the primary instruments in acquiring this kind of knowledge: with sight mainly used as a kind of touch. But Hans's attempts at discrimination are not so abstracted. Outward characteristics are bound up in his mind with questions of potency. Seeing a railway engine release water, he wants to know where its penis might be. Hans's father, acting under supervision from Freud, appears to have stimulated this unproductive line of thought.

Elsewhere, Freud frees himself from this theory and asserts another view about the origins of knowledge. It is one that has had a long and varied history in European thought. At its starting point, it presumes that the seemingly naive linking of the question, 'How are babies made?' with the question, 'How are things made?', has the widest possible ramification.

The birth of his sister Hannah probably increased Hans's tendency to classify prematurely.

> Later he was taken to the kitchen. He saw the doctor's bag in the front hall and asked: 'What's that?' 'A bag,' was the reply. Upon which he declared with conviction: 'The stork is coming today.' After the baby's delivery, the midwife came into the kitchen, and Hans heard her ordering some tea to be made. At this he said, 'I know! Mummy's to have some tea because she is coughing.' He was then called into the bedroom. He did not look at his mother, however, but at the basins and other vessels filled with blood and water, that were still standing about the room. Pointing to the blood-stained bed-pan, he observed in a surprised voice: 'But blood doesn't come out of my widdler.'[5]

(Freud's text in German has *wiwimacher* for widdler. It means wee-wee maker and can apply to either sex.)

Inside the kitchen, and perhaps a little identified with such important figures as the cook and the doctor, Hans feels confident in predicting a birth from seeing the bag. We may be uneasy at taking this as a straight inference. The linking of bag and stork comes so close to his later conjectures about uterus as stork-box, that it implies a much richer diversification in thought.

In his paper on Leonardo, Freud distinguishes between the

[4] Freud (1909), p.9
[5] Ibid, p.10.

abilities of the scientist and the reveries of the artist. The Freudian scientist classifies by outward characteristics; he believes in the existence of certain knowledge; he pursues a higher calling than the artist. Science deserves better than this. Yet someone like the Freudian scientist exists in most of us.

Hans's thoughts about birth are those of an artist; especially when they are tinged with longing. He keeps looking out of a window to glimpse a girl who appears at a window across the courtyard – he is very much a boy who looks out of windows. In this, he touches on something in Freud himself, who returns to a variant on this kind of incident in his essay on *Gradiva*. What we think to have lost is always there, at home within us, if only we can look in the right direction.

Freud's prose is most vivid when it describes birth reveries – as when Hans watches thought a window horses having their wares unloaded at a customs station across the road from his home. Freud relates the patience of these beasts, and the dependence of society on them, to the unacknowledged burden borne by women in pregnancy and childbirth.

'Where do babies come from?' – here, for Freud, is the unconscious meaning of the Sphinx's riddle. Uncertain about the value of birth reveries, he claims at one point that Hans uses reverie as a form of lie, intended as an act of revenge against his father (for daring to be potent). True though this observation may be, it goes against the view stated elsewhere that such reveries are a mode of research, ways of arriving at the meaning of knowledge. The Freudian scientist sees thinking (or enlightened reasoning) as opposed to reveries. He dismisses reverie as superstition. He sees misconceptions as necessarily entailing bad motives and tending to block mental development. Freud thinks that Hans disbelieves the story that storks bring babies – it is as though Freud wanted Hans not to believe it. Hans keeps returning to the story without provocation; he elaborates on it with the satisfaction of a believer.

He consistently gets the facts wrong. Like the dreamer who lost her baby in a swimming pool, and joined up with a conjuror, he slides into magical solutions when faced by the puzzle of a birth in which he takes no part. We know that his mother was not coughing. She will not need tea to relieve her non-existent cough. Blood and water in her room will tell us nothing about the facts. In the face of a breakdown in knowledge, Hans retreats into omniscience.

On occasion, the same might be said of Freud. He has to ignore information. Hans suggests that the crumpled giraffe in a dream represents his new-born sister – a hint which his father, and Freud, pass over in silence, as though they had not heard it.

Misconception as an element in development

A woman who suffered from depression and a difficulty in being able to sleep, found it intolerable to think about the thoughts that passed through her mind. She dismissed as 'ridiculous' any attempt to find them meaningful, or to relate them to each other. When she did begin to entertain these thoughts, she became frightened that she would be invaded by night terrors. As it was, she reported that people would ring her up, or call on her, at all sorts of improbable hours in the night – comings and going that took on the quality of obsessional thoughts, especially in the form of intrusive erotic images.

When asked if she had read fairy stories in her childhood, she said no – except that her father had once read to her 'The Tin Soldier'. She went on to say that she had not been able to read until she was ten. She had been called lazy. At her first school she had learnt to write 'loopy' writing. She had then been sent to a school of some reputation, where she had been obliged to print out the letters separately. Her ability to write had so deteriorated that she had been one of the few girls in the school not be given, as an award for trying, a hymn book. She had been very upset over this failure.

The school of some reputation sounded like commonsense itself. But commonsense without the capacity for understanding. It appeared this this sibling-like institution could not tolerate her right to be 'loopy', or allow her to give rein to the loopy thoughts crucial to imaginative development – and she had deteriorated. And because of this, she had been punished. She had been denied a husband or lover, in the form of a him/hymn book.

By nature she was a successionist. She wanted a world of seamless surfaces. But the fabric had deteriorated, at least in her night thoughts. Unwelcome presences, like newborns, broke into her sleep. She had projected her hostility for the new and the unpredictable into her teachers at school and so felt disabled by their criticism. Through the agency of the school, she was able to exercise hatred for her own considerable talents. She hated herself as though she were hating the potential in a new baby.

Learning and mediation

Oedipus acquires a language and a symbolism too easily. He exercises a form of gangsterism. His ability to answer the riddle is bound up with the killing of a baby (actually, a potential in himself) and the implanting of his own seed in his mother's womb. Short cuts may be useful in learning by rote. In other kinds of learning, we have to come to terms with the mediatory. The instant gratification of wishes leads to dissipation – the brutality of instant gratification tends to rebound – in the case of Oedipus, with catastrophic effect.

A woman complains to me about her difficulty in following any shift from the figurative to the abstract, in thought and in painting. She relates this difficulty to the wearing of clothes. She wishes she could see more of me than my face. She is openly greedy about this, like a daughter enraged because she cannot be the wife. Her inability to see any distance between us is disconcerting. She seems to believe she owns me: why, then, can't she have me? She is furious. She begins to talk about clothes in an increasingly contemptuous way – ending up with an attack on Salvation Army girls who look like prostitutes.

She holds the unexamined view that any ability to move from the representational to the non-representational depends on some information that is being withheld from her. What she is allowed to see is so little, as opposed to what she has good reason to believe is there. What I give is not enough; she wants to devour everything. The figurative and the representational appear to be identified with the nipple you suck at and the breast you are allowed to see; the abstract and the non-representational with whatever exists beneath a mother's clothes – her body and the contents of her body.

She reported a dream which gave a fuller picture of her relationship to knowledge. In her dream, she came to see me in a waisted white dress. I told her casually to go home and to listen to a radio programme for 11-year olds. She found herself listening to the programme. It was about a Spanish painter, Joan Miro. She was struck by the oddity of man being named Joan.

She gave me various associations. She thought of Miro's

pictures – of which she knew little – as squiggles. They reminded her of noughts and crosses: which, in turn, reminded her of hugs and kisses. She thought of a child who is learning to read – and Miro brought to mind a book, recommended by a specialist in reading problems, called 'Sounds Travel Too'.

We tried to understand the dream. At the time she began to menstruate, at the age of eleven, she had become conscious – as though for the first time – of how hostile she could feel towards her mother. However, the dream indicates that however painful it may be to learn that your father rejects you as a bride (the waisted/ wasted white dress), you can achieve gratification of a different and more mediated kind at the breast or its equivalent (the radio programme/the aural experience of being analysed). Her gangsterism had been blocked. It was founded on the false belief that if you marry your father (or, if you are Oedipus, your mother), your greed will at last be satisfied. She was put in touch with the belief that if she was to gain anything worthwhile in life she needed to work at it (sucking at the breast) – and she needed to have her work directed through some convention or mode of symbolism (the analogy for this mediatory process being the valve function of the nipple). Being able to enter into the intial stages of learning entails her having some experience that modifies devouring greed. In the dream she did not break into the privacy of the parental couple. She came to knowing about them indirectly, through the figure of the painter: the Joan mother + the admired or (ad)Miro father.

Oedipus responds to the cryptic violently. He seeks to destroy opposition. The dreamer has begun to realise that the cryptic is not inevitably malign. The resistance it offers her helps her to make discoveries in thought – It gives her something to grip onto, something to engage with. It allows her to have experiences.

Chapter 3

REVERIES OF THE EXCLUDED SELF

> The unsophisticated observations of our predecessors, the residue of which is preserved in the term 'hysteria' (derived from the Greek word for 'uterus'), came nearer the truth than the more recent view which puts sexuality almost last.[1]

The solitary will, or sibling dispossessed by its junior – call it little Hans – embroiders a myth out of its isolation. The source of this myth is ancient and world-wide in its influence – although each of us embroiders it in our own way. It concerns the difference between men and women.

Men are allowed to be omniscient. They have magical powers. Their actions are touched with divinity. Women are associated with indefinable forces also. But they have no independent power. They are linked to some lawless and dissolute element in nature, inchoate matter itself. Men claim to discover forms, laws and regularities. They fight a hopeless battle to render female disorder less dangerous. Their struggle probably begins in reveries, a child's way of coping with the inevitable disorder and bloodiness of the birth process. It gives us one (wrong) idea of how we derive knowledge.

(A note of caution: I am writing about men and women not in terms of gender difference, but in terms of the masculine and feminine component that potentially exists in all of us.)

Male reverie

For a long time, learned men believed that mental disturbance in women could be located in an organic malfunction of an unusual kind. They had no equipment to scan the inside of bodies. They

[1] Josef Breuer; see Freud (1895), p.247

were sure, however, that they could descry movement in the interior, like astrologers predicting changes on earth from looking into the depths of the night sky.

In looking out, they were looking in, like an infant dreaming to look through skin into some imaginary site located within the breast: within its mother, a staging of the night sky. We are considering a male reverie, of general occurrence, based on the wish to give a 'causal' explanation for everything – especially for actions that challenge powers of conceptualisation. Many of the learned men thought the uterus was unanchored. They reached this conclusion by scholastic inference. Some of them (including Galen) believed that it was lightly held by ligaments, from which it could easily free itself. They assumed that the uterus had its own capricious life.

The association of femininity with fickleness and with the random element in matter often takes on the force of a metaphysical principle. It argues: this is how the universe comes into being. Women need men in order to give form to their babies and to defuse a certain combustible and dangerous quality in their natures. Areteus claimed that the uterus was an animal (that is, an anima or breathing entity) that could wander upward, downward or to either side. Little boys are sometimes horrified because they cannot control their mother's sexuality; she is the cat who walks the tiles. The anima-uterus is such a mother, seeking to be free, like breath released from the lungs. The body that holds it in place has a quality of the little tyrant about it.

In the *Timaeus*, Plato has the Pythagorean scholar Timaeus describe the uterus in the following way:

> In men, the organ of generation can become rebellious and masterful. It is like an animal, unable to obey reason. The sting of lust maddens it. It attempts to gain absolute sway. The womb, or matrix, in women is similar. It is an animal within them, desirous of procreating children. When it continues to be unfruitful long beyond its proper time, it becomes discontented and angry. It wanders in every direction through the body and closes up the passages of breath. By obstructing respiration, it drives women to extremity, causing all varieties of diseases in them. Until at length love brings together men and women. Love plucks fruit from the tree. It sows animals in the womb, like seed in a field – animals unseen because of their smallness and their being without form.

> Separated and matured within, they are finally brought out into the light: and the generation of animals is completed.[2]

Plato argues that male and female sexuality have something in common: body sensations may be similar, and emotionality can seem to trap the individual in either case. Sexuality in both men and women is identified with an explosive force – a pubertal and limited view of sexual human relationships. The learned men believed that when sexual forces were blocked in women, disorders ensued. They did not believe this to be true of men – for the simple reason that men, by their nature, do not allow their appetites to be frustrated. A man who sickens through sexual frustration betrays his nature: he becomes womanish.

Men fill the world (or so the ancient view goes). Men realise themselves through domination. They are expansive. A true man bestrides and bestraddles. He preens and boasts. Women are different, even in their styles of vanity. They tend to be circuitous and circumspect and concealed in their interests. They are not only like nature: they are an aspect of nature itself, beguilingly guileful. They live out the biological truth that a seed, falling into a fold in the ground, may or may not become a fruit-bearing tree. The act of germination is not visible and (until recently) could not be tampered with. The subterranean nature of this disclosure is typical of femininity.

Male sexuality is externalised. The male organs of generation are unconcealed. Timaeus sees male sexuality as similar to politics. It belongs to the public domain, to the market place and not to the olive grove. The penis becomes rebellious and masterful. It asserts itself tyrannically or, if tyrannised, incites rebellion. Orgasm is vigorously compared to slaves who overthrow a tyrant, then become tyrants themselves and then, in turn, are overthrown. The politics of male sexuality are monotonous, narrow and flavoured by sado-masochism.

In women, the organ of generation is inside the body and unverifiable by the senses. The *intelligible* idea of the wandering uterus throws into disarray any *sensible* idea we may have of physiological space. In terms of natural space and time, we find ourselves puzzled by the thought of an organ being able to move about inside a body, when a body has no gaps or secret passages. The uterus is perplexing in another way: it affects the organs it comes close to not by contact but by a sympathetic or magical

[2] Plato III, p.675

influence. It operates by remote control, gravitational in manner. We begin to wonder whether the myth of the wandering uterus is an unimaginative confusion – or a bold attempt to master a body of essential if elusive truths about human nature: what we might call the inner world of our feelings.

Subversive voyages

Male sexuality lends itself to a mechanistic view of the world, overt and unsubtle – in which Democritean atoms collide and bounce off each other. It lends itself to Cartesian assumptions about body as machine, or Hippocratic theories in which body organs are insulated from each other for the sake of diagnosis. Female sexuality junks such theories. The uterus slips from its moorings and glides though the body like a moon that unstrings the tides.

The compacted male self sees these dockings and departures as mysterious. The learned men might have anticipated, in body terms, the kinds of mental displacements which Freud was later to describe. The subversive voyages of the uterus are startling in ways which bedim the revolutions of male sexuality. They insinuate doubts in us about the plenum and about a God thought to achieve a maximal creativity with the minimum of effort – a plump and fulfilled world in which there are no gaps in matter or kind, and in which theories of succession, both natural and political, are given a divine authority.

Breuer considered the earliest of his (and Freud's) speculations about hysteria as marking a return to ancient conjecture. Most of the earliest physicians, Greek and Arab, saw womb displacement as sexual in origin. They were divided in their opinion as to whether it happened because of too much sex or too little. Nearly all of them agreed that it was something they could afford to be censorious about. Paul of Aegina thought that womb movement afflicted women 'prone to venery'.[3] The womb is set in motion by its being engorged by semen – or other putrid matter. 'Engorged', as well as putridity, gives an unflattering picture of women's insides (as well as of semen). The ancient Greeks often described sexuality in intestinal terms: in males, as a form of evacuation; in females, as a swallowing.

The followers of Hippocrates observed that womb movement

[3] Paul of Aegina, p.634

usually afflicted widows and elderly virgins. Many of them advised sexual intercourse as a 'cure'. Or they would recommend breathing exercises. A profound importance was attached to certain types of breathing as expressive of sanity – can we suppose some underlying, lost relationship between ancient Greek and ancient Indian culture?

To get the uterus to return to its proper place you had to apply something that smelt foul to the nose and something that smelt sweet to the vagina: a stick-and-carrot treatment intended to shift the uterus downwards: a possible derivative for smelling salts, with their cruel pong. Cures were usually punitive. 'Some have brought to the nose a chamber-pot containing stale urine or faeces,' wrote Paul of Aegina.[4] Hot cupping instruments were applied to the groin or lower abdomen. Enemas and carminatives (flatus-inducing medicines) were zestfully thrust up anuses. Ligatures, writes Paul, might be 'applied to the extremities'.[5]

Sydenham and Locke

The wanderings of the uterus disturbed all attempts to work out a coherent theory of medical practice. Doctors were baffled and irritated by the nature of hysteria (which they often identified with femininity itself). Their discipline was undermined by it. They made sense of it, if at all, by drawing on the language of demonology. Wishing to describe a strange overlap in body and mind, they seldom allowed for the fact that the actions of mind, when described in body terms, result in mysterious phenomena.

Maleness was easy enough to understand – maleness being body enactment and body fulfilment. Physical laws and theories of outward characteristics made sense of it. The female was more elusive. Its regularities, if any, exist in a domain beyond the physical – in the domain of anima (the self that is all breathing, all air-pulse), the domain of mind. The regularities of body and mind, though they have something in common, widely diverge.

Thomas Sydenham, the seventeenth-century physician, wrote a remarkable letter to William Cole, in which he insisted that hysterical symptoms are so unlike other symptoms that we might think them simulated. In the case of a hysteric person, the enflamed or diseased area of the body in no manner indicates the source of distress.

[4] Ibid. [5] Ibid.

A person under the spell of witchcraft is cut off from the meanings of their actions; they are possessed, disembodied, a witch being responsible for their actions. A hysteric person is similarily under an influence – through the actions of a bodily organ. As the uterus roves about the body, pain and tension increase or subside with it – and tempt the inexperienced doctor into a wrong diagnosis. The enflamed or diseased area of the body provides no clue as to the source of the illness; it is a little like the idea of referred pain, which so fascinated Descartes. Placeness, succession, are misleading ideas in this context. Sydenham thinks a doctor is ill-advised to localise the origins of a problem. He needs to look at symptoms – and also at occurrences remote from the symptoms. Sydenham reformulates demonology in naturalistic terms. Hysteric symptoms are quirks of the flesh. They indicate remarkable mental processes and (although Sydenham does not say so) ways in which the laws of mind differ from the laws of body.

A demonologist might reflect this approach, thinking of these symptoms as evidence of a devil – who has the power to assume a pleasing or unpleasing shape as he so wishes. The devil can turn into best friend or worst enemy, wife, husband, parent, child. He informs parts of your body, becoming your leg or eye or genital. He can be the incubus or succubus who saps you in dreams. He can vanish or appear. He has the powers of an artist who has gone to the bad. 'For I conceive that the devil gets into their body,' asserts Henry More, '...and makes it pliable to the imagination.' A Shakespearean imagination, no doubt. Such abilities were limited to women thought to be enthralled by the devil – until the late nineteenth century, when Charcot scandalised the public by insisting that robust males could be victims of hysteria.

Sydenham's caution in diagnosing symptoms was reflected in the scepticism of his close friend, the philosopher and qualified doctor, John Locke. Our capacity for knowing, Locke insists, is limited and modest. Sources of knowledge are often not available to us. A quotation from Ecclesiastes (11:5) is the epigraph to the fourth edition of his *Essay concerning Human Understanding*: 'As thou knowest not what is the way of the spirit, nor how the bones do grow in the womb of her that is with child: even so thou knowest not the works of God who maketh all.'

The pregnant uterus is a suitable emblem for one of our

difficulties in understanding. The little Hans in us is baffled by its mysterious nature: something of a tantalising and supremely creative importance is happening within it, which cannot be directly known. During Locke's lifetime, impressive engravings were made of post-mortem dissections, demonstrating the uterus with a foetus inside it. No one had access to the living culture in which a foetus grew. The living culture was like the workings of God's spirit in nature, indubitable and yet inaccessible. Locke does not concur with those learned men who believe that we arrive at truth by projecting a causal explanation of visible mysteries into an unknown and possibly unknowable area of the uterus.

He wrote his *Essay* at a time of heated controversy concerning the nature of sexual generation. Improvements in lens-making, and in the design of the microscope, inclined some embryologists into wrongly thinking that they had made discoveries. Some of them did make discoveries. Some of them discovered less than they thought they had done. The quality of lens, although improved, was less fine than they had supposed: and glass distortion was more than once taken as evidence for improbable theories. Swammerdam misinterpreted grains on his microscope lens as animalcules, or tiny men, thought to be suspended in seminal fluid. Hypotheses were raised on next to no evidence; and in no time at all, the hypotheses were converted into 'facts'. The question of how knowledge is arrived at called for rigorous examination, as Locke saw.

The uterine model arouses complicated feelings, which he somewhat avoids. He skirts the theme of uterine dread and the issue of occult causes. An important argument concerning certainty in knowledge depends on whether we find meaningful three concepts that relate as much to the uterus as to the structure of nature in general – these concepts are latency, potentiality and innateness. Locke doubts the value of these concepts in any theory of knowledge. He believes that a true theory should depend on a picture of the self as a coherent entity, conscious in its coherence – a system in which each agency in the self has a reasoning access to other agencies. He does not allow for hiatus or a mutative element.

According to these beliefs, hysteria remains unknowable – as would any other form of mental dissociation. Locke claims that the sleeping self cannot have experiences that the waking self knows nothing of. He rejects dreams as mere jumbles. He acknowledges that the pregnant woman can intimate the mystery in nature – while at the same time he thinks that what she has to offer is contrary to the discovery of sure knowledge. The pregnant woman is an emblem of the double self in one body: or, transposably, of a double self in the mind. The unborn sibling that Oedipus feared becomes, in Locke's view of the world, the stirrings of an unconscious that he would rather know nothing of.

Systems of meaning

In Plato's cave, watching the shadow-play, we are so positioned (with a clamp to the neck), that we cannot look away from the spectacle. We wrongly assume that the representation before us is the total reality. A benign mother allows the infant at her breast to experience the idea of play – of fiction, of conditionality. In Plato's cave, the baby in us is swaddled and given no choice. We are unable to see that there are other options – in a sense, that we are living through a modality of experience.

Our failure to recognise a convention has something to do with the nature of sense perception itself. The senses have the strange power of insisting that they, in themselves, have the authority of truth. The ancients often compared the power of each of the senses to erotic compulsion. To some extent, they exaggerated; but only a little. It is hard to believe that systems of meaning are not necessarily engendered by the senses – or by the continuities in consciousness that our senses would seem to provide.

The blind man, moving about his room, asks himself whether touch alone precipitates meanings. The pads on his fingers nurture definitions. His fingers bring the bookcase into being! From another view, touch (and the other senses) merely confirm or deny expectations already secure in the mind. The senses claim an ancillary relationship to systems of meaning. At most, they underwrite the truth or falsity of these systems.

One argument against the belief that the senses in themselves precipitate meanings is that meaning is disabled if we isolate the impact of the senses; we would somehow be lost within the sense. Condillac imagined a statue whose awareness was limited to a capacity for smelling. One day it met a rose and was forever lost in its first impression of fragrance. There was nothing to extricate the statue from its being engulfed. A rapt infant might be lost in some particularity of its mother's appeal, which its mother playfully and gently might release it from. It needs something behind, or beyond, or beneath the raptness to release it.

The Lockeian view of mind as conscious in its communication between various agencies, does not allow for some agency in the mind that activates change. A mind given over to consciousness would be immobilised by the presence of the first thought to enter it, as Leibnitz believed. There would be no means by which unknown and possibly uncontrolled thoughts could enter into knowability. A mind that was wholly conscious would be unable to wake from sleep, however much it was stimulated by outward events. When I wake in the morning, I do so because something (or someone) inside me wakes me. A ground must be supposed for changes to occur, either in mind or in the physical world: and this ground is probably an unbounded and unknowable space.

Condillac proposed a mythological explanation for the dissociation of meaning-systems and sense impression in the mind. Original Sin shackles us to a body that misinforms us. Before the Fall from Grace, Adam intuited systems of meaning, the Godhead itself, in which there were no confusion. After the Fall, he was left to untangle sense information that often beguiled and lost him in sensuousness. For all that, Condillac believes empirical investigation remains the likeliest source of truth for fallen man. He does not (nor should we) overtly blame Eve – or femininity – as the corrupting factor in sense impression.

Breathing

Myths concerning some lost key to understanding are widespread. At one stage in his life, Descartes was convinced that mind contains innate truth-yielding ideas. By a certain method, the investigation of these ideas would discover whole systems of lost, non-sensuous meanings. He thought that mathematics – algebra especially – brought us close to this recondite knowledge: a knowledge once better understood than it is now.

At some time there had been a conspiracy, in which certain authors suppressed all knowledge of the true techniques of understanding: '... my opinion is that these writers with a low sort of cunning, deplorable indeed, suppressed this knowledge...'[6] We can rediscover it, he asserts, if we allow ourselves to introspect a sense of (possibly spatial) proportion in ourselves – a sensation of structure which underlies all knowledge.

One way in which we can approach a Cartesian investigation. Consider a figuration emerging from a void – the idea of non-physical points arising from some non-sensuous ground. Pythagoras is thought to have been the first to draw this picture. None of his writings remain extant. My knowledge of Pythagorean teaching, originating in rumour and neo-Pythagorean commentary, is largely based on Burnet's commentary in *Early Greek Philosophy*.

Pythagoras

Points and figuration come into being out of a *void*. In the first instance, *void* is a Greek conception of *air* as darkness, mist, vaporous condensation (with powers of contraction and dilation), as well as a kind of nothingness. Burnet looks to the night sky as inspiring the Pythagorean belief that all phenomena can be defined in terms of units and measurements.

A dome of brilliant and space-defining stars appears out of a black and unending nothingness. Think of the awe that overwhelms us when we look up, and abandon ourselves, to the constellations of a country sky at night. Proportions appear to take form before our eyes out of a context of the immeasurable. The loss of any sense of distance, combining with an awareness of awesome spatial harmonies, make our heads spin. We cannot look up into the sky for long.

Another Pythagorean analogy is of an empty field in which you place boundary stones – so that space takes on definition in terms of numbers. The assumption is that quantification depends for its existence on a ground that is possibly infinite. There is some likeness to Leibnitz's belief that conscious thoughts require for their movement an unconscious and unbounded ground.

The night sky and the unbounded field provide the

[6] Descartes (1628), p.12

Pythagorean with two models for the emergence of thought. A third model – based on the fact that we breathe – is more urgent. By the fact of breathing we gain a sense of measure. Breathing parcels out the diffusions of air. It is a pulse that grasps and transforms, the closest organic equivalent to the act of thinking.

Plato compared breathing to eating. The analogy holds to some extent. The infant measures out its nourishment in terms of suck – a muscular and sensuous activity that puts it in touch with disturbing (and disturbed) attributes of the feeding object. Breathing is more abstracted and primordial. Having our suck disturbed puts us into a rage: having our breathing disturbed puts us into a panic.

Breathing demarcates self from non-self less securely than sucking does. It is in the nature of breathing that we may come to believe that since we breathe, everything must breathe; the pulse of life is everywhere; and the universe itself can be heard to sigh. Many of the ancient Greeks, including Plato's Timaeus, believed in an *anima mundi*: a world soul which, being soul, had to breathe.

The relating of breathing to our capacity to put out thoughts into the world, or to take them into us, is probably one of the earliest of human assumptions. 'The act of breathing, so characteristic of the higher animals during life, and coinciding with life at its departure, has been repeatedly and naturally defined with life and soul itself' (E.B.Tylor).[7] Beliefs concerning the nature of selfhood and mind originate in theories about the nature of breathing.

Choking

Consider some determinants for bad and good states of mind. For bad states of mind consider choking, or being choked – thought processes as hysteric in nature, snarled up, unsure of convention, buffeted back and forth in some zone between psyche and soma. (The founders of psychoanalysis hoped to free their patients from this condition.) For a good state of mind consider breathing, pulse, the discovery of spatial proportion – definitions arising out of an unbounded ground. Plato's Timaeus puts this in a slightly different way. Of the discontented uterus,

[7] Tylor, vol. 1, p.432

he said: '...It wanders in every direction through the body and closes up the passages of breath. Obstructing respiration, it drives women to extremity, causing all varieties of diseases in them...' Blocking the passages of breath recalls the state of the neck-clamped spectator in Plato's cave. You cannot release yourself into reality, you cannot breathe, if you cannot use fictions, conventions or other forms of mediation. We feel that capacities for symbolisation – and for knowing that we symbolise – are as essential to us as breathing.

Timaeus contrasts choking with the love which brings together men and women. Love sows the seed which releases further breathing in the womb (the foetus as animal). Every moment is potentially a moment of birth, of revelation – at least in the understanding; and all births, physical and mental, are potentially dangerous. Every moment is metaphorically an encounter with either a bad or good mother: a mother who kills us as we move down the birth passage, or perhaps a mother who is helpless at our dying; or a mother who enables us to embody life. Plato indicates that our being able to sense the existence of enablement is bound up with the coming together of man and woman in love and of our having evidence for an unseeable and unknowable knowledge concerning the 'animal' within.

We stare up at the blackness of the night sky and out of nowhere, seemingly, appears an awesome constellation of stars. A Pythagorean would liken this experience to the gradual forming of a great chord of music out of silence. Our sensations are pre-verbal, seeming to begin in muscular co-ordination. As against this, failures in the process of inspiration (or respiration or aspiration) underlie the bodily distortions – the disembodiment – of hysteria.

Coming into being

Anaximenes adds to our knowledge of the night-sky as a model for inspiration. Observing processes of condensation and rarefaction in the natural world, he was to suggest (according to Hippolytus) that '...infinite air was the principle, from which the things that are becoming, and that are, and that shall be, and gods and things divine, all come into being...'[8]

[8] Kirk, Raven & Schofield, p.145

Through air the Gods come into being and pass away. Air can rarefy or condense; and so can the object of aesthetic perception, as Freud was to observe in his descriptions of mental functioning in dreams. (He uses the term condensation.) Out of a void, ex nihilo, emerge the most complete and satisfying representations of reality – this is a profound truth about the ways in which mind operates. God-entities emerging from the void cannot be explicated: but their coming into being in an inconsequential way is fundamental to the beauty that Socrates believes is mind's prime function to apprehend.

Mind intuits ideas that cannot be located in the continua of nature – the discontinuities of absolute beauty, absolute goodness, absolute beauty. (And in the twentieth century, we would add, absolute pain.) These are some of the givens of mind: the ground for embodiment, that always await re-discovery. In the natural world, we find them through processes of gestation. Weak at the knees, we look up at the night sky. In Renaissance paintings you will frequently find a sky of radiant blue, out of which an ascending figure seems to emerge, like a distillation of air. The radiant blue concentrates itself in the figure. The infinite, or unbounded, gives birth to the defined object and to definition itself. Out of breathing, out of pulse, we gain a sense of measure. We begin to discover order. Cellular proliferation, as breath follows on breath, begins to seem universal. We rock ourselves to sleep in our own pulse. Cosmic order appears to extend out of a condition of narcissistic satisfaction.

Breathing as a defence against otherness

A man spoke and behaved in such a way as to indicate that he believed his breathing, by its rhythm, could control a couple imagined to be in intercourse within the breast. Sucking at the couple in the breast made him feel powerful in his bowels. Sucking was a diuretic that transformed moist faeces into dry ones. He could imagine himself as pregnant – at the expense of feeling under attack from the couple he had separated.

His solipsistic mythology asserted a kind of order. It was self-protective. But he feared attacks on his capacity to breathe. One session began with a painful and obstructed breathing; he was deeply upset; his mother was dying of lung cancer. On another occasion, he found himself speculating on whether blue babies suffered from a poisoning or from being suffocated. He knew that incompatibility of blood systems in two people dependent on each other's systems brought about blue babies. It was being dependent on others who did not satisfy his wishes – they sometimes importunely died, for instance – that undermined his confidence in steady breathing. Grief breaks in; and grief delayed can take the form of choking.

Pulse used in the service of narcissism does not invalidate pulse as a possible unit in universal coherence. I like to imagine the foetus, with its diminutive pulse, finding a reassuring correspondence in the larger pulse of its surroundings. Breathing releases us from narcissism if it puts us in touch with unlike.

Some of the ancient Greeks saw breathing as an umbilical cord that relates us to the outside world. Sextus Empiricus quotes Heraclitus as asserting that through breathing we become rational. In sleep, breathing continues as 'a sort of root',[9] drawing in nourishment from the natural world.

Heraclitus discounts any significance attached to experience in sleep. Our senses close down; we lose the power of memory. Our dreams, at most, give actual glimpses into the landscape of after-life; we have the perceptions of the dead, as though we had entered into them. (To use a modern jargon: all dreams for Heraclitus entail that the dreamer enters into states of projective identification.) We think we can turn to a private wisdom – when it is in the nature of wisdom that it should be accessible to all.

The complacence of believing in a universal regularity is important, at least for a while. It gives us time enough to establish a capacity for mentally tuning-in to things. An infant with some experience of stability in both feeding and the pre-birth period will be prepared a little to ride the turbulence of maternal incoherence – the 'madness' of a mother who will not obey its wishes, stemming from a so-called uterine disorder, her relationship with the infant's father and with future siblings.

Reveries of universal order – or of disorder – are equally valuable. One does not invalidate the other. The danger is that one way of looking at things will assert itself at the expense of the other. Visions of order that deny the importance of hiatus, incompatibility, or states of incoherence that are sometimes mutative, easily become demi-tyrannies that emprison us. At

[9] Burnet, p.152

the same time, visions of disorder, commitments to perceiving life as miraculous and inconsequential, can blind us to the importance of free-standing otherness and biological sequence in any theory of human development.

Burnet informs us that the Corybantic priests used to purge patients of hysteria by having them listen to music and attend to dance: a far less punitive cure than smelling salts. But would music and dance have been adequate in the face of a terror that destroys the ability to make discriminations? The Pythagorean belief in generalisation – the relating of particularities to some general cosmic pattern – must have been disabled by knowledge of *globus hystericus*. Blocked wind-pipe, invisible fingers tightening around your throat, no breath, no life – terrible premonition of a weaning worse than any weaning. No wonder that Plato's Timaeus associates the closing up of the passages of breath to madness in women and the eruption of many illnesses. In the moment of our being choked, we unfairly accuse our mother of being the one who chokes us. The Pythagorean stars sink back into darkness.

A parable about the relationship of breathing and life

At one aberrant moment in history, breath was taken as evidence of life – with dreadful consequences. The 1623 Law against Bastardy proposed that if an abandoned corpse of an infant was found, and the infant demonstrated to be illegitimate, then no more evidence was called for – the death was a murder. The likelihood of a natural death in childhood was discounted. Mothers were sentenced to death. Many of them were hanged.

In time, there was a reaction to this barbarism. Critics insisted on the need for careful autopsies. Indeed, the procedures of the post-mortem were established because of this barbarism – but at first catastrophically.

One of the procedures related to the question of breath as evidence for life. William Harvey revived an experiment of Galen's, in which it was thought that the lungs of an infant would float on water if the infant had drawn breath, if only once. The experiment was improperly conducted and the hypothesis believed verified. Many women were convicted on its evidence – and put to death – before it was shown to have been unreliable.

It recalls witch-ducking. If you float, you must be a witch; if you drown, then those who outlive you will remember you as innocent. I suspect that anxieties about moving down the birth canal become related to an elder sibling's fear that breathing space at all times is drastically limited. If your breath fails to sustain itself at birth, consider yourself an innocent with a guilty mother (guilty of being inadequate, at least, if not a killer.) If you dare to continue breathing, you must be a monster – since (according to the lore of the elder sibling) all comings into beings are a violation of a preformed and limited universe. On this assumption, each breath I take expensively buys me identity. It confirms more deeply my criminality and guilt at living at someone else's cost. The dead and the unborn prey on the living and weigh them down with guilt.

Issues of personal identity and breathing are hard to sort out. Glanville Williams wrote:

> In medical works, respiratory action of the child, whether initiated within or wholly without the maternal parts, is taken to be indicative of life before birth. But this is not the legal view, for as a matter of law what happens before birth cannot indicate the position after birth. What the law requires is life after birth, not life before birth.[10]

Medicine and mutation

> I see men become mad or demented from no manifest cause, and at the same time doing many things out of place.[11]

De morbo sacro (Concerning the Sacred Disease), an essay written by a member of the Hippocratic school, possibly Hippocrates himself, marks a watershed in the history of medical diagnosis. For the sake of convenience, I shall take its author to be Hippocrates – and somewhat amplify his argument.

He is concerned with the treatment of bodily events that are seemingly uncaused, spontaneous and tending to strike terror into the heart of the spectator: events that appear to be bound up with states of suffocation. The art of medicine has its beginning in the investigation of mutative phenomena. Their nature tempts us to explain them in supernatural terms. Naturalistic expectations, biological processes, do not seem to apply.

The subject of the essay – the sacred disease – is epilepsy.

[10] Williams, p.22 [11] Hippocrates, p.179

People who witness an epilectic fit can be frightened into a belief in occult causes. They may come to think of the epileptic as a holy person, someone set apart, in taboo. Convulsions communicate a horrifying power. Hippocrates describes '... many persons in sleep, groaning and crying out, some in a state of suffocation, some jumping up and fleeing out of doors, and deprived of their reason until they awaken...'[12] Possession occurs 'from no manifest cause'. (We might think the sufferers are possessed by dream logic.) 'I see men become mad or demented from no manifest cause, and at the same time doing many things out of place.'

Such events attract supernatural explanations – and healers who lay claim to supernatural powers: medicine men, thaumaturges, wizards. Often the holy men display symptoms of the disease they set out to cure: they practise miracles (i.e. exhibit events that have no natural cause), have vision-inducing fits, boast in a way that a present-day Hippocratic would label schizoid.

Hippocrates denounces them as frauds. He proposes medical techniques that take the heat out of the situation – and allow the physician to cope soberly with a frightening situation. The cure of bodies differs from the cure of souls: doctors are not priests. It is on this point that the essay marks a watershed in treatment. It establishes an orthodoxy in medicine which is with us still.

Hippocrates' handling of his theme applies to more than his observation of epilepsy. It covers any bodily act which projects a state of violent inconsequence into the spectator. It offers us a technique for regaining our executive self, so that we should not be paralysed by the authority of the illness.

The projections he writes about deny body boundaries. The one who suffers the act and the one who observes it become mixed up with each other, choked. I am no longer able to observe my illness. It has somehow managed to become alien to me, incomprehensible, and yet it has swallowed me up. In a similar manner, through the very fact of proximity, a discontented womb is thought to infect sympathetically, gravitationally, a healthy organ. The 'holy' disease attracts a 'holy' physician who becomes vertiginously indistinguishable from the sufferer of the

[12] Ibid.

disease. A 'mad' disease attracts a 'mad' doctor – in the vortex of group process.

'Mad' disease, 'mad' doctor: the first therapeutic relationship

Hippocrates does not mention the best-known case of such a coming together. (It is less a case, perhaps, than an improbable myth of huge significance.) Thomas Laycock, a nineteenth-century specialist in female (as opposed to male) insanity – a distinction thought important in those days – saw it as the first recorded example of someone being 'cured' of hysteria.

One day the Sicilian magus Empedocles was out walking. He came across the corpse of a woman who had been dead for thirty days. (We do not know why she had been left unburied for so long.) By some means, also unknown to us – perhaps resuscitation by breath? – Empedocles raised the woman from the dead.

Possibly, he practised some kind of breathing cure. The fourth-century physician who records the miracle relates it to the sage's talent for pneumatology. Empedocles claimed to be able to control the winds – and he carried out various experiments in testing the power and uses of air pressure. He sought to demonstrate that a vacuum could not exist.

The legend sounds like a menstrual variation on the myth of conception by ear. The woman presumes herself to be infertile. Her thirty-day periods leave her feeling like death. She becomes pregnant when the right man appears; and the breath of life in the womb is like a resurrection. Such a reading of the legend is consonant with the view that wombs become discontented because they remain unused. In terms of mind: femininity in both men and women goes mad if it remains uninseminated. Thomas Laycock would have disagreed.

The recognition of masculinity and femininity as mental traits, appropriate to both the sexes, is a recent discovery. Laycock would have been shocked by this idea and he would have rejected it. Importantly, for our purpose, Empedocles and the dead woman anticipate Josef Breuer and his therapeutic relationship with Anna O., officially the first psychoanalytic patient. In other ways, they anticipate Laycock and his approach to hysteric women.

Laycock did not believe that men could identify with femininity. Men embody reason, women unreason: this is the way of the world. Masculinity and femininity are metaphysical polarities, opposed in the same way as order and disorder are opposed. Femininity is ungraspable, inchoate, identified with gaps and spasms. Women survive by being cunning. They live by disloyalty. The hysteric symptom epitomises their condition. It is a form of deceit. Empedocles did not practise a miracle: he was sorting out, in a quite practical way, a case of hysteria. Empedocles' woman was not dead. She was merely simulated the condition of being dead – a typical strategy for the hysteric.

Organs swell and shrink. Neuralgias, aphonias and paroxysms appear and disappear. Laycock and his contemporaries believed that hysteria was a female illness – indeed, all female mental illnesses were subsumed under it. All eating disorders – anorexia, bulimia and pica (see below, p.163) were hysteric, or womb-derived, in origin. Hysterics are dominated by insatiable hungers. At other times, they can do without food, seemingly forever – and yet, mysteriously, they do not lose weight.

The Laycockian woman is pure subversion. Using a startlingly modern phrase, Laycock directs our attention to 'the difficulty in studying the semiology of hysteria'.[13] This is his position. He was not taken in. Or was he? Some women, he insists, can exist for seven years without defaecating. (A bold stand against the regularities of nature.) Some women can urinate through their eyes.

Laycock remarks on this astonishing proposition in the 1840s. Fifty years later, with a change of tone, and even more extraordinarily – considering his sensitivity to the feminine – Charcot repeats this observation in his Salpêtrière lectures.

Shaman

Laycock would have been disinclined to see – as recent commentators have been inclined to see – that Empedocles mirrors the strange condition of the woman he raises from the dead. Empedocles enjoyed just as dissociated a relationship to his body as the woman did. (I owe the following controversial information to E.R.Dodds's *The Greeks and the Irrational*.)

[13] Laycock, p.354

In 1936 a Swiss scholar suggested that we should see the activities of medicine men, like Pythagoras and Empedocles, within the folk-traditions of shamanism – which apparently exist to the present day (in Siberia; or at least, in a Siberia of the mind). At one time, the culture of shamanism extended from Scandinavia, across the Eurasian land mass, as far as Indonesia.

Its cult figure, the shaman, is someone reputed to be of unstable mind (and therefore sacred). He is Laycockian woman in a man's body. His peculiar, feminine relationship to food is rationalised in terms of a need to practise a religious vocation. He must fast; he must observe various rites – a training intended to liberate him from the regularities of nature. Through his training he becomes free to quit his body at will and to be in two places at once. (High in anyone's list of mad beliefs must be the one that you can be in two places at once. It goes in the same category as the wish – to re-phrase Hamlet – that you can both be and not be.)

The shaman changes sex when it suits him. He practises divination and medicine of a religious sort. He is expected to write religious poetry. All these qualities have been ascribed to Empedocles, in legend at least, as well as to other religious leaders.

The wandering uterus finds its male analogue in the shaman, as he migrates from body to body. Hippocrates put paid to such wizardry when he denounced the religious exorcists as 'conjurors, purificators, mountebanks and charlatans'.[14] From now on, in the mainstream of medicine, physical events will be given physical explanations. But the unpredictable, seemingly causeless paroxysm will not be forgotten. It will continue to tantalise the neurologist.

Hippocrates

Hippocrates isolates facts. He disconnects. He locates aches; he scrutinises body stuffs; and he does so with the intensity of a priest contemplating the entrails of a ritually-slaughtered beast. He does not make a prediction, though – nor does he tell us what he is thinking.

A woman of Cyzicus gave birth to twins after a difficult

[14] Hippocrates, p.179

labour.[15] Birth took place at the time of the plague – was the plague relevant to her subsequent condition? Hippocrates reports that her lochial discharge was insufficient. It was common practice (until sometime in the nineteenth century) for doctors to believe that problems in lochia often indicated impending madness. The woman becomes fevered. She complains of chills and of pains in her neck and head. She cannot sleep. Plague symptoms – or symptoms related to a difficult birth? She is silent, sullen and 'disobedient' (Hippocrates' word). In parenthesis, he adds that her urine is thin and devoid of colour. She has a continuous thirst. She wants to vomit: her bowels seize up. On the sixth day of her illness, as night falls, she becomes incoherent. She may stir fear in her physician – the fear a child might feel when it sees its mother lose power over her tongue. (But Hippocrates does not register such anxieties.) She is unable to sleep. On the eleventh day, she is possessed by a wild delirium – which soon abates. Her urine turns black, oily and thin. She has diarrhoea. Convulsions seize her on the fourteenth day of her illness. Her body grows cold. She is unable to urinate. On the sixteenth day of her illness, she loses all powers of speech. She dies on the next day.

Hippocrates certifies that she died from phrenitis, a brain fever consequent on the act of giving birth. (From the condition of which, we get the adjective phrenetic.) He inclines to believe that he was describing the deterioration of a plague victim. It is surprising to realise that he was reporting on a terminal case of puerperal fever; even more surprising to learn that Esquirol thought this case to be the first recorded example of someone in the grip of a puerperal psychosis.

We feel the pain in this death. Reveries about coherence underlie sanity: coherence is imbued with maternal feeling. Destroy it – and we can deny that it ever existed. We can argue that all we ever had was waste matter or a collocation of atoms. For all that, the fragments of the lost coherence hint at their former desirable condition. They yearn to re-find themselves.

In the *Charmides*, Socrates recalls a Thracian doctor who once told him that the doctors of Hellas were unable to cure many diseases – because they 'were ignorant of the whole'.[16] Doctors

[15] Hippocrates, p.78

[16] *Charmides*, 156, 157

separated soul from body. Socrates believes that soul diseases can be cured by a talking cure. Headaches, and other physical symptoms, are curable in this way. Socrates marvels that a pain in the head may impel a man to wish to improve his mind. Hippocrates does not share this view. 'Every man preens himself on finding the whole,' thought Empedocles. 'Men only believe that upon which, as individuals, they chance to hit as they wander in all directions.'[17] Hippocrates might have agreed. He establishes a tone in diagnosis which is with us still. Clipped style. No time for reverie. He keeps us at some distance from the woman of Cyzicus. She is seen as a patient – as someone less than human. He enters into a transaction with a physiological disorder, not with the woman herself.

'Les formes frustes'

Freud praised Charcot for his ability to classify types of hysteria – he was especially gifted, Freud thought, in defining 'les formes frustes'[18] (a term from numismatics: coin faces rendered illegible and valueless through blurring). Charcot would contemplate a patient for a long time in silence. Bystanders could hardly bear the suspense. Eventually Charcot would make a classification. Hazarding a guess, I think his skill depended on his having intuited that the subject for observation was not hysteria but the more unusual properties of femininity – in either woman or man. His silence was the silence of someone looking inwards to his own femininity. Arguably, he anticipated the Freudian hypothesis that femininity is as essential an element in the realised masculine self, as masculinity is in the realised feminine self. We all aspire (hopefully) to embody a good couple: we are both embodied and disembodied at the same time, prisoners of gender endowment and yet free.

Charcot comes close to this line of thought – as when he proposed that robust railway workers were suffering from hysteria. Less unusually, he admits to a connection between femininity and slyness and acknowledges a debt to Sydenham's views. Almost in an aside, he compares the subterfuges of the hysteric symptom to the styles of an artistic movement then

[17] Burnet, fr.2 p.204
[18] Freud (1893)

much to the fore – and in which doubts about sexual definition played a considerable part. Hysteria, he tantalisingly intimates, puts him in mind of the Art for Art's sake movement.

Neurologists have long been aware of some element of hiatus, or disjunction, in a whole range of phenomena. In his masterly study of 1907, *The Border-land of Epilepsy*, W.R. Gowers groups together (with epilepsy) faintings, syncopes, vagal attacks, migraines, vertigos, night terrors and sleep disturbances such as nacrolepsy – a sudden and irresistable falling into sleep, characterised by vivid dreams. A loss of consciousness is a frequent event in this range of experience. Gowers looks for a neurological understanding of it, while at the same time reporting the psychological and, on occasion, metaphysical responses of his patients.

Oliver Sacks, referring to Gowers in his study on migraine, pursues a similar theme. A patient thought that there was a relationship between nightmares and migraines. Sacks thinks that 'the fact of association is clearer than its interpretation'.[19] He sees some connection between epileptic and migraine cycles and 'the more leisurely cycles of sleeping and waking' or, more distantly, 'the excitatory and inhibitory phases of some psychoses'. He adds: 'Gowers placed migraines, faints, sleep disorders, etc., in the "border-land" of epilepsy; we can with equal justice reverse his words and locate migraine and migraine-like reactions in the border-land of sleep.'[20]

Intolerable images reside within us – mutative changes often misread by us in terms of dying and death. To save our sanity, we may put the images into others or into the general pool of culture. We do not know what images of terror Anna O.'s dying father put into her at the time when she was nursing him; but later, when she moved into the care of Breuer, she discharged into him images and terrors associated with death – one such being the frightening hallucination of a skull. It seems that she had to defuse herself of some terror, perhaps put into her by her dying father. Inability to project or defuse the self of such images – failures in mourning, in other words – can result in the kind of choking Gowers describes: 'With the dyspnoea (breathing difficulties) or cardiac sensation, or both, is often associated a

[19] Sacks (1971), p.158
[20] Ibid, p.122

sense of impending death, so intense that no recollection of its falsity in preceding attacks prevents the conviction of its present reality... Another occasional feature is a sense of unreality in what is seen.' A 28-year-old woman had suffered nine months from attacks, which had been heralded by early morning headaches. 'Some time in the forenoon she suddenly found that she could not fix her attention on any subject. After this had lasted an hour or so, a sense of sleepiness came on; then suddenly she felt wide awake, with an intense feeling of fear, extreme coldness of the hands, feet and legs and inability to move.' Within moments, she feels she is being suffocated; her heart beats violently. The attack gradually subsides.

In another case, the subject was an officer in the army, aged 30, two of whose sisters were insane.

> He had been in especially good spirits... Quite suddenly, a dreamy mental state came on, a reminiscent state, the well-known feeling that whatever was happening had happened before. It was not momentary, as in epilepsy, but continued... His hands and feet became cold; his own belief was that the mental state came first. With the coldness his face became increasingly pale, and physical prostration set in, speedily reaching such a degree that he was scarcely able to move. If he tried to sit up, he fell back at once. His extremities became icily cold, even to the observer. So great was the prostration that he could only utter one or two words at a time... His pulse became smaller and smaller, until it was hardly perceptible. There was not a moment's loss of consciousness throughout. His own sensation was that he was dying, gradually passing out of physical existence.[21]

Death, as an endured experience, does not exist in consciousness. The projection is probably of something contiguously related to ideas of dying – mutative and inconsequential and more terrifying than any assessment of death itself.

Breuer

On two occasions, and no more – and then only marginally – Breuer states that Anna O. had a mother. He mentions her father often. Her father is important. He states that her father's terminal illness (from a peripleuretic abscess) largely induced her collapse. He makes two passing references to her mother. He

[21] Gowers, pp.20-3

points out that she, as well as Anna, had nursed the father. And he points out that the mother had gone away, briefly, at the time of Anna's black-snake hallucination.

The mother's absence does not strike us as odd. We probably do not notice it. The oddity is that we fail to notice the absence. Anna somehow lulls us. She comes over as the primary inspiration in the case, someone who has taken over the maternal presence by pushing out an actual mother. Breuer writes about Anna with the millimetre attention of an infant too close to its mother's skin. There is no distancing.

His uncertainty reflects her confusion. He has been projected into by her. Can we approach its meaning? When Hans's mother gives birth, the little boy, deeply perturbed, feels the whole world is falling to bits: and he retreats into omniscience. Faced by the anima, the dangerous principle of unpredictability, of a third factor emerging – new baby, new idea – most therapists tend to feel like Hans. Breuer is their pioneer in his capacity to carry creative bewilderment. In the face of turbulence, he does not take flight. Learned men in the past had thought of hysteric women as pests and relegated them to some sub-human category. Shattered by his meetings with her, Breuer was tempted to describe certain episodes in Anna's life in the same way. He found them bewildering and believed them unavailable to reasoning. But he did not betray their possible significance by in some sense destroying them within himself.

In a moment of insight, Freud later realised that Anna's hallucinations and markedly distorted physical condition could be made to have sense within a normative conception of humanity. In so recognising this, he had begun to defuse her illness of its malign power. It was possible to approach hiatus, the emotional, with reasonable understanding. Freud saw Anna's condition as an arrested and unusual form of mourning – unusual because the mourning process had actually begun before the death of her father. Events in the mind and facts in the world often diverge.

Processes of mourning flow like unseen currents within us. They only tend to surface into the conscious mind at times of death and birth, when traces of the process can be frequently confused with madness. Mourning is a type of learning, possibly the most painful. It obliges us to work through, or revise constantly, the mutatives of arrival and departure. Some would argue that mourning is less an act of working through than of being worked over, less an act of making than of being made. Anna's attempt to mourn was to tell herself stories: or rather, she allowed the stories to tell her. An inspiration seemingly from without brought her alive as a story-teller.

Story-telling

Story-telling is as much of a symptom as hallucination or physical paralysis. It differs in one way: it offers direct access to personality. Personality is not opaque. It must symbolise to live; symbolising being a mental counterpart to breathing.

Doctors have always listened to patients telling their stories. The tradition that medicine and poetics are (each of them, in their own way) curative has never been quite forgotten. Breuer brought to it open-mindedness. He allowed himself to be fascinated by his patient. He in Vienna, Charcot in Paris, sensed a kindship between femininity and art. It was clear that the relationship between the sexes was undergoing a change. Nineteenth-century novelists had begun to attend to women, as well as write for them. The cultural atmospheres of Vienna and Paris must have encouraged both men – in attaching importance to women, and in presuming that professional men will naturally be humanists, familiar with the idiom of ancient Greece and Rome.

Breuer pities Anna. She lacks scope to exercise her gifts; is inhibited by a paternalist culture; is so immersed in a stream of consciousness that she is liable to be drowned by it. We have no reason to go along with his views. Anna was no mouse. Even at the age of twenty-one, she had authority. She had not timidly bowed to the wishes of her father. On the contrary, she had entered into her breakdown shortly after she and her father had had a blazing row. Uncrushed by paternalism, she responds to the challenge of being in the male company of Breuer; and she and he together discover psychoanalysis.

Breuer leant towards literary stereotype – seeing Anna (I suspect) as a victim of 'bovarysme'. 'Madame Bovary, c'est moi,' thought Flaubert, the qualities of femininity transcending gender. But Anna was more disturbed and talented than Emma Bovary. She often sounded sibylline. Breuer was impressed by her knack for attending to people, while at the same time conducting a continuous flow of story-telling – in what Breuer calls 'the private theatre'[22] of her mind. He did not observe insincerity in her split consciousness. It seemed evidence of remarkable abilities.

His method was intentionally cathartic, a Pythagorean purgation. His allusion to the theatre is appropriate; but he does not work the idea too hard. We never learn who the players are, the scene shifters, the dramatist or the audience in Anna's private theatre. Breuer is more concerned with the artistic policy of the theatre – and the conditions under which the policy is changed. She has to enter into a condition of auto-hypnosis, trances – forms of inspiration (Breuer thinks) that can be precipitated when someone falls in love, or (strange juxtaposition) works too hard as a night nurse. She tells him at first stories that remind him of Hans Christian Andersen. After her father's death, the stories grow more sombre. They then break down into discrete, horrific images: this is after a meeting with a specialist, who blows smoke into her face while she is lost in an hypnotic trance and brings about her collapse. Her feelings of horror lessen when she reports the images to Breuer. Breuer is impressed by how the act of 'chimney-sweeping'[23] (as she calls it), of story-telling, seems to relieve her symptoms.

In the mind's eye, body is not irreducible fact: it is a mode of symbolisation. Body symbolism does not draw attention to itself because it is conducted within a deterministic context. Body imperatives – the need to eat, sleep or relieve discomfort – assert themselves, misleadingly, as more crucial to our well-being than the need to dream or to seek for definitions. A paralysed arm is an unwelcome fact that you will probably have to live with always. Breuer and Anna demonstrate that such a fact can be transformed into story, and in this way modified – if only we can find the right story.

Her interest in story-telling is comparable – in its intensity – to the extremities of her physical state. She underwent muscular seizures that (on one occasion at least) left her close to total incapacity. She suffered from extreme disturbances in vision. She experienced crises of a sort that recall Melanie Klein's woman in mourning. People began to look unreal to her. The

[22] Freud (1895), p.22
[23] Ibid, p.30

walls of her room appeared to cave in. (Our need for a private theatre increases if the actual world seems to collapse about us.)

She was convinced that she was living in the wrong room. She did not think she had a misconception about where she should be. She thought the room had a misconception about her. Her family moved house. She was convinced she had not left her former bedroom. She hallucinated her former room with stubborn conviction. When she wanted to go to the door, she banged into the stove.

She projects herself into an idea of her former bedroom (as though entering into, and controlling, a womb). She uses time and language in the same way as space. She escapes from the present moment and locates herself at exactly the same moment one year before. Extracts from her diary show that she lived out the previous year moment by moment in the present, and with absolute accuracy.

She uses her formidable powers of memory as a defence against having experiences. Her illness is a massive sulk. She forces space and time to bend to her wishes. Illness plays the same trick with her powers of speech. She finds that she cannot talk; sentences fragment in her mouth: syntax disjoints. She loses any hold on her native tongue. She becomes a mute. After a while, she begins to speak once more – but only in English. (Her nanny's tongue?) Most of her conversations with Breuer are conducted in English.

The ancients thought of eating disorders as forms of hysteria. For generations, their successors agreed with them. The guile and occult influence of the hysteric was thought to be essential to any definition of the feminine. If the world oppresses us, we change it in our minds to suit our needs. Anna's use of her powers of symbolism – making (in thought) this room into that one – is typical. Eating disorders are, in the first instance, difficulties in ingestion and digestion, whether mental or physical.

Keeping spaces barren

I recall a patient who thought of experience in general as being like an authoritarian father and retreated into some idea that she had of being a 'good girl'. She came into therapy in the hopes of getting further cues of this kind – therapy as a consumer guide to the better life. She listened to what I had to say with the intention, primarily, of learning about my life style. She wanted to know about good shops, good swimming pools, good schools, fashionable ways of behaving.

She had her great secret. Outwardly imprisoned in social convention, inwardly, in her mind, she could do what she liked with the outside world. She appeared to bear out the ancients' opinion of hysteric women: that they can live outside the pressures of physical exigency. She thought she could survive without eating – and so on.

She preyed on me. She would give me no space. She haunted the park where she thought I went over the weekends. Once, she thought, she had seen me with a pramful of babies. She was shattered. She had seen a ghost: no, she had seen worse than a ghost. She had seen an actual presence. We agreed that she should try and avoid the park. Soon, she claimed this to be a punitive prohibition. She had nowhere else to take her children over the weekend. Without the facilities of this particular park, they would pine away, as though locked in an empty room.

She now had a dream in which she found herself in another park, where a dreadful murder had taken place. By her associations, it became clear that she had converted the park, where she had believed she had seen me, into the other park (where she could murder my pramful of babies without being caught out). She knew that what we do in our minds exists outside the laws of the land.

She lived a phantom existence. Anything could become anything else in her mind. Her conversions of reality were unrewarding. She was like Madame Bovary. She ate rubbish. She feared a Bovary death. (A brown, faecal-like liquid pouring out of the dead woman's mouth.) She had no trust in the idea that otherness might be nourishing. She had no trust in the possibility that some food might be good for her – because she was able to convert anything that came to her into good or bad, as she thought fit. All converted goodness turned out to be an idealised form of badness. It was like the reveries of Madame Bovary, whose truth was revealed in the manner of her dying. She was terrified at the thought of being discovered: to be discovered would be to have an experience. Her conversions were subtle and elusive. Both she and I found them hard to delineate.

Most hysterics feel childless, although they may be the mother of many children. They feel possessed by a discontented womb, that malignly and at a distance influences everything. They cannot enjoy experience and they cannot eat with pleasure. Experiences are often thought of as cages or empty rooms, analogues for the barren womb. Hysterics unconsciously believe that the womb they keep barren is not theirs: the bodily pangs they feel are of someone else's babies being denied.

Oppressed by experience, they doubt the authority of otherness. They see no value to it. Anna loses touch with her mother tongue. It becomes a phantom and vanishes. She goes mute. She begins to acquire a tongue that is not really hers. She speaks a foreign language, as though internally taken over by someone else.

Language and inspiration

Language is identified with deep oceanic places, tempestuous seas, calm streams, the tantalising drop of water on our lip – by which our imagination seeks to prefigure the infinite possibilities of the uterus. To speak is to become witness to the oceanic, symphonic and yet elusive presence of the procreative site. (No wonder that Shakespeare should have been enraptured by water, music – and language.)

All this has been long understood. Nineteenth-century psychologists had a dab hand at analysing language transpositions. Coleridge, who knew all that presumably needs to be known about the liquid flow of language and music, tells in a celebrated passage in *Biographia Literaria*, of how – on a visit to Germany – he had heard of a peasant woman who had lost all powers of native speech. She had awoken one morning speaking Hebrew.

The extraordinary nature of the case, and the manner in which it was elucidated, became a *locus classicus* for the nineteenth-century psychologist. Sir William Hamilton thought it decisive in demonstrating the existence of a latent mind. Leibnitz had been right after all.

Theories of latent mind suppose – and this one is no exception – that mysterious events in the present can be acounted for by some reference to the past. And so it was in the case of the Hebrew-speaking peasant woman. A young doctor – a precursor of Freud, perhaps – discovered that, years before, the woman had worked as a child-servant in the house of a scholar clergyman.

Her bedroom was next to his study; and, half-consciously, she had listened to his reading aloud of Hebrew texts.

The explanation is moving – at least if we allow ourselves to imagine the child as listening in awe and love to the enunciations of a mysterious tongue. At the same time, it does not do justice – nothing can – to the magnificence of the event that it attempts to explain.

Coleridge accepts the explanation at face value. Yet he, if anyone, should have seen how little bearing it had on the miraculous aspect of the case: the inspiration of waking one morning, bearing the riches of an unhabitual speech. He himself claimed to have had this experience. Whether he experienced inspiration in this way or not is marginal to his having given us authentic proof of the riches that inspiration brings. He claimed to have awoken from a dream and written down its content in the form of a poem, *Kubla Khan*.

Many of us have written down our dreams, thinking them visions, and looked at them on the next morning and found them rubbish. Coleridge wrote down a dream that, on the page, has the power in itself (and for perpetuity) of generating the visionary glow. The poem has acquired the inexplicable properties of language itself – of Hebrew perhaps, the language long thought to precede other languages, the holy language infants utter before they are struck dumb by the need to trade in daily speech.[24]

Each morning we wake with the language of inspiration on our lips – potentially, at least, if we do not betray the inspiration.

Rocking ourselves to sleep in our own pulse

Consciousness modulates. It moves on different levels of awareness. It shifts. It calls on different modes of expression. An important, unexplored psychoanalytic theme establishes itself from the moment of inception, the very paragraph in which you can see the whole enterprise of psychoanalysis coming alive.

Breuer reports that Anna's sleep routines had been disturbed by her need to nurse her father at night. She would sleep during

[24] Coleridge's own father, whom he much loved, was a Hebrew scholar. In his theory of inspiration, Coleridge looked deliberately to the idiom of Old Testament revelation. He was opposed to Greek or Roman theories of inspiration.

the afternoons. Her rest during these times would drift into states of something like hypnotic trance – a getting inside of something.

> After the deep sleep had lasted about an hour she grew restless, tossed to and fro and kept repeating 'tormenting, tormenting', with her eyes shut all the time. It was also noticed how, during her 'absences' in day-time she was obviously creating some situation or episode to which she gave a clue with a few muttered words. It happened then – to begin with accidentally but later intentionally – that someone near her repeated one of these phrases of hers while she was complaining about the 'tormenting'. She at once joined in and began painting some situation or telling some story, hesitatingly at first.[25]

Breuer is impressed by the observation that consciousness is something to be jostled or broken into. 'The whistle of the train bringing the doctor whom she expected broke the spell.'[26]

Walter Benjamin has remarked (in an essay on Leskov) that good stories tend to come into being accretively, by repetition. Old women at spinning wheels, yarning thread and threading yarns: story-telling as a kind of breathing, the yarning and the shearing as emblems for fate itself. Sanity requires stories to articulate lives. Emotions exist in time and fill a space. The mind needs metaphors, as plants need water and air. On some basic level, suspiration and inspiration are one. The unfurling of a story is the fulfilling of a potential. Physical symptoms – it could be all illness – are botched potentialities, failures in mental poetics, unwritten chapters in an autobiography. Out of muttered words, 'tormenting, tormenting', are rocked words and phrases and stories – a psychic cradle in which Anna's cramped and distorted limbs can stretch out.

[25] Ibid, pp.28-9
[26] Ibid, p.39

Chapter 4

AT EVERY MOMENT THE WORLD RE-CREATES ITSELF ANEW

Two's company, three's a crowd. The shock of the mutative is the shock of a third factor – new baby, new idea – breaking in on the security of the self as feeding infant. It leaves the infant within us in states of extreme perturbation: either we will choke or we will continue to breathe and to develop. Breuer is almost annihilated by confusion when he comes close to Anna; but enduring the experience leads to discoveries. In *Hamlet*, and in the slightly later writings of Descartes, mutative anxieties are described against the background of infinite space. It is as though Anna's domestic stagings were to be given a cosmic setting. The man at the funeral, the possible dissembler, transformed, re-appears as the Ghost of Hamlet's father and as the fictive tempter at the end of the first *Meditation*, who places Descartes's narrator in a condition of extreme doubt.

Nightmare and unresolved mourning

Hamlet suffers from bad dreams. He does not tell us the content of his dreams – merely that they are bad. 'Oh God, I could be bounded in a nut-shell, and count myself a king of infinite space, were it not that I have bad dreams.'[1] They sound claustrophobic, uterine, as though the prince thought himself an ancient Greek, climbing into some incubatory place in order to dream. A nut-shell would be infinitely preferable. His step-father, the King, sees his brooding as incubatory. 'There's something in his soul/ O'er which his melancholy sits on brood; and I do doubt the

[1] *Hamlet*, 2.2.257-9

hatch and the disclose/ Will be some danger.'[2]

An incubus is a nightmare in which a devil presses down on you. To incubate means both to press down and to hatch – to procreate and give birth at the same time, often to bad issue. A blocked abdomen can induce nightmare if we think of the blockage as a failure in mental digestion. The girlish prince is pregnant with thought (often stinking, soiling thoughts). His girlishness is hysteric. He would like to get rid of his femininity. Surmisably, he would like to put it into Ophelia – in the form of a being abandoned, of going mad, of drowning: one reason why, in a despairing fashion, he is so cruel to her. (Sarah Bernhardt was to impersonate the prince, Laforgue to write poems celebrating his feminine grace, at the time Breuer was seeing Anna.)

The amount of mental space you have does not (within reason) condition the quality of your thought. It is possible to live like a Renaissance prince – to be without fixed points, a Giordano Bruno, a king of infinity – within the nut-shell of a provincial court. But how? The ancient Greeks believed that if you slept in a holy place your dreams would be purged of 'badness'. Holy places included caves, or shrines to Asclepius, the first doctor, slain by Zeus and brought back to life as a ghost hero.

Hamlet is convinced that the content of his dreams is identical with the sensations we have in life after death. 'Dream' and 'after-life' are two names for the same space. He refers casually to this assumption: so much so, that we might think his audience to have been steeped in the idea. He uncovers a kinship between sleep and death: both are times in which we have dreams. And he puts over the disputable point – that the dead have dreams – as a statement about reality, not as a mild fancy. 'For in that sleep of death what dreams may come...'.[3] According to Tylor and his followers, the ancients believed that the image of a dead father in a dream was no different from the actual presence of a dead father. Both were evanescent. 'It cannot indeed – this airy substance – be grasped or held like the one visible self; and hence comes its name, the "psyche".'[4] Corpses are sleepers who have lost their dream-self.

Dream-selves, divorced from bodies, congregate in the underworld; and in the underworld dream-selves enter into

[2] Ibid, 3.1.167-9
[3] Ibid, 3.1.66
[4] Rohde, pp.7-8

dream categories, by the positions they take up. Nightmares – believed to trouble the dreamer early in the night – gather about the entrance to the underworld, where a triple-headed hound, with six rows of teeth, stands guard. (The ancients appear to have assumed that nightmares were bound up with excessive oral aggression.)

If my father dies and appears in a dream, where does he come from? The dreams of the living are thought to be, not representations of our inwardness, but the arrival of shades who often bring with them anything but the fullness of corporeal life. To dream is to open a window on the underworld – or rather to have the window thrust open before us. We see angels, devils, and the souls of the departed: the beings of those who have no-being. At such moments occurs flashpoint: there-and-then becomes here-and-now.

After we have died, we shall become apparitions in the dreams of the living. We may find ourselves lost, and with no powers of control, in someone else's nightmare. We shall probably find ourselves dreaming dreams of a hellish kind. Separated from our body, we dream the dreams allotted to dead persons. Hamlet suggests to himself that if dreams have the same relationship to sleep as the burdens of life have to life, then dreams are (by this fact) intolerable. The living of life, however painful it may be, is preferable to the pain of dreaming dreams. He rules out any escape from pain through suicide, since our lot in the after-life, painful dreaming, is worse. 'In that sleep of death what dreams may come/When we have shuffled off this mortal coil/Must give us pause.'[5] The dreams of the dead are so terrible that even to consider their existence paralyses action.

A Cartesian might reasonably want to distinguish between the dreams we have when inside our bodies – and the dreams we have when outside our bodies: something like a Homeric swoon. The possibility of leaving our body and travelling about as an apparition of our bodily self is, in fact, accomplished by Hamlet's dead father, a ghost who trumpets a great deal about the anguish of having to live out a dead man's dream.

Hamlet senior is a Cartesian mind, divorced from body (as Descartes on at least one occasion liked to imagine mind as divorced) – tormented by bodily desires and jealousies. Body

[5] *Hamlet*, 3.1.66

haunts him, without giving him its executive powers. In death, he is a little like his son in life, unable to implement feeling by worldly action.

He makes unworldly claims. Divorced from body, he is also separated from his wife (he confuses body and wife a little, like an adolescent). He calls his wife's second husband an adulterer, as though he were still married to her. He forgets that in death we lose marital status. His reactions are appropriate to a living person, a Hans or Goldilocks, who feel pushed out, and rendered semi-invisible, by the birth of a younger sibling.

Drowning

In most murder cases, we find ourselves asking: where is the body? We have no idea where the corpse of Hamlet the elder might be. The problem of the body (invoked by an allusion to funeral meats?) is somewhat hidden from us by displacement: as in Hamlet the younger's ruminations over Yorick's skull and the exceptional amount of time he devotes to the issue of Polonius' guts. The ghost curdles Hamlet's blood with a description of his death pangs. The dreams of the dead are full of bodily yearnings and bodily torments, as skin-enflaming as an Elizabethan swaddling (which kept the infant in urine and faeces).

Hamlet broods over 'the dread of something after death/ The undiscover'd country from whose bourn/ No traveller returns.'[6] The Ghost died without last rites. Presumably, he was not allowed to enter the undiscovered country and kicks his heels in some ante-chamber to hell.

To the living, all deadlands are much the same. It would be fair to say that the action of the play ironically does qualify Hamlet's assumption: a traveller does return from the unreturnable bourn and brings with him discoveries that unhinge his son. (The pun on bourn/born makes us pause. The date chosen to celebrate Shakespeare's birthday, 23 April, happens to be the date of his deathday. Could it be that those who chose the date believed that genius apprehends the running out of its biological clock?)

A difficulty in mourning is that we hunger for the dead to return to us – on our terms, not theirs. Hamlet has to sort out the

[6] Ibid, 3.1.78-80

difference between his passionate filial love and the more sobering assessment required of a father's reputation. He has scruples about his father's crimes, 'broad blown, as flush as May'[7] – and not only because his father died unconfessed. The brother of Claudius was probably as much of a villain as Claudius himself. It is an old story. One tyrant replaces another – and suitably reaches for the first tyrant's wife. Hamlet complains because the courtiers soon forget decorously to mourn the dead pirate; he does not allow them good reason to carouse. Mourning, as a form of loyalty, is a lonely business, maintained against the odds. Hamlet, an only child, feels isolated in guarding a son's love.

His loyalty is put under strain by a grotesquerie in the action. He has put a brave, courtly face on his father's death and has uttered the slightly awkward sentiment of an obituary, 'I shall not look upon his like again.' He is confident in his epitaph – he does not as yet believe that 'the devil hath power t'assume a pleasing shape'. Horatio unintentionally undermines his confidence with an unsuspected comicality. 'My lord, I think I saw him yesternight.'[8]

Hamlet collapses. He is thrown into convulsive doubt. He does not understand the meaning of his intense feelings. He begins, perhaps, to live out a popular and age-old misconception: that femininity is a species of masochism. His response to the Ghost has a tinge of a perverse craving about it, as though he willed the Ghost to destroy him. He sees his troubles as like a sea and correctly enters into mixed metaphor as a means of expressing his disorder. Horatio fears the Ghost will lead Hamlet to walk over a cliff's edge and have him fall into the dismembering sea beneath. Our manner of understanding the fear of this disintegration – the way in which it represents feeling – is important to our understanding of the play as a whole. It anticipates Ophelia's drowning. And in turn, Ophelia's drowning (I would suggest) is an analogue for an experience many women have in labour – of a helplessness in fate, of a giving over to the unfolding of a reality over which they have no control: that may, in its extremity and wonder, make them feel some kinship between birth and madness. Creativity (in other, more halting

[7] Ibid, 3.3.81
[8] Ibid, 1.2.188-9

words) is opposed to complacence. At some stage, it supposes a coming apart, an entering into disintegration, not unlike a drowning.

Deathdays

Hamlet's meetings with the Ghost and his ruminations over Yorick's skull are so different, as pictures of the past within the framework of the present, that we might think they came from different plays. A religious, apocalyptic imagination and a naturalistic, proto-scientific imagination lie side by side, one giving way to the other in the audience's mind, as at the moment when Hamlet returns from England.

Meeting the Ghost is here-and-now, flashpoint, conversion – at least as an idea. The Elizabethan stage did not have the equipment to communicate *terribilità*. And Shakespeare brings out the bullying, terrorising side to the Ghost too well to have us quelled by any claim the Ghost might make on authority. We have to accept, as realised, the possibility that the Ghost might have the power to induce madness. Mourning as here-and-now collapses all sense of past and future. It renders the world insubstantial – truly an underworld of hallucinatory shades.

When Hamlet returns from England, it is as though a storm had passed. The gravedigger, who throws up Yorick's skull, works with real earth. He digs a credible grave. The nightmare, and the cataclysm, have moved away; and he finds a reassuring world refreshed by first light. No *terribilità* here. A real world is about us, of a nature touching the senses: a sustained and sustaining series of natural processes.

Hamlet responds to it as though he were an eighteenth-century gentleman elegising in a country churchyard, fastidious, holding himself back a little from earthiness. His memories of Yorick are warm: the closest the play comes to a naturalistic picture of a father and son together. 'He hath borne me on his back a thousand times.'[9] We wonder whether this is how Shakespeare imagined his small dead son Hamnet, in the sleep of death, as dreaming of him.

The elegising Hamlet is an antiquarian; he has that sort of distancing from the past. The play catches a curious moment in

[9] Ibid, 5.1.180

the development of theories about the relationship of mind and body – and it anticipates at least one future trend. The emergence of history as a conserving and conservative activity, an institutional activity about institutions, something we meditate on in churchyards or Roman ruins or at court (meditating on burial customs, former greatness and courtly intrigue, as well as studying the records) can only be managed by splitting off the a-historical and the apocalyptic into aesthetics, romantic theology and a misconceived psychology concerning madness.

The Ghost carries these split-off elements. He is not so much the disembodiment of an actual father as the ambassador for a fantasticated internality, a creature of our wishes. He performs the same function for Hamlet as Laius and Jocasta do for Oedipus. He might be a presence inside a mother – not so much a dead father (whose life has been spent) as an unborn foetus-monster, or a wandering uterus, magical in its catastrophic influence. The Ghost's appearance is ruinous: it brings down everything with it.

Or so we jealously surmise. As the child outside the mother, we think of the ghost as the foetus inside the breast/underworld, who maliciously contaminates our feeding with toxic jealousy – for where else, we ask in helpless naivety, would these noxious feelings inside us come from? Boundaries break in jealousy. We think that the foetus poisons us; and in a desperate reversal, we hope to poison the foetus. All conceptions of inside and outside give way to an image, in perspective, of a foetus in a breast being poisoned by another foetus in the breast, moving on into infinity. We travel down the perspective to lose our sense of guilt. The jealous feeder at the breast feels exculpated.

The Ghost complains that his brother poured poison into one of his ears while he was sleeping in an orchard. Himself poisoned, he now pours poison into Hamlet's ears: accusations, horror stories about the after-life, that overwhelm the prince. It gives us a clue as to the nature of Hamlet's bad dreams.

He dreams of being poisoned – surely, he acts out the content of the dream in having the actors present the 'dumb-show'. The dreadful act of poisoning by ear is transfigured into a symbolic (and interpretable) action. Put together the Ghost's description of his own death, and the action of the dumb-show, and we have the narrative content of the dream. A 'leperous distilment' coursed through 'the natural gates and alleys' of his body (he tells his son) – 'and with a sudden vigour it doth posset/And curd, like eager droppings into milk,/The thin and wholesome blood; so it did mine,/And a most instant tetter barked about/ Most lazard-like with vile and loathsome crust/All my smooth body.'[10]

Indigestion, nightmare and jealousy stand, as a triad, at the entrance to the underworld. Colic in infants, the posseting of curdled milk, the spasms of indigestion, enact jealousy – a form of poisoning which we would like to think had been put into us. The psychosomatic volatility of jealousy is enacted when a baby spews up stinking, soiling, half-digested milk.

Similarily a skin complaint can embody some failure to feel jealous disgust. (We have bodies to carry the feelings we cannot think, as well as to implement the feelings we do think.) The Ghost's vile and loathsome crust sounds like some form of eczema, or heightened nappy rash, a convenient representation of distressed emotion. Jealousy becomes tangible: decay, abrasion, decomposition; something you can touch or scratch; something that chokes you, something perceivable under a microscope. Its toxicity spills over into Hamlet's bad dreams – but then being intoxicated is his fate.

He is offered a poisoned chalice at the play's close. In its one heroic, truly cathartic moment, his mother takes the chalice and drinks the poison, a futile sacrifice. Saved from one poison, Hamlet dies from another. Gertrude's sacrifice is, at most, consonant with other moves towards redemption in the play. Christian belief has a mother witness her son die a terrible death: the son dying to redeem the mother (and all mankind) from Adam's sin. A variant on this belief would have a mother dying to redeem her son: a familiar notion in former days – when mother and infant went through labour at extreme risk. Birthdays were liable to be deathdays.

Innateness

Hamlet is as shocked by the Ghost's appearance as is Hans by the birth of a sister. Nothing can be taken at face value. Can the Ghost be trusted – indeed, who is the Ghost? Faced by the

[10] Ibid, 1.5.64-73

metaphysical, Hamlet turns empiricist. How can he test out the Ghost's statements as evidence? He sets up a primitive scientific experiment – the 'Mousetrap' play. Then the epistemological question dissolves into another question, the change-about occurring around about the time that Polonius is murdered, the new question being: what value should I give to innate thoughts – ie. to dreams, apparitions and other images that cannot be verified? As Shakespeare's treatment of the action takes on a naturalistic diffidence, Hamlet's questionings acquire a non-worldly, theological vigour.

The innateness question goes through two stages of transformation. It first dwells on the fact that a king can pass through the guts of a beggar. Kings must die and be rubbished in the end; but more than that – the question recognises – we have the privilege to ingest beings superior to ourselves. The foulest of minds, in logic (if seldom in reality) has access to the kingdom of infinity – or to thoughts of the most sublime kind. Something better than ourselves can enter into us at all times. Perhaps they have always been there. Optimism finds its starting-point: in mind, a wondrous world is re-created anew at every moment.

The speculative powers of a historian might be stirred by such clues. Hamlet looks at a skull and wonders what kind of personality (and profession) it once enfleshed. His contemplating of the skull has often – and rightly – been taken as emblematic of the whole play: except that his contemplation is imaginative and not morbid (as it is sometimes supposed) – less a dwelling on death than on the nature of a former life. The Ghost gives us nothing to catch onto; it has no body. A skull is a fragment of evidence, a residue, something to begin from. Hamlet, as the aristocrat-scholar (presumably brought up among the castle servants), looks at the skull, and allows himself to think about the activities of a one-time lawyer or merchant, a member of the new rising classes. (A family he might have married into, if Ophelia had not died.) An archaeology of the mind, history itself, the precious inheritance, is easily enough dug out of the ground – the grave-digger in most of us is careless in our handling of it. Pondering on tactile evidence, imperceptibly allows us a non sequitur: we find ourselves touching on a spiritual otherness. Stones begin to speak. A skull becomes all that it is not: living flesh. Hamlet's ruminations could be as much about the future as about the past. He thinks of other lives, and, thinking of otherness, allows thought to rise out of time. An infant contemplating its mother's full contour might infer whole realms, both past and future: the former procreation and the impending birth – timelessly resolved into one idea.

The epistemological question

Hamlet does not raise the possibility of an autopsy, let alone insist on an investigation. The corpse of someone who had died in the throes of poisoning would (appallingly) exhibit the manner of death. If the murdered king had been buried secretly, the nature of his death would have been guessed at. No rumour of a suspected murder percolates through the court – at least not so far as to Hamlet's ears. He is convinced he acts alone. No one else wishes to bring anyone else to book. We, the audience, may vaguely think of ourselves as some court of last appeal. Our ineffectuality in this regard heightens the sense that justice, as an institution, does not exist within the setting of the play.

The crime has two witnesses. A court of law would find the testimony of neither satisfactory. One witness is the all-powerful murderer himself, the tyrant who does not speak publicly on these matters, and whose confession (overheard) is intended only for God. The other witness is the victim himself – who deigns to speak only to his son and whose evidence, anyway, is suspect.

The Ghost claims to have been asleep when the poison was administered. He may have awoken during the agony. His report of the crime suggests he did not awake. How did he know then that he had been murdered? He might have dreamt that he was being poisoned by ear, and while he was dreaming of his death, was coincidentally – a large coincidence – murdered: a possible interpretation of Hamlet's fear of the dreams we dream 'in that sleep of death'. Or he may claim that he has hindsight. In the after-life, all things shall be known. He does not explain why omnipotent knowledge should be so limited in its power – why he must seek out an agent among the living to carry out his revenge.

Miraculous organ

The play is full of talk. Language and action do not quite connect. Language is seldom used directly, as a means of communication. People speak to fend off each other, to disguise their motives, to gild surfaces or to propose false arguments (even to themselves, in soliloquy). Courtly language has the same function as courtly clothes: to self-aggrandize and to conceal.

Hamlet is the most eloquent of Shakespeare's heroes. The more he speaks, though, the more he strikes us, in some real sense, as muted. He uses talk in a way that suggests he is caught up in some pre-verbal experience. His considerable power in the court is as a dumbness, an anomaly among the chatter, grieving, clowning (the best clowns are speechless, like death itself), inky-cloak'd among the high colour, an embodiment of the equation 'king-clown-death'. If he impresses us as potent, he does so as a silent remonstrating presence.

He describes himself as inarticulate. We may think that he is a clever lawyer, claiming to be too honest to have the courtier's way with speech. But he speaks truthfully. Words become devalued in a court given over to lying, to flattery, to hypocrisy. Verbally, he is powerless. If he speaks out, he does so in soliloquy, confessionally, like Claudius in prayer. He is overheard by us, the audience. We respond helplessly, as any divinity might. We might want to help him, but we cannot. The verbosity of the actors adds to the sense of useless talk. By contrast, the silence of the dumb-show clamours. Dreams speak – often without resorting to a single word, and the dumb-show is like a dream. Words in dreams tend to be used unobviously, to reveal unexpected gleams of meaning that the tyrant in us would prefer to conceal.

Hamlet informs us that a tongueless murder will 'speak out with most miraculous organ'.[11] The re-enactment of crimes, as a means of extorting a confession from criminals, finds its original (I surmise) in a conception of purgatory, as a place where we must be brought to realise the extent of our wickedness – by a re-living of the past. The Ghost puts the idea into Hamlet's mind, by informing him that he has been condemned by day 'to fast in fires,/Till the foul crimes done in my days of nature/Are burnt and purged away'.[12] Hamlet would like to incinerate his uncle a little. The fires would be pointless if the Ghost did not go through some re-enactment of his past while they burnt: the

[11] Ibid, 2.2.598
[12] Ibid, 1.5.11-13

whole enterprise is intended as a painful re-living and regretting.

The laying on of a 'cunning scene' is disquieting. Hamlet's puritanism gets between us and our pleasure. In the totalitarian atmosphere of the court (which Hamlet lends himself to), theatre becomes show-trial. You look for a catharsis – and you end up by being purged. Shakespeare, also, lays a cruel mouse-trap for his hero, by having him (in his sorrow) obliged to meet the impossible challenge of the Ghost.

Mice

Bernardo: Have you had a quiet guard?
Francisco: Not a mouse stirring.[13]

A colloquial nothing, perhaps, or clue to a possible meaning of the Mousetrap theme? We do not know much, if anything, about Elizabethan mouse-traps, so we cannot picture Hamlet's intention. Put together with the 'cunning scene', the trap implies a barbarous representation of female sexuality. Rodents keep being alluded to. The Queen reiterates bitterly (what T.S.Eliot, in another context, was to observe resonantly) that the murdered Polonius can be compared to a rat behind the arras. She uses 'mouse' as a term of endearment.

'– Not a mouse stirring.' Children who suspect their mothers to be pregnant can become intensely suspicious. They look for the least indication of change. Adults in therapy, going through a similar phase, will approach a meeting as though they were tight-lipped detectives. Their senses rake the scene for a good mile around the meeting place, looking for clues – as to what, they are not sure.

Hamlet intends to undermine, and possibly to destroy, the couple on the dais. My conjecture is that he has feelings about a couple that liken it, as structure, to a mother with foetus (the mouse within). The narrative of the king's exposure does not give direct evidence to support this view. However, a scene in another, later play, by another author, echoes the structure of the Mousetrap scene with such fidelity that we might read it as an inadvertent commentary on Hamlet's intentions.

[13] Ibid, 1.1.9-10

Abricocks

Ferdinand, the jealous tyrant in Webster's *Duchess of Malfi*, does not want his twin sister, the Duchess, to have a relationship with a man – if he is not allowed to arrange it. He has his creature, Bosola, spy on her. Bosola is convinced that the Duchess is pregnant. He determines to test out his belief by having the Duchess eat 'abricocks'. If the Duchess eats the 'abricocks' greedily (which she does), she will demonstrate the avidity which Bosola believes generates a pregnancy. Confusing fertility with greed, he gives credence to the ancient Greek belief that pregnant women abandon themselves to 'pica' – as we have seen, the magpie desire to eat extravagant or perverse substances. The desire informs him about the nature of their sexual inclinations.

The foetus inside them, a distillation of their greed, has seized power and now rules over an expansive and expanding maternal empire. The swelling stomach of a pregnant woman, he assumes, is the same as the swelling stomach of someone who eats too much. He is unable to sort out differences in outwardness – and in inwardness. He confuses orifices: vagina with mouth, the mouth that eats the 'abricocks' – like the trap that devours the mouse. He is a Hans devoured by jealousy and gone to the bad. His hatred of women probably derives from a desire to be one of them. He is fascinated by the ways that contours can change. He recalls a young waiting-woman. She had a monstrous desire to see a glasshouse. 'It was only to know what strange instrument it was should swell up a glass to the fashion of a woman's belly.'[14] Contours change because of the glass-maker's breath playing inside them.

He gives the Duchess the 'abricocks'. She promptly goes into labour and begins to sweat, coldly. Terrified, like Claudius, she calls out for lights – as though needing divine inspiration to make some primary definition: let there be light! She is swept out of sight – into an unseen place, into the mystery of the birth-act.

In a sense, Bosola has precipitated the labour by giving her the 'abricocks'. The stigma of conception has moved from one parent to the other. A father, in his lechery, tricks a mother by his offer of fruit. The actual father of the Duchess's child disowns parentage, fearing danger. (He has reason to.) He accuses Bosola

[14] Webster, 2.2.5-10

of poisoning the fruit and of stealing jewels, as though shifting a curse. Like Hans or Hamlet, Bosola is not privy to acts of conception, pregnancy and birth. He infers mysterious processes. Out of a fabric of inferences, he creates a body of pseudo-knowledge. He too becomes a procreator, of a kind.

Places of birth and slaughterhouses reek of blood. Imagination easily confuses outward forms. Hamlet identifies conception with infanticide. He sets a trap for a mouse. He may want to kill it: he also wants to confirm its existence. Testing out pregnancies, predicting the gender and condition of the child, is a primitive sort of science: science conceived of as certain knowledge. The 'cunning scene' has us attend to an act of procreation and knowing; indeed, to identify with it. The king is expected to confess his sins: in the same way, Christian women attend a Churching to give thanks and to pray forgiveness. Claudius' confession echoes Hamlet's wish to mourn at the beginning of the play. Both men hope their hearts will not harden.

Hamlet shares with Hans the presumption that every birth entails a death (the elder sibling's feeling that the birth has killed his heart). He tries to trap the mouse with a cunning scene to ensure his own survival. He hopes that the dumb-show will warn the couple that the foetus is killing him – so would they please kill it?

Ingesting Rembrandt

At the time when Descartes was dissecting corpses in Amsterdam (with an ever-increasing fascination), Rembrandt painted 'Dr Nicolaes Tulp Demonstrating the Anatomy of the Arm' (1632). Seven spectators stand by the doctor, as he demonstrates the arm. All of them are men and all of them are similar in feature. All of them resemble the corpse a little. It spreads before them like an unwelcome banquet. They respond to it with fascination, shock, disquiet, anger, elegaic melancholy, solid fatalism. They seem to be looking at their own reflection in death. Tulp himself is impassive, possibly withdrawn in thought. One of his hands touches the dissected arm with a scalpel. The other hand delicately seems to recoil from the act of dismembering, as though signalling its absence (in kinship) from the corpse's hand. We see evidence of a conflict in these faces:

between a belief in the disinterested nature of scientific investigation and a talion fear at having tampered with a sacrosanct deadness. Looking into entrails tends to spell catastrophe.

Rembrandt does not engender the corpse through resonant paintwork. The corpse is Cartesian extension and little more. Disquiet is heightened by the linear *trompe l'oeil* mode of representation – and by the cool conceit of having the content of the dissected arm look as though it were oozing out of the dead man's insides, like some unlatched concertina.

It has been suggested that both here, and even more obviously in 'The Anatomy Lesson of Dr Deyman' (1656), Rembrandt went to Mantegna's 'Dead Christ', for style and pictorial structure. The appeal of scientific naturalism – strong in the seventeenth century – has us say: this is all there is to a corpse, dead matter, impassive style. At which point, another voice breaks in and demands that we place the experience within some context that allows for awe and terror – even though the impersonality here, and in the Mantegna, keeps channelling us back to naturalistic expectation.

Corpuscular philosophy had become an unavoidable climate of opinion. Rembrandt probably found it uncongenial. But he had to contend with it – as here, with Dr Tulp. A corpse has no part in the spiritual drama of life. It is not like the face of an old man or woman, Rembrandt's maps of the spirit. A corpse can be used – briefly, anatomically, as a source of information. Fundamentally, it is discard, awkward, to be got rid of as soon as possible.

Matter, as an idea in itself, can be responded to in various ways. Decomposition can be a redemptive source for rich and warm painterly textures, as Rembrandt realised, in 'The Slaughtered Ox' of 1655. Or we can think of it as a self-contained activity, a suspended animation, existing out of time: in a milieu of dusty museum-pieces, air too thin to breathe, uteruses blighted by spells. Many Dutch still-lifes, including some of Rembrandt's, have an atmosphere of a-temporal sterility, more inert than any corpse: of water in beakers that lips will never touch.

The corpse before Dr Tulp becomes an icon for a new faith: an artificial and pedagogic conception of death, which the urge towards scientific naturalism insists is the only appropriate conception. It is a pressure of this kind, as well as a need to be distinct and clear, that moves us into Cartesian dualism: envisaging body as extension, mind as thought.

The artist, using the new faith as a starting point, has to douse feeling. Naturalistic descriptions of death and of the body-husk tend to be grotesque, if they are not dispassionate and factual. Infused by feeling, descriptions of this type lend themselves to fantastic and volatile representations of the spirit, as in Descartes's description of mind in truancy from body. Reveries about inert matter, if passionate, usually lead (in an un-denominational manner) to acts of resurrection.

The spectators convey an atmosphere of perturbed thought. The corpse emits an atmosphere of brute power, bringing a sense of vivid compulsion to a frigid scene. The source of its power is unclear. Does the corpse carry our fear at the prospect of dying? Psychosomatic transformations intensify, as manifestations of body and mind become absolutely themselves. James Joyce took a religious term 'epiphany' – meaning the manifesting of a divine or superhuman presence – and applied it to moments in daily life when random and fragmentary impressions glow with significance. Theories of momentary revelation can counterpoint the effects of scientific naturalism.

Rembrandt's 'The Slaughtered Ox' is epiphanic. Wending through the brilliant night streets of Amsterdam, we see (in the warm blaze of a butcher's shop) an apparition of multi-hued meat. Of the Ghost in *Hamlet* we had asked: where is the body? In the painting, all is body – a body of paint, in a process of transformation, a body of paint indicating the torso of a beast. The force of the painting only marginally depends on its bringing out an iconographic likeness between the hanging of an ox and a traditional view of the Crucifixion.

Rembrandt demonstrates a flayed beast, a turning of an inside outward, without stirring revulsion or sadism. He frees the spectator from the wish to project badness into other people's guts – so that, for a while at least, he can see what is truly there. The messiness is not a messiness he has put into the inside: it is, he begins to learn, the embryo of an order which he does not yet understand. Rembrandt demonstrates how flesh, blood and fat have the quick properties of paint. His matter is a mode of spirit – in a sense that Spinoza might have recognised. Paint, as substance, has a life in it, awaiting release. The carcass, as substance, has a life in it which we would deny. The carcass does not represent a dying God. Rembrandt frees us from the fear that dead bodies might acquire living faculties: that images of decaying flesh might transform into growing foetuses. The carcass is sufficient in itself, and grows in fulness, in its being what it is.

Matter unsymbolised (i)

An 11-year-old boy makes an inch-high chair out of plasticine. I ask him why he wants to make a chair – and why a chair, rather than anything else. He answers noncommittally. A chair is nothing more than a chair. The idea that an act of making is a form of interpreting has no place between us; it withers in the bud. I doubt whether I actually had the idea (of making as interpreting) during the meeting: that way of thinking – that way of working the mental plasticine – had been withheld from me. I was stupefied; and stupefaction was the only experience that the atmosphere in the room allowed me to have.

We sit side by side at a table. An atmosphere of hesitation between us – impossible to imagine that the careful making of a plasticine chair might indicate something about our relationship. Someone in the room is voiding significance from the mainspring of development: the experience of 'you and me in the here-and-now'. There is no sharing between us. An emphasis on physicality blocks thought and dissociates feeling. A thing is no more than that which we (in good sense) think it to be. The fact that the chair is made out of plasticine – a substance which is not chair-ish – cannot be acknowledged. He chops up the plasticine in an automatic way. He says that chopping reminds him of times when he has played at being cook with his mother. She gives him orange peel to chop up. He thinks his mother does not take his cooking seriously. (He may think I don't take him seriously either – because I cannot understand the meaning of his actions.)

He is small for his age. No one takes seriously his potential for aggression. He conveys no apprehension of damage or possible harm in his chopping up. It carries little or no feeling. It appears unsymbolic and unsymbolising.

(First interjection. The child's parents had separated. He probably could not tolerate the pain of allowing himself to think about the meaning of chopping-cooking: of a couple coming together to chop up a marriage (orange peel/orange blossom?). Second interjection: within weeks of the 'chair' meeting, he began enthusiastically to report his dreams. He became absorbed in the activity of understanding the meaning of his dreams and the nature of their representations. Shortly afterwards, his father arranged to chop off the therapy.)

He holds onto the idea that a chair is a chair with such tenacity that I lose sight of the fact that the idea of a chair is an idea, and not a chopped-up bit of indifferent matter.

An infant holds on to a nipple with such tenacity that we think it holds on for dear life. We may think it cannot let go because it fears to fall to bits. But the boy making the plasticine chair wants things to be in bits, at least in my mind. He cannot let go, in case things come together. The meaning of his holding onto an extrusion is related only by accident to its outwardness (or to the need to classify things by their outward characteristics, as Freud thought). It bears on inwardness. The infant holds on – in order to control life within: the threatening, non-normative, non-sensible, non-predictable condition of experience within the uterus. To insist that a chair is nothing but a chair is to enter into an act of conservation – to maintain a delusional theory of sanity as unchangeability. It is to claim territorial rights over a dangerous zone, a mother's uterus, a zone often identified with the here-and-now. The boy clamps down on whatever it is that generates meanings in the self. He does not allow the here-and-now to exist. His claim that a chair is a chair and nothing else sounds like an assertion of materialism. He presumes that a world of unchanging material things exists beyond the bounds of consciousness. Such an assertion, arguably, is a consequence, and not a source, of the claim that a chair is nothing but a chair. The source is an attempt to usurp a creativity localised in the uterus, and to misuse its powers, by asserting that reality is inert, unchanging matter. The boy blocks an impulse towards foetal life.

Matter unsymbolised (ii)

Another, seemimgly different case throws light on his condition. It concerns a young woman, whose parents (like the parents of the boy) were in the process of divorce. She dreams that she is in a sparely-furnished room in her parents' house. When she turns her glance away from any piece of furniture – and then looks at it again, she finds that it has vanished. She magically relates her powers of perception to the comings and goings of objects. If she looks away, for instance, the pieces of furniture appear to be wiped out.

Her powers of perception are thought to modify the existence of the furniture. There are a number of possible modifications; one of them being that she believes her powers of perception are able to sustain the furniture. She is as omnipotent in her claims as the boy who insists that a chair is nothing but a chair. The God both of them represent is a jealous God who will not brook change – or allow the generation of creativity to others.

To maintain that a chair is an unsymbolisable entity, existing as matter in perpetuity outside consciousness, is to insist that our anti-symbolic view of the world underwrites the existence of a world of this nature. It is similar to the belief that the world contains objects, whose comings and goings depend on our perception of them. The vanishing of bits of furniture in the dream mirrored one of her most cherished assumptions: that she could enter into her mother, and control events, as though from inside her mother, by seeming to vanish into thin air. (Air was presumed to have some kind of aperture in it.)

She had almost died in the first weeks of life – from attacks of vomiting and an uncontrollable diarrhoeia. She was thought to have been 'allergic' to the taste of mother's milk. Whenever she began to recognise herself as existing outside her mother, she felt attacked – as in a dream in which she felt herself to be pecked at by a gigantic bird. In the face of terror, she would retreat into semblances of her mother once more (dreams in which she was lying in pear-shaped swimming pools). She tended to believe that she possessed her mother's inside places, at the expense of a mother who seemed to be collapsing and dying.

Here-and-now

Anna sits in her room with Breuer. The room she sits in is different from the room Breuer sits in. It exists in another house and at another time. Breuer thinks her room existed at this moment, exactly one year ago. Anna walks to a door that does not exist and bangs into a stove whose existence she denies.

Breuer thinks that she would have us believe that the there-and-then is the here-and-now.

The stove bruises her ankle. She might argue against it that the here-and-now need not be physical immediacy. It can be vision (and vision cannot be readily sorted out from states of delusion). Plato's pilgrim found that life in the Cave was one of an unremitting torpor. The sun, burning his eyes, was the experience of an here-and-now idea communicated by other than by the senses. Breuer too recognised that something other than a shock of the senses, an intelligibility, might impel Anna from the there-and-then into the here-and-now. Through an innate idea, he embodied passions concerning a dead father. It was as though the voice of the dead father had spoken through Breuer, as the voice of Apollo speaks through the oracle. But with one important difference: Breuer modifies the tone of the dead father's voice and the meaning of its words.

Blake

William Blake looks into the sun. 'What,' it will be questioned, 'When the Sun rises, do you not see a round disk of fire somewhat like a Guinea?' O no, no, I see an innumerable company of the Heavenly host crying, 'Holy, Holy, Holy, is the Lord God Almighty.'[15]

Blake's sun, like Plato's sun, is index to what we have always known (somewhere in our minds). Its incredible power offers a metaphor for the primordial energies innate to mind – the extent of whose intensities we barely begin to acknowledge. His equivalent to the shadow-play is mercenary calculation, the Sun as shining guinea, a worldly frame of mind, merely reflecting phenomena, unable to understand why a caged robin red-breast 'puts all heaven in a rage'.[16] The shadow-play, mind merely reflecting phenomena, the caged robin red-breast – these are parsimonious images, of the uterus as a prison. The uterus, as unpredictable and inward creativity, is stirred into rage by acts of misrepresentation.

Blake doubts the value of bridging passages between perceptions. He faces extreme juxtapositions: air/Gods; grain of

[15] Blake, p.370
[16] Blake, *Auguries of Innocence*, p.333

sand/ world; puny son/towering Ghost. Anything might happen between moment and moment. There is no legitimate succession in space and time. At every moment, conceivably, the world is re-created anew. Anything can happen in the here-and-now, immersed as we are in a drowning sea of aliveness. Babies at birth, 'immersed in the element', often lose touch with intuition, lose innate skills and faculties for a while, become incoherent.

To be in the here-and-now is to recollect there-and-then as though it were a fiction, the realm of the therapy waiting room (although those who suffer the fictions can find them painfully real). Apologists of the there-and-then deal in alibis. They live justified lives. Someone living in the here-and-now will think of history as a succession of excuses – and hold irrelevant all attempts to account for pastness. From this viewpoint, all pastness is a carapace to keep nowness at a distance.

Accountability lies in nowness. All experience is face-to-face encounter, with something – some unknown variable, sacred imminence imbued with dread. All vulnerability is infantile vulnerability: utter helplessness, utter floods of anxiety. If we open ourselves to the immense forces inherent in the immediate moment, we have reason to fear that we will be blotted out.

Immersed in the element

To describe here-and-now (the meeting with a Ghost, the look into a Platonic or Blakeian Sun) calls for a diction either biblical or psychotic. Language tends to deaden, or to look fadedly grotesque, in any attempt to describe the here-and-now encounter, including transference encounters.

A woman arrived for a meeting in a tormented frame of mind. She believed her left eye was twitching. She felt she had a bolt through her head – and she recalled a story, in the Bible, about man who put a bolt through a woman's head. She thought of three black children in care. The mother was reputed to be psychotic. She was always going away. Her lovers were certainly criminals, possibly murderers. Whenever she came back to the children, she had an extreme effect on them. One would go into convulsions, another would excrete.

I take these thoughts to be there-and-then thoughts that can be converted into a commentary on the here-and-now, and the feelings the woman is having about immediacy. It seems tenable to see me (in transference) as both the man who puts a bolt through her head and the psychotic mother who induces extreme somatised reactions in her children. The mother has intercourse with murderers: presumably, she has penile bolts lodged in her. The intensity of the equation of mother and murderer is such that it cannot be contained – and the mother ejects something of the murderousness into the children.

In the lightning flash of the here-and-now, the equation ramifies; it becomes multi-determined; a uterus in the throes of an activity beyond our ability to be able to evaluate it. The bolt through the head becomes a murderous penis in the mother; a piece of stool thrust out of a child's anus; a bolt-penis-stool thrust into an eye, spasmodically twitching, etc., indefinitely. It recalls the Ghost's horrific description of the states his body underwent at the time of his being murdered (whatever 'being murdered' means).

To explore the equations a little allowed the condition to become tolerable. Mind was less given over to somatisation. The woman was then able to report a gentle incident – terror had been diminished. She was about to leave the building in which her office was situated, when she met an admired senior colleague, whom she hardly knew. The colleague spoke to her in a friendly way and addressed her by her first name. She felt moved – perhaps more moved, she thought, than the occasion justified. In the here-and-now, the situation had improved. She was able to tolerate me as an encouraging maternal presence, and (by extrapolation) to allow the here-and-now mother some relationship with a father who was not a murderer.

Eyes pregnant with a mother's babies

A man in a state of there-and-then tells me of a recent meeting with a group of women – with whom he has a professional association. He had observed among the people in the group a blind woman and two women who were noticeably pregnant. He had been acquainted for some time with the blind woman. He tended to think of her blindness as a hysteric symptom.

He thought of her as being full of hatred on this occasion. He did not consciously relate his intuition about her hatred to any feelings he might have had about the two pregnant women.

We invite a there-and-then anecdote to re-form in the

here-and-now. The matter-of-fact becomes disturbing, a threat to any security that exists between us. I am inclined to think that the voice that speaks out for the present moment can be located as a blind woman in the man who observed the scene. The blind woman in him articulates the moment by saying: 'The nipple-eyes you take away from me become babies inside my mother's breasts. I am blind now and I am filled with blind hatred.'

Another voice, the mother's voice perhaps, answers: 'The fact that I can take the nipple-eyes away from you probably allows that they are returnable to you at the next feed. Your blindness is not organic or irreversable. If I return the nipple-eyes to you, you might (in a moment of insight) allow yourself the biblical rapture of thinking that: "My eyes are implicitly as rich in their insight as the goodness in my mother's breast".'

A tentative conclusion is approached: if I attack the baby in the breast (or two babies, one in either breast, represented by the two pregnant women), then I damage my eyes and diminish my capacity for perception. Conversely, my eyes will be pregnant with my mother's babies. I might be allowed a Blakeian insight.

Creative play

> I saw that I could conceive that I had no body, and that there was no world or place where I might be; and yet for all that, I could not conceive that I was not.[17]

At the time his mother gave birth to a sister, a disillusioned Hans entered into a condition of doubt. He did not turn against the experience. The meaning of the games he later played with his sister focused on birth, on mystery, on a mother's interiority. He was able to enter into creative play.

Descartes and Cézanne

Joachim Gasquet recalls how one day he came across Cézanne seated before the Mont Sainte-Victoire. Cézanne was painting. They entered into conversation. Cézanne pointed out to Gasquet how deceptive the sight of the mountain could be. You could

[17] Descartes (1637), p.101

easily confuse convexes with concaves. Sense impressions are deceptive. Cézanne alluded to Plato's Cave. In painting – continued Cézanne – he sought to find integration, of mind and body. He latched the fingers on either hand together, to demonstrate how he sensed a quite physical co-ordination. The emerging of coherence, in paint, on canvas, he called the discovery of the 'motif' – or motive.

To discover the motive, he needed to uncover (at least to his own satisfaction) the geological foundations of the observed scene. He had contemplated the mountain and found himself dreaming about its Roman past, its classical qualities, its Virgilian resonances. From dream, he slipped back (in thought) to more primordial times. He felt the world to come into being – out of a dance of two atoms. He felt himself threatened by a sense of chaos; he intuited the infinite; he entered into despair. Lost, in despair, he dimly began to apprehend a structure, a geological ossature. The geometric vision became suffused by tender feelings – and by colour, light air. For a while, he was assured of a sense of integration. Briefly, he was able to catch onto some intimation of a 'motif'.

> Outside myself, in addition to extension, figure and motions of the body, I remarked in them hardness, heat and all the tactile qualities, and, further, light and colour and scents and sounds, the variety of which gave me the means of distinguishing the sky, the earth,the sea and generally all the other bodies one from the other.[18]

Cézanne describes a rebirth of the world through the act of painting. The quotation precedes him by about two hundred and fifty years. It comes from Descartes's sixth *Meditation*.

Against verisimilitude

In a dialogue entitled *The Search after Truth*, one of Descartes's characters advises master painters not to try to make art out of the botched work of apprentices.[19] A master painter might reclaim a little from ineptness. He will be unable to transform the painting enough to satisfy expectation. In a similar fashion,

[18] Descartes (1641) p.187
[19] Descartes (1701) p.312.

Descartes's speaker counsels us to throw out our apprentice misjudgments about the nature of the world. We should reconstruct an understanding of it from an entirely different starting-point.

Descartes does not spell out the meaning of his analogy. From some of his views, stated elsewhere, we may infer that he believes the master painter and apprentice function differently: one thinks in terms of a non-representational type of truth, the other in terms of verisimilitude (*du vray-sembable*) – a notion of likeness that gets in the way of our understanding the truth.

The master painter closes his eyes, as it were, to achieve insight. His intuitions are kinaesthetic. The apprentice abandons his eyes to mimicry. He fails to see that consciousness must communicate with some innate idea of coherence – if it is to interpret phenomena. The content of bad art equals whatever it is that dreams (and hallucinations) have in common with the look of daily life: a certain adhesive surface, an unceasing flow of sense data that acts as a thought-inhibiting skin. The sensuous surfaces of life get in the way of us and the truth.

Cézanne swoons before his subject. He thinks of the swoon as feminine. During the act of integration, he feels the heat of the sun to penetrate him. The heat of the sun fertilises him. He gives up definition, in the hopes of discovering the 'motif'. He risks losing everything – he has deliberately committed himself to a mourning process. In a dream, Descartes finds himself blown about like chaff in the wind. Out of helplessness, there emerge configurations – like the whirlwind itself.

Blindness and insight

A young man has come to the end of a therapy. He has entered into a process similar to a weaning or mourning process. He is tormented by the thought that his enemies will crowd in on him – and that he will lose his sight. He is disgusted by the state of his skin. (He has scratched it to the point of rawness.) He worries about the possibility of harming his girl friends and about the condition of an aunt who has gone blind. In the here-and-now, he wants to punish the departing source of nourishment, and (at the same time) to identify with it as an object attacked.

Our final meeting adds to an understanding of his anxieties. He had been listening to the radio programme 'Desert Island

Discs'. The guest on the programme had been a writer who had gone blind. The writer had described how he had been operated on for the blindness. After the operation, he was told that the prognosis was grave. He had been filled with despair. He had turned on the radio by his hospital bed.

He realised that he was listening to a Housewife's-Choice type of programme. He felt contemptuous. He had been about to turn the radio off, when the announcer said that the next record – which had been asked for by a housewife from Liverpool – was a piece by J.S.Bach for piano and flute. He paused for a moment. The music began. He felt moved. He became aware that his despair had begun to recede.

The patient said he had been to Petty France today to have his passport renewed. He wondered how he would feel in ten years' time, when he would return to have his passport renewed once more. He had reached a turning point in his life: a moment, too, in which he could think to look over its entire span. For years he had relied on my mental eyes, or insight. Now he was about to lose the eyes. If he could suffer the loss, without giving in to his persecutors, he might undergo some shift in mental dimension – represented by a shift in symbolism, from the optic to the aural (optic=fears about blindness/aural=listening to the radio programme).

An outward-directed man was about to turn inward. Outward-directed thoughts tended to centre on proprietory claims, about gaining or losing things. He had worked on loaned equipment, allowing me to identify the therapist's eyes (or insight) with some concept of an external source of nourishment. Inward-directed, he found himself in a different field of experience. He had ingested the idea of a couple – Bach and the Liverpool housewife – a couple that exists outside space and time and observes different regularities from those that the outward-directed man thinks of as habitual. (I would argue that the coupling is necessary: it only seems accidental insofar as we meddle with it, or the music.)

A rich internal centrality modulates our being

Descartes fears likeness. Our senses lend themselves to an automatic use – at a cost. I have to de-humanise myself when I use my eyes to register images as though they were photographs.

I become identified with an impersonal machine. I may submit myself to this identification, so that I can dissociate myself from the acts of cruelty, which I photograph with my eyes, and which I myself may have engineered. The I-am-a-camera claim is one of the strategies of sado-masochism.

In the first hours of her life, a newborn girl used her eyes (it seemed to me) to look carefully at whatever it was that happened. She was intent. Her eyes were focused. They had an intelligent look about them – they appeared to be taking in whatever they saw.

She lost this way of using her eyes. Other kinds of eye-use took over. Her eyes stood out, startled, as though she were pushing images out of them (i.e. hallucinating). She may have been using her eyes to gobble up the visual world.

She had been born – she had been doused in aliveness. Had the shock of immersion induced incoherence? I thought it more probable, in the light of observation, to argue that the experience of being immersed in the element had strenuously begun to exercise her capacity for symbolisation. It seemed possible that she was trying to work out some likeness between the ways she used her eyes and the feeling manner in which her mother gave her the breast. She used her eyes to take in. But she might have imagined her eyes, which are able to stand out, to be like nipples feeding the world. Descartes has a dream, or a hallucination or an experience (we cannot be sure), in which his eyes eject sparks. We feed with our eyes – and we are fed. We may imagine our eyes to be like mouths (often unsteady, anorexic mouths), the entrance to a digestive system.

If we consider our senses to be acting as agents for our internal objects, then there is congruity in our expecting eye function to be interchangeable with other organic function. Eyes can reasonably digest or gobble, put in or put out, pierce or veil, soil or cleanse, clutch or release, penetrate or recoil. Optic metaphors often insist on being taken literally.

Descartes assumes that some innate idea of perfection underwrites the possible truth of our perceptions. The young man leaving therapy found within himself a blind writer – who in turn had found hope through the unlikely conjunction of J.S.Bach and a Liverpool housewife.

A soldier reports (in Shakespeare's *Antony and Cleopatra*) that the god Hercules has abandoned Antony: a loss registered by strains of music drifting away beneath the stage. The sensuous wonder of the music hints at the sumptuous quality of Antony's life. Its passing away anticipates his death. A rich internal centrality (the music) modulates our being. We have no authority over it. Our eyes are pregnant with our mother's babies. Our mother, in having babies, quickens our eyes.

Cartesian dreaming

On the night of 10 November, 1619, Descartes (then aged twenty-three) had a series of dreams. He thought them important and kept a record of them. During the previous days – and much taxed by the effort – he had arrived at certain conclusions about the nature of knowledge, and the method he intended to use in carrying out his life's work. He had decided that he should call all claims to knowledge into doubt. He would clear the ground, in the hope to discover the indubitable – some fact (or facts) that could not be refuted. He believed that if he followed the method he had worked out, he would need only one certain fact, as a starting point, to be able to build a secure and unified foundation for all the sciences. He was convinced that one authority alone should co-ordinate the enterprise: he himself.

Cézanne had wanted to have himself re-formed by the world so that he could be witness to a natural coherence – as it emerged (in microcosm) on a canvas. Descartes hoped to discover a secure foundation for a world of deceiving sensation, by reliving the first act of creation itself.

His biographer, Baillet, reports that he went to bed on the night of the dreams fevered with enthusiasm. He was *en-theos*, God-possessed: and resembling God in his global ambitions. He later claimed that his dreams had been God-inspired. He went so far as to say that he had been told their content before he had dreamt them. (By whom, we do not know.)

He is walking through streets. Certain shadowy shapes appear (phantoms?): he is terrified. He is unable to lean on his right side. Ashamedly, he turns on his left side (in his dream, or actually, in a half-awake state?). He tries to straighten himself. A whirlwind sweeps him up. It spins him around, three or four times, on the pivot of his left foot. He feels frightened. He is even more frightened by the thought that he might fall at every step.

He seeks refuge in college grounds (perhaps La Flèche, the Jesuit school he had attended). He enters by an open gate. He tries to reach the college chapel: he hopes to pray there. He sees that he has passed an acquaintance, whom he has not greeted. He re-traces his steps a little to make up for his inattention – and the wind flings him against one of the chapel walls.

About this time, he sees another man, also in the college grounds. The man informs the dreamer that if he goes in search of Monsieur N., he will be given something. But what? The dreamer imagines the gift to be a melon – brought to him from some distant country. He is surprised to see that the man who speaks to him (and various other people around the man) stand on their feet steadily. The wind has begun to die down. He continues to bow and stagger as he moves about. He awakes and feels a pain (in which part of his body, he does not say). He is convinced an evil genius is set on seducing him. He turns over on his bed, from left side to right side, and prays to God for protection. For the next two hours he lies awake, in meditation, mostly thinking about the existence of good and evil in the world.

Interpreting the dream

He has the unnerving knack of interpreting his dreams while still asleep. He thinks the wind represents an evil genius. He was brought to the chapel by God. He was unable to find refuge there. The evil genius got in his way – the evil genius threw him against the wall. He thought the melon represented the charms of solitude – quite what he meant by this he does not say. Does he mean masturbation? We might want to draw a comparison between a capacity to envisage imaginary worlds as forms of criticisms, or hypotheses, about the actual world, and an inclination to hallucinate images and scenes – to make up a world to suit our wishes.

He goes to bed in a state of elation; he wakes from the dream in a sober and fearful frame of mind. He had been confident that he could discover a basis for science. Now he has scruples about the conflict between good and evil and about knowing one from the other. He had thought himself God-inspired. In the dream, he finds himself devil-haunted, isolated, a target for criticism. He conveyed such remorse that Baillet was moved to ask whether he had been drunk when he had fallen asleep (it had been a night of national festivities). Descartes, shocked, said that he had not touched a drop of alcohol in three months. Inspiration alone had enflamed his enthusiasm during the previous three days – and communicated the content of the dreams to him, even before he had dreamt them.

The dream is here-and-now, flashpoint, a little like Hamlet's meeting with the Ghost. It puts us in touch, in a slightly tawdry way, with eschatological concerns. Descartes (like Cézanne) wishes to reach out for otherness, for the free-standing, for permanence, for sureness in knowledge – for some conception of the classical. His dream gives him a wilful response. It is baroque, apocalyptic, disturbing, confusing, primitive in its allusions, over-impetuous in its disorganisation. The wind bloweth where it listeth. All certitude, all familiar perspectives, are lost: they might never have existed. He has no one to share whatever bearings he might have had. He is surprised to see other people in the college courtyard standing steadily on their feet – while he bobs and sways in a manner that might have had any reasonable person ask: Are you drunk? – Are you having a mad fit? Within a few years, Sydenham will write to Cole about the mystery of referred symptoms in hysteria and the subterfuges of the body; and Thomas Willis will give the first neurological description of convulsions, hysteric spasms, tics and arcs. We wonder how Willis might have described Descartes's movements in the dream, if – like the other figures in the courtyard – he had not seen or felt the wind. What would anyone conjecture about a man who aimlessly pivots on his left foot, or bows and staggers in all directions?

A voice says: Descartes is arrogant, Descartes is mad, Descartes thinks he is God – it is not surprising that he should feel constrained by polite society. A kinder voice asks whether Descartes is identified with a depressed or damaged object when he drags his feet, or is lost in a manic object when he is pivoted about on his foot. These are conventional voices, anxious to proscribe the untoward. The same voices are raised when Blake informs us that he has been talking to angels in his garden.

The language of inspiration cannot be translated into the language of the conventional. Descartes's bowings and staggerings are emblems for the manner in which a genius talks to himself – as are his hubristic, devil-defying claims to god-status. His arrogance is small, when compared to the impertinence of the conventional voice, seeking to diagnose his condition. The courtiers in the dream, aspects of Descartes's 'conventional' self, seek to play down scandal. To be blown about by the wind is to be displaced – and to lose social and physical status. The world of surfaces and textures and sounds whirls about us, past us, and flies away like a shed skin. The Aristotelian structure collapses. As Cassirer saw, infinity seeps into the ego – and the ego is engulfed by infinity.

Consciousness no longer inhabits places. Descartes describes a hypothetical position in logic; in doing so, he also describes a condition in mind. 'I conceived that I had no body, and there was no world or place where I might be,' he asserts – intentionally or not, putting himself into a madman's position. He adds, with profound emphasis, 'but for all that, I could not conceive that I was not'.[20]

Hamlet's 'To be or not to be' is less antithetical than we had assumed. *Not to be*, having no body or place, is acknowledged as an embattled assertion of *to be*. I exist, in spite of having no physicality or location. In moments of inspiration, you cannot be sure you are right – nor can you be sure you are wrong. Descartes identifies the wind with an evil genius. He may have been wrong; or it may have been a conventional part of himself that made the interpretation. Hamlet was alone in hearing the Ghost's communication – and the wind may indicate an inspiration that only Descartes can be buffeted by. If this is so, then the norm for human aspiration no longer lies with courtiers or schoolmen; and it is not Descartes who behaves abnormally in the dream.

Through unusual body movements, he articulates the freedom of exploratory thought – a type of thought unbounded by considerations of space. He celebrates a new kind of knowledge in the dance of body-in-mind. He is a gravity-defying astronaut of the intellect. He gesticulates a non-representational experience.

It is not he who is unreal – it is the un-named city, the phantom-haunted streets, the college and the chapel in the college courtyard which (in their shadowy nature) are like stage scenery in an abandoned theatre – as the night-watchman puts out the last lights. The polite gentlemen, not Descartes, are the ones who hallucinate. Sensible minds live in a constant state of – if not hallucination, delusion.

[20] Descartes (1637), p.101

Bodies articulate thought: thought finds its expression in body. The conventional and generous (melon-giving) deportment of the gentlemen is compared to dislocated movement, expressive of thought, stirring embarrassment. But Descartes will consciously reject this view. He will speak out against the notion that body movement is a kind of thought. He will write in *The Passions of the Soul*: 'We have no conception of the body as thinking in any way.'[21] He has no conception of body thinking. Also: body has no means of conceiving thoughts.

Spinoza will differ from him, arguing that body and mind, each in their own way, manifested the divine substance. Mind stands amazed at the actions of the body, as body exhibits thought in different ways from the ways mind does. (It is as though body and mind each had a different unconscious, joining each other at some indeterminable point.)

The determinations of body

> No one has thus far determined what the body can do... nor need I be silent concerning many things which are observed in brutes which far surpass human sagacity, and many things which sleep-walkers do which they would not dare, were they awake...the body can do many things by the laws of its nature alone at which the mind is amazed.[22]

For Descartes, mind is angelic: body is machine – a self-perpetuating system. He will insist that bodies are like watches and other automatic instruments. They function properly, or not at all. A watch that runs backwards, or hesitates, threatens any sense that we might have of meaning. The watch analogy – when applied to human behaviour in general – would have us see people in terms of functions. If they fail to function, they become incomprehensible. They are liable to be labelled by an incomprehensible label – 'mad'.

In all probability, Descartes did not have our fear of machines. He, and other Renaissance scientists, thought of the inside of watches as beautiful – and as appropriate representations for the mysterious order of the cosmos. As he grew older, he began to

[21] Descartes (1649), p.332
[22] Spinoza, *Ethics* III.2 (note)

look to the interior of the human body as the source of a revelation that he had once sought to find in dreams.

As a source of truth, he distrusts body. He distrusts the corporeal in every form. He distrusts nature – which is a congregation of bodies. At the same time, he loves human anatomy. He finds the order of bodily structure beautiful. He deals with the conflict in interest by transfiguring corporeal meaning. He studies the inside of dissected corpses in a manner that suggests he is contemplating the architecture of the perfect city (an idealised Rome, perhaps: or the city of God). In the 'Discourse', he writes about the circulation of the blood with the impassioned flair of an architect – and with the kind of attention that he had once brought to the recall of dreams. He observes otherness. He writes about otherness with a feeling that allows us to think of it as being as much of a symbolisation of his life as any other. (He looks into the inside of bodies with the intensity of an infant looking into the breast – for the meaning of knowledge.) He is assured by the order and regularity of this interior. He does not see it as coldly automatic, as the watch analogy might imply. He is reassured by it as he might be by knowing that meals take place at fixed times. Descartes died in his early fifties. By his medical researches, he had hoped, poignantly, to change the tempo of the biological clock: he had hoped to extend the human life span. To compare the body to a watch is to remind onself insistently that a body exists in time – and in time will cease to exist.

He associates body (by likening it to clockwork) to the movement of stars and to the idea of timeless patterning itself. He does not see it as given over to generation and decay: he does not conceive of it biologically. He sees it as functional: an architecture of sluices and vents, neo-classical – if you wish, he anticipates Ledoux's bland moon-like designs for an imaginary sewer works.

Theories of function impose a rectitude on human behaviour that human behaviour does not invite. It can be cruel – as when we apply it to the question of insanity. If something malfunctions, force it back into a correct function (as by electric shock treatment). Assume that you know the correct from the incorrect. Assume that mind should be assessed in terms of equilibrium rather than in terms of its capacity for development – an equilibrium often maintained at the expense of development. Descartes's conception of body as automatic becomes the psychiatric orthodoxy – and it is with us still.

Prelapsarian

Gesticulations and shapes in dreams reveal the thoughts of a culture as well as of the individual. Plato, Aristotle, had been fascinated by the idea of a sphere – and by spheroid shapes. At the time of the Renaissance, a sort of doodling in reverie brings about a deliquescence in shapings. The vacuum (it is feared) might exist; to-be will be swallowed up in not-to-be; the universe to fly apart at the seams.

Artists begin to consider stains on walls, accidental contours, as the gist of inspiration. In a notebook Leonardo, preoccupied with centrifugal and centripetal forms, relates whorls of water to whorls of hair, as though contemplating Ophelia, and the downward spiral of a drowning girl. Descartes postulates a universe whose composition depends on the dynamics of the vortex – a whirlpool (whirlwind) hypothesis that an enraged Newton took pains to expose as false.

Descartes awoke from the whirlwind dream in a dreadful state. Two hours later, after some painful meditation on the actualities of good and evil in the world, he fell asleep again – and found himself entering once more a baroque and apocalyptic (here-and-now) atmosphere.

He heard a sharp and piercing noise. He took it to be a clap of thunder. That was all – that was the second dream. He awoke from the dream into a situation more dream-like than any dream. His eyes were showering forth fiery sparks of such a luminosity that he could see objects in a darkened room. He realised that he had been through an experience of this kind at least once before. Was he hallucinating? He seemed to be malfunctioning – in the way a watch malfunctions. Night (a sensible commentator will presume) is no time for steady thinking. Night is the time when we lose points of sensible reference. Descartes, clearly, has lost all fixed points. And yet it was, in some such obscure setting as this, without compass, without maps – the universe seeming to fly apart – that Cézanne came to believe that he might seize on the 'motif'. The Renaissance scholar Julius Scaliger (whose views on innate ideas are considered by Leibnitz, in the *New Essays*) identifies innate ideas with *semina aeternitatis*, or seeds of eternity, or *zophyra* – 'meaning to say living fires, flashes of light, hidden within us, but caused to appear by the contact of the senses, like the sparks which the shock of the flint strikes from the steel'.[23]

The young Descartes is interested in images of this kind. He writes (in *Cogitationes Privatae*):

> There are in use seeds of knowledge as in a flint: philosophers extract them by reason, but poets strike them out by imagination and then they shine more brightly.[24]

Mind exhibits immense muscularities: or so thought the neo-Platonist Ralph Cudworth. The uses we put mind to in daily life are trivial and slack in comparison to our mental inheritance – which largely remains untapped. Cudworth, de-evolutionary, believes that man is a fallen angel, and nature a ruined kingdom, hinting at visionary possibilities. Theories which limit memory to passive recall – or perception to acts of automatic registering, cramp potentiality.

Epistemological mimicries are misuses of mind. Human beings are like giants, lulled into drowsiness by a seductive nature. The giant stirs – and seeks to realise himself through the language of nature. He learns that nature has provided him with a tongue inadequate to his needs. He must turn to non-representational modes of articulation. To realise his inheritance, he must turn to the generative powers of symbolisation – in language, mathematics, fiction-making, dreams.

Underlying the view of mind as immense muscularity is an image of mind as uterine, in labour, contracting and dilating, a Platonic interior, a place where Hamlet dreams. One aperture leads to the world that admits us at birth, the other opens out onto an intolerable sunlight: the primal couple comes together in a blinding fusion. Mind is angelic essence, a meteor fallen from a realm that precedes the Fall. Its genetic analogue is preformationism. Adam's semen, the *semina aeternitatis*, contains all mankind. No stray seed of suggestion: the seed was there at the beginning.

Descartes, too, is convinced that 'germs of truth' reside in

[23] Leibnitz, *New Essays* (49)
[24] *Cogitationes privatae*, pp.11-13

mind innately. Truth germs can be intuited aesthetically: in the proportion of the geometer and the architect. In the cave of Asclepius, he finds himself inside an Adamic prelapsarian coitus. His eyes hugely spark *semina aeternitatis* – seeds to father a new philosophy. In the first dream, he had felt helpless in the face of an omnipotent power. The position no longer holds. He is the one now to claim the omnipotence, perhaps delusionally.

'There seems no real room in his system for the concept of learning.'[25] The prejudice that our eyes give out rays of light, eye-beams, is deep-seated – and false as a statement in optics. Is it false as an expression of the belief that inner life, or inner light, spills over and radiates outer life? Descartes was convinced that if we use our attention in a certain way, we will begin to perceive thoughts in our minds that we had not previously realised were there. 'I for the first time perceive things which were already present to my mind, although I had not as yet applied my mind to them,' he writes in the fifth *Meditation*. The things perceived were numbers, figures, movements – 'I discover an infinitude of ideas of certain things which cannot be esteemed as pure negations'.[26]

He distrusts there-and-then knowledge. He has no sympathy with the belief that we might achieve an imaginative identification with the past through the available evidence: the shards, the languages, the half-forgotten institutions, that invite us to conjecture about the past. He doubts the value of all conceptions of pastness, and of knowledge acquired from books or through traditions. He thinks that the study of history should be avoided: it is too much like travelling in foreign parts. 'One becomes a stranger in one's country,' he writes in the *Discourse*, 'and when one is too curious about things which were practised in past centuries, one is usually very ignorant about those which are practised in our own time.'[27] History is something into which you enter and then cannot escape from. Some people – Breuer's Anna, for instance – have a similar fear about the here-and-now. History swallows us up, we lose our powers of judgment.

He thinks the present is a proper subject for study. He admires and learns from men who thrive in kinds of *doing*: navigators, soldiers, watch-makers, scientists (or at least the idea of

[25] Kenny, p.103
[26] Descartes (1941), p.179
[27] Descartes (1637), p.84

experiment – as practised by himself). His contribution to optics and geometry was considerable. He is haunted by the idea of foreign countries and the fear it invokes in him. His distrust of history relates to his distrust of 'placeness' as an Aristotelian concept. He wishes to replace theories of 'placeness' by theories of function. History is a kind of placing; and all thought dependent on place is misleading. Eudoxus, his representative in *The Search after Truth*, says, 'My mind at its own will disposing of all the truths which it comes across, does not dream that there are others to discover.' Eudoxus compares himself to the king of an isolated country – 'beyond his frontiers there was nothing but infertile deserts.'[28] The post-Aristotelian universe, being homogeneous, is the same at every point in space. It seems no longer meaningful to think in terms of fixed points.

He did not live out his theories. Reclusive, introspective, he spent most of his life on the move – travelling through foreign countries. In Amsterdam, where he dwelt for twenty years, he changed lodgings thirteen times, to cover his tracks. He has something of Hamlet's restlessness. 'In the following nine years,' he writes of his early manhood, 'I did nought but roam hither and thither, trying to be a spectator rather than an actor in all the comedies the world displays.'[29]

Decoding ciphers

He dreams. He comes across a dictionary on a table. He opens it – hoping to find it useful. (Without warning our concentration will now be broken. The first book is forgotten.) – He comes across another book, an anthology of poems. He reads in it the line, *Quod vitae sectabor iter?* ('Which path of life shall I follow?'). As soon as he looks at one book, it changes into another. The more attentively he looks, the faster the books transform, one into the other. The intensity of his attention increases – by projection – acts of rapid self-transformation in the object.

The books he looks into (in the dream) are eminently ones to dip into: for tips, recipes, clues or facts of a slightly disreputable kind. He prefers books that you can control, manuals – or books

[28] Descartes *Search after truth*, p.308
[29] Descartes (1637), p.98-9

you can misuse, as magical puzzles, runes, oracular strategies. He does not envisage books as journeys through space and time, nourishing the reader and bringing about a change in outlook. Cartesian texts – indeed the Cartesian world – present ciphers to be decoded. They may turn out to be more convolutedly cryptic than the original code. Possibly there is a right message: but you doubt whether you can discover it. Descartes's prose masks complexity; its beauty is guileful. For him, duplicity informs science and nature. Learned societies should be secret societies. In the *Cogitationes privatae* he writes, 'The sciences are today masked. They will appear in all their beauty once the masks have been removed.'[30]

A man in the dream presents him with some verses beginning *Est et non* – and recommends the verses. Descartes assumes that the verses (by Ausonius) are in the anthology. He opens the anthology. The man asks him how he came by the books. Descartes says he does not know – and he observes that the dictionary has disappeared. It now re-appears, in a different guise. He cannot find *Est et non* in the anthology. He recommends the *Quod vitae* poem to the man. Looking through the anthology, he comes across several fine, small portrait engravings. He says that this is a handsome edition, and new to him. The man and the books vanish.

He attempts to interpret the dream while still asleep. He presumes that the dictionary represents the sciences – and the anthology a union of philosophy and wisdom. He then affirms the special power of poetic inspiration over philosophic deliberation.

Books involute pastness: huge tracks of time devoted to their writing – the writer's history; huge tracks of time covered by the subject matter. They have the property (in Descartes's dream) of vanishing and re-appearing, or of giving up only a fragment of their meaning, in relation to what he says or does. A book disappears – when he says he doesn't know how he came by it; his interlocutor, and all the books, vanish, when he praises the beauty of a certain edition. The actual world trembles on the lip of his consciousness: its comings and goings are dependent on what he says or does. He must walk with fragile step. By its nature, a text available for elucidation contains the past – and

[30] *Cogitationes privatae*, p.5

the future. A Latin poem, written centuries before, gives him clues as to how he should conduct his future career.

A story told about Augustine so resembles the events in the third dream that we wonder whether Descartes was identified with the saint, or (if he had not heard the story) in some similar psychological pattern concerning inspiration and contingency. Leibnitz tells the story in the *Theodicy*.[31] Augustine was in doubt about the truth of Manicheism. He asked himself which side he should join. In a raised voice, he declaimed Ausonius' tag, *Quod vitae sectabor iter?* 'What path of life shall I follow?' At which point, he heard a cry from a neighbouring house. *Tolle, lege*, cried the voice, 'Take, read'. The saint opened Holy Scripture at random and read a passage (unknown to us), the content of which convinced him he should give up the Manichean cause.

He presumes that God reveals his wishes through random events rather than by systematic reasoning. Inspiration is mysterious in its operation – the whirlwind blows where it listeth. Acts of procreation are haphazard. The voice in the neighbouring house inseminates the saint, like a voice crying in the wilderness, preparing the way for the Word made Flesh. A conception by ear. The first insemination prepares the saint for a second insemination – by Holy Writ. Someone inspired in this way owes nothing to reason for their inspiration – nor do they think of themselves as open to refutation by reason.

Descartes concludes that he should follow the path of poetic inspiration. He leaves unresolved, as did Hamlet, the question as to how he will know whether he is inspired by God or the devil – 'The devil hath power t'assume a pleasing shape.'

Beauty

> They say the heavenly bard (i.e. Virgil) set for the phantoms of sluggish sleep a place beneath the elm-tree's leaves, and appointed there two gates. One, which is arched with ivory, ever pours forth upon the air a host of deceptive shapes. The other is of horn and sends forth visions of the truth.[32]

In the realm of images, how do we know the true from the false? A child observes its mother. It scrutinises suspiciously any

[31] Leibnitz, *Theodicy*, p.178
[32] Ausonius, vol 2, p.29

change in her clothing, hair style, make-up. It wonders whether she has taken a lover or, worse, become once more pregnant. Hamlet distrusts pleasing shapes; he believes the devil might have entered into them. Like all dissimulators, he is a prey to the fear of being dissimulated. The decision to stage the 'cunning scene' triggers off anxieties about the devil's powers of dissimulation – the devil mirroring the prince's intentions, the prince mirroring the devil's intentions – in an ever-increasing rebound.

Nothing in the here-and-now is impersonal; not even matter is inert. When the here-and-now provides us with the shock of beauty, we have reason to be disconcerted. Beauty cannot be as good as it looks; it must be some form of guile; or seduction. Both Shakespeare and Descartes created texts of a disturbingly beautiful kind. At times, they must have been perturbed, as well as awed, by the burden of their immense talents – and wondered if they were in the devil's fee. Consider the sequence of projections beginning with Hamlet's 'rogue and peasant slave' soliloquy.[33] The actor playing Hamlet informs us that the actor standing before him (and playing the part of an actor giving a performance – in a 'dream of passion') can feign intense feelings over nothing – 'What's Hecuba to him, or he to Hecuba...?' With every cue for passion, he, Hamlet, must keep quiet, 'unpregnant of my cause'. Unable to be pregnant, he compels himself to be a 'whore' and sets up the 'cunning' scene. He begins to worry about the devil's skill in dissimulation. The King and Polonius try to trap him, using Ophelia as bait. The King compares his plot to 'the harlot's cheek, beautied with plast'ring art'. In the next scene, Hamlet denounces Ophelia. Her power of beauty transforms honesty into a bawd. Through her, he tries to divest himself of the responsibility of playing whore to the King. He rails against her ability to breed, and (by way of rhetoric) dramatises a child's hostility to the fact that women change – often in the subtlest ways – when they become pregnant.

Descartes informs us, in the first *Meditation*, that he has detected many false beliefs in himself:

> All that I have accepted as most true and certain I have learned either from the senses or through the senses; but it is sometimes

[33] *Hamlet*, 2.2.552-609

> proved to me that these senses are deceptive.[34]

Who does the proving? And where does the deception lie? Not, surely, in the senses themselves. My senses are not courtiers; they do not have the capacity to deceive. I can only believe I am deceived by my senses if I enter into a here-and-now understanding of experience and think that some antagonist (implicit in the metaphor of experience as an encounter between two minds) has infiltrated my senses. My touch, my taste, my sight, my smell have been possessed by the enemy and work against my wish to perceive the truth. A belief of this kind might arise naturally in puberty when we are unable to shake off sexual thoughts. But thoughts of this kind derive from earliest infancy – as in the fear that our mother will be invaded by some alien presence. In puberty, the senses seem to have been taken over by an enemy.

Descartes gives three examples of sense deception, so unusual that they tend to disarm the reader. First example: a man thinks he is a pumpkin. Second example: a man unable to tell the difference between dream images and waking perceptions. Third example: a man looking at a piece of paper in his hands as he sits beside the fire. How does he know that this is not a memory or a hallucination? The first two examples disturb us because they present unknowns as established truths. I would dearly like to meet a pumpkin-man, or a man who could not tell dream from waking perception, but until then I feel reluctant – and shall yet override my reluctance – to generalise about them.

The third example has bearing on our understanding of the here-and-now. Descartes sees no reason why we should not think of experience as nowness.

> ...from the fact that I was in existence a short time ago it does not follow that I must be in existence now, unless some cause at this instant, so to speak, produces me anew, that is to say, conserves me. It is as a matter of fact perfectly clear and evident to all those who consider with attention the nature of time, that in order to be conserved in each moment in which it endures, a substance has need of the same power and action as would be necessary to produce and create it anew... the distinction between creation and conservation is solely a distinction of the reason.[35]

[34] Descartes (1641), p.145
[35] Ibid, p.168

In the here-and-now there is no past, no future. We originate in, and are sustained by, something in the experience itself – as by some falsity or truth. Descartes describes falsity and truth in supernatural terms. He sees all experience as being like some encounter with a human being. He has a here-and-now preference for isolates, sports, mutations. He resists the appeal of successionism – the chronological flow of history, the seamless content of books, the naturalistic unfolding surfaces of things, the unceasing business of making up plausible there-and-then excuses, lies, works of fiction.

In a *coup de théâtre*, he turns these dangerous aptitudes against themselves in order to discover a point of indubitability. He invokes a fiction – which may have been given to him by the content of his first dream, the one about the whirlwind. He imagines an evil genius with the powers of a supreme artist, who differs from other artists in being able to make or unmake the world absolutely: and to bring about states in others similar to psychosis.

> I shall consider that the heavens, the earth, colours, figures, sound and all other external things are nought but the illusions and dreams by which this genius has availed himself in order to lay traps for my credulity; I shall consider myself as having no hands, no eyes, no flesh, no blood, nor any senses, yet falsely believing myself to possess all these things...[36]

I recall a man whose so-called closest friend offered him a sweet. The sweet contained an hallucinogenic drug. It brought on a state of psychotic disintegration and a physical incapacity that lasted for about two hours. During this time, the man thought he was lost forever in a nightmare. Anyone, or anything, could have assaulted him. The idea of the evil genius raises this sort of threat – to exist without being able to live. It lies at the chilled heart of the mutative experience; it is the moment of mutation itself.

The evil genius puts the self into a logical position where mind can find no reference point for itself in body – in effect, the self finds itself in the same position theoretically as the pumpkin man. The pumpkin man denies the existence of his actual human body (which continues to exist in spite of his denial). In

[36] Ibid, p.148

place of a body, he has the embodying projection of the thought, 'I am a pumpkin.' He finds meaningless the question: 'What does it feel like to have an invisible rind?'

The powers of the evil genius are limited. He cannot dissolve the real world; he can only produce the delusion of its dissolution in the mind of the narrator. He is a fiction – imbued with all the dreadful force of human omnipotence. He is a logical operation intended to help the narrator separate out the sensible from the intelligible. He operates by making fictions of an overwhelming kind. He is not God-like, since God (according to Descartes) is no man's fiction. God is not available to the inordinate powers of human transformation. Men make fictions. God does not make fictions. He creates – and his creativity occurs whether we believe in it or not.

'I am looking at my hands.' The evil genius answers: 'You are deceived. You have no hands. What you see is a deception.' We have no power to refute the evil genius. As he challenges each of our commonsense assumptions, we are gradually pushed back into a last-ditch proposition. We assert that if the evil genius does not grant us the right of being conscious, then he will destroy everything, including our relationship with him. He will therefore lose his powers over us. He can only continue to enthrall us by granting us the slight concession of our having a consciousness. In doing so (Descartes believes), he gives away everything. From this slight point, and by stages, we discover confidence in the being of the natural world.

Being baffled by the meaning of experiences which have no context is different from trying to conceive of experiences which are beyond the scope of imagination, although we may find metaphors for extreme states of mind – like thinking I am a pumpkin – appropriate to our being able to appreciate spaceless and timeless thoughts. I do not know what it is to become a pumpkin, but my imagining of it puts me into a frame of mind in which I lose bearings – and become aware of how adhesive and repellent is the *trompe l'oeil*, which Descartes called verisimilitude. (In this sense, the present-day Cartesian will find all photographic reproduction vacuous.) Dream images, hallucinations, delusions and *trompe-l'oeil* art have – in common – a quality of feigning a likeness. They give us a deluded impression of knowing where we are. They are examples of the mind's capacity to clone appearances – in the service of self-deception.

Idea and representation

In dreams we can find ourselves isolated from other modes of awareness. An unfamiliar and disturbing painting, if we cannot ignore its presence, will seem to take us over and to estrange us from familiar points of reference. We may be driven into saying, as Descartes does, that the painter uses colours we have long known – as in the case of that patch of red. We mislead ourselves: the patch of red in this context is no longer the idea of the colour we have cherished. It has been transformed by its context.

Verisimilitude is globally invasive: it can swell up and possess us. Jean-Paul Sartre's disgust at the adhesive nature of surfaces (as described in his novel *La Nausée*) is Cartesian in inclination – as is his concern with the theme of being and nothingness (a distinction that engages Descartes in the third *Meditation*). I conjecture that Descartes, like Sartre, would have distrusted a kind of art practised in the twentieth century, in which the seductions of surface likeness are used as a trick to shock us into recognizing that we have been seduced. One instance of this is the surrealist sugar cube, made of marble, which feels far heavier than any sugar cube. Sartre denounces the trick in an essay on art and revolution. Hallucinations are made out of stuff like this.

Cézanne and (issuing out of him) the art of Cubism, have a Cartesian inspiration. The Cubist does not confuse the idea of a violin as a three-dimensional presence with some mimicry of three-dimensionality. The idea is clearly an idea in two dimensions. It is demarcated from volin textures and bits – which often are presented in the picture as actual stuffs. A Cubist work of art does not rely on verisimilitude.

Descartes's belief that a patch of red paint should remain indomitably a patch of red paint, whatever the transformations in meaning on the canvas surface, is a tenet of the modernist aesthetic. He has not been acknowledged as one of its originators.

Misrepresentation and murder

The meeting with the evil genius is flashpoint. It is comparable, as a type of fiction, to the dingy theatricality of Hamlet's meeting with the mad-inducing Ghost. Here-and-now meetings bring about a loss of all history, all recognition. The baby looks into its mother's eyes and cannot find its own reflection. 'No hands, no eyes, no flesh, no blood, nor any senses...' Charcot recalls a man who looked into a mirror and could not make sense of his own reflection. Visiting his native city (Paris), he believed he had never been there before. The evil genius appears to us at some crucial moment of hiatus, when we are filled with distrust at the failing regularities of the world. He disorientates us in regard to our understanding of the object that feeds us. He destroys all indicators. He is the stranger at the funeral who says that the dead man is not our father.

He is the here-and-now antagonist who destroys definitions. Who I am, and whomever it is I meet, and whatever it is I shall become, are labile identities. We have no guarantee that we will find some defining 'motif' or Cartesian God. Meaning disappears from memories, maps, dictionaries. Past and future are voided.

Our fear at becoming incoherent is added to by the fear that the friendly antagonist, who criticised definitions, should now turn out to be a committed liar – lying being, I would suggest, a mental equivalent for the wish to commit acts of infanticide. Truth, like pity, is a naked, newborn babe.

A dream brought home to me the severity of the lying assault. The woman who dreamt it found that she was looking down at her legs – she was sitting on a beach, her legs stretched out before her. Each time she spoke, her legs grew more and more swollen and suffused with blood. She knew that the content of what she was saying at this moment in the dream consisted of lies – the issue of blood being related to the uttering of lies. She gave, as an association to the dream, a report that she had read in a magazine. She had read that Soviet troops in Afghanistan were spraying Afghan partisans with 'a yellow powder', which brought on haemorrhage. The yellow powder was extracted from wheat that had gone mouldy.

Whether the report in the magazine was true was a there-and-then concern – if possible calling for a there-and-then investigation into the facts. In the here-and-now, the report communicated a truth about a mental state. The wasting of nutriment (of wheat being allowed to go mouldy) gave lethal powers to invaders who wished to destroy the inhabitants of a country. The dreamer had doubts about the ability of the Afghans to resist the invaders. Consciously, she identified with neither side. The dream implied otherwise: her wasting of opportunities in therapy was bound up with murderous wishes against babies felt to be inside the Afghan therapist mother. Her way of isolating herself from the meaning of the attack was by identifying with its target. She was the victim of haemorrhage. Destroyed were certain essential tributaries in her body – veins and arteries: the sluices and vents of Descartes's beautiful city. Destroyed, too, were certain essential structures in her mind – a complex of definitions, references and judgmental dispositions, on which her capacity to develop as an adult depended.

When she had first menstruated, she had feared she would never have babies. She had believed that the menstrual blood (like the haemorrhage in the dream) indicated that her murderous wishes against her mother's babies had prohibited her from ever becoming a mother herself. She would forever be confined to bleeding (and lying). She was desperate. She had little to hold onto – except a lover who willingly acted out her wishes that he should be unfaithful to her.

The Cartesian encounter with the evil genius, as a misconception in the service of exploration, allows us to investigate theories about space and time. It frees us from fixed points. As a malicious misconception – similar to the yellow-powder blitz in Afghanistan – its wiping out of fixed points results in our feeling mad.

Liars – and the haemorrhage dreamer is no exception – cannot see why this, or that, must be as it is. Liars are like phantoms who do not know whom (or what) they belong to – they are like Goldilocks, who thought of her home as a strangers' house and the members of her family as members of a different species. Liars lack the ability to be dependent on other than bad objects. Their condition is different from the condition that faces anyone in the flux of the here-and-now. Treachery is second nature to liars, because they have no first nature.

Chapter 5

THE LEYDEN JAR

Etienne-Dominique Esquirol's impressive psychiatric survey, *Des malades mentales*, was published in 1838. It contains a chapter on post-natal breakdown entitled 'De l'aliénation mentale des nouvelles accouchées et des nourrices' – a pioneering essay on the subject, exemplary in its seriousness of approach, scholarship and depth of reportage. Esquirol gives lengthy observations of how women behaved in breakdown while in a mental asylum. He took most of his notes – which he appears not to have embellished – during the years 1811 to 1814.

> A woman has a good experience in childbirth. The next day she sprays her bed with sweet-smelling liquids; her lochias are suppressed; her milk does not rise; madness breaks out the same day; she does not recover for about ten months; and then only after a bout of para-typhoid.[1]

It does not read like direct observation: it might be a hearsay report, or a quote from the newspaper. He communicates a series of non sequiturs. Perhaps he imagines them to have some meaning in their disconnection; he does not indicate the meaning. We want to fill in the gaps and to feel at less of a loss. Discontinuities threaten us: we look for explanations. He tunes into frequencies inaudible to later generations. What can we pick up now on our sensitive antennae? Aristotle's theory of residues might account for the assumption that the woman was deranged by failures in lochias and lactation. 'Sweet-smelling liquids' alludes (possibly) to the ancient Greek belief that different kinds of smell move the uterus. Failing this type of explanation, we tend to say that the woman went 'mad' – whatever 'madness'

[1] Esquirol, p.120

might mean in this case: a hold-all, perhaps, for any type of startling incongruity.

Five other cases he clusters together. They are similar to the first one in their discontinuity:

> A woman gave birth one evening. The next day, her husband threw a bucket of water over her. She went mad – she never recovered.
>
> A girl, aged eighteen, became pregnant. She somehow managed to conceal the pregnancy from her parents. She gave birth to her child in an attic – during very cold weather. She had to climb a long flight of stairs to reach the attic. Her periods did not return. She went mad. She recovered after a year; and her periods began once more.
>
> A woman feeding her baby at the breast was frightened by a storm. She began to run; she was agitated; she grew over-heated. She waded across a river: the water came up to her knees. Her supply of milk dried up. She is now in a permanent state of melancholia.
>
> A mother feeding her child was startled by a clap of thunder. Her milk dried up. She lost her reason.[2]

They are all tragically catastrophic. Or rather they are not tragic in the strict, Aristotelian sense. They do not stir pity or terror. They leave us distanced from the condition of being alienated. They do not draw us into the heart of inconsequence – or invite us to take discontinuity seriously, as an alternative to our usual intuitions concerning space, time and the order of experience. They put pressure on us to believe that feelings are somehow determined. We have to work against a matter-of-fact tone to realise that their discontinuity puts us in touch with a permanent sense of puzzling discontinuity in ourselves – which we usually manage to avoid, in part through our thinking ourselves able to trust (misguidedly) in the truthfulness of memory. Esquirol is writing about something that he finds disquieting and wishes to keep at some distance from himself. He wants to dissociate it from his understanding of what it means to be a human being.

We cannot avoid discontinuity entirely. It surfaces in our dreams. In dreams, we unquestioningly accept an often cryptic syntax as the idiom of a language long ours and usually

[2] Ibid, p.120

suppressed. As in dreams, anything might happen at times of birth and death. We become credulous – we fail to ask questions. We do not know why the husband threw a bucket of water over his wife. Esquirol does not say why. He implies that breakdown is a familial, social, even climatic conspiracy. His impassive tone is weighty with implications that we cannot work out. In spite of himself, he communicates a sense of the random; he is an unwitting agent for the Id. He does not appear to design the order in which he puts together his notes. There is little narrative and the order is non metaphoric, a placing together of unreflecting surfaces. Sharp incongruities, one after the other, are the hallmark of his style. He looks at his patients as the editor of a newspaper might look at the world – as a series of bulletins, whose impact as truth is increased by the incongruity of juxtaposition. The world is thought to be true if it is seen to be made up of discrete bits, related to each other without any conscious meaning.

Only a literalist (a madman or a literary critic, perhaps) would read the page of a newspaper for its presumed coherence – and stumble on the truth that with the passing of time, the pages in a newspaper do seem to become stylistically coherent, in the same way as dreams do. We think about the world, and select its facts, in a way that with the passing of time appears dated and eccentric – and consistent.

'A mother feeding her baby was startled by a clap of thunder. Her milk dried up. She lost her reason' – she is not unlike the mother who fed her baby by a river, was frightened by a storm, waded deeply through the water and found that her milk had dried up. Esquirol presumes the need for thoughts to be equilibrated: abrupt disturbances bring about derangement. He finds a kinship between the need gently to decant thought – and an idealising picture of nature as a non-mutational, seamless fabric. He gives the same value to claps of thunder as to mental bolts out of the blue.

Giorgione

In Giorgione's painting, *La Tempesta*, a woman breast-feeds an infant by a stream. Lightning flickers in the sky. A man watches the woman from some distance: the quality of his watching is hard to define. He might be looking at her protectively; or he might be looking at her dispassionately. The landscape conveys a calm timelessness, Esquirol's conception of nature as a seamless fabric. The woman's unconcealed, almost flaunted breast-feeding, her uncovered groin (inviting and, in the context, inappropriate), the summer lighting (with its dangerous, silent excitement), the man's look – these are unusual elements that draw attention to themselves.

They disturb a reticent and equilibrated nature. They encourage us to wonder whether, in their disquieting difference from the other aspects of the depicted scene, they are intended to set up some kind of equation among themselves. The summer lightning, for instance, possibly reflects the feelings that pass between the man, the woman and the baby. We cannot be sure. A tranquil scene consolidates mystery. We waver in our understanding – between the perceptions of the man and the perceptions of the feeding baby.

Brusque weanings

Esquirol tends not to demarcate different levels of understanding: a climatic occurrence (thunder) an organic change (milk drying up) are given the same dimension as the intimacies of breast-feeding and of going mad. He follows Hippocrates – who did not distinguish climates and environments of the mind from actual climates and environments. The notes invoke Greek medicine. They invoke also the animism of *Oedipus the King*. Wells dry up: people go mad. Natural catastrophes and catastrophes of the spirit are identified.

He focuses awkwardly on his subject. In the aftermath of a psychic catastrophe, a detached part of the self thinks to observe its own confusion; as represented by another part of the self, which cannot separate inner from outer – events in the mind from events in the world. (In the same way, the man in Giorgione's painting contemplates, at some distance, the perplexing fusion of the feeding couple.) Esquirol tends to identify with the detachment in his patients – to avoid becoming lost in their confusion. He becomes lost, rather, in their distancing or callous disregard for their own well-being. He endorses, with some reservations, the theory that failures in lactation induce insanity. He does not go so far as to agree with those of his predecessors (he names many of them) who think that mothers go mad because milk leaves the breast and rises up into the brain. He believes, wholeheartedly, in another theory, widely accepted in his time, if not now – it accounts for many of the disjunctions he describes.

Brusque weanings, he insists, damage both the infant – and the mother. Mothers after childbirth require a period of lying-in (as though the act of birth itself were a weaning). They are prone to any shock, however slight. They must be insulated from any tremor that might upset psychic balance. One in four breakdowns in childbirth – he declares – occur because of post-natal shock: and he adds, almost defiantly, that this has always been known. (The knowledge has been lost since his time.) In Rome, women are kept in confinement at home. A crown, or garland, is placed on the front door to notify the passers-by that the house has become a sacred place. In Haarlem, the law requires that at the time of a birth a notification of the event should be placed on the front door of the house where the mother is confined, so that the police, or the military authorities, will not disturb her by attempting a break-in – for other reasons.

A woman in childbirth becomes a sacred object. She transforms her surroundings into a sacred place. Esquirol believes that she and her surroundings can be easily profaned – as, he thinks, by a husband wishing for sexual intercourse. There is doubt whether she has been set apart to be protected, or in order to protect those who might wish to intrude on her. A mother about the time of confinement is thought potentially to be someone who loses all coherence if intruded upon. The intensity of the fear that she might be profaned is bound up with the fact that birth does entail a violent and often public entry into a woman's private parts. Her insides, as it were, are turned out. Birth comes so close to a socially-sanctioned enactment of rape, so close to impropriety, that it must be veiled in religious interdiction.

The arousal of awe is expedient only in part. It touches on a genuine intuition. In some primitive cultures, a woman is truly observed to swell in charisma as well as size during pregnancy. Scatterings of psychic power unite and enter her forbidden person. She herself will probably feel helpless in the act of giving birth; she may feel she is anticipating the sensations of her own death bed – but to those who are with her, she has become an authoritative presence. Obstetricians, midwives and husbands attend her as though they were courtiers, or initiates in some tribal rite.

The immense powers of nature have imperiously taken over at the moment of labour. Everyone feels drawn to serve them. A mother-to-be is nature's intermediary: helpless, and yet touched by a mysterious divinity. Acts of birth invoke a rightful sense of religious ceremony – as well as summon up the half-lost memory of some violation.

The Ophelia girls

Esquirol proposed that brusque weanings, hiatuses, breakings of the flow, induce the disorder known as madness. He would divert the disorder by setting up special conditions: post-partum lyings-in, or other forms of confinement. He placed value on seeing women in breakdown in a hospital setting – without their newborn babies.

Prisons and asylums of various kinds exercised an unusual appeal at the time he was writing. If criminals were for prisons and lunatics for asylums, then art was for museums and animals for zoos. (The Paris zoo was founded in Esquirol's lifetime.) The dangerous had to be defused, the unclean purified, the eccentric and creative made orthodox and safe. A key metaphor for dangerously creative flare-ups was drawn from a new field in science: that of electricity. If you wished to scrutinise the insane or the disordered or the creative, you would first have to insulate their agents.

In 'Between Heaven and Earth' – a section of one chapter in *The Golden Bough* – Frazer brings together a fine collection of myths about confinement. Doubt has been cast on the anthropological accuracy of some of his sources. Less questionable is the imaginative vigour of the myths, and the light they throw on a nineteenth-century atmosphere which in many ways is still ours. Frazer sees myths as means of coping with moments of mutation in the process of generation and decay. If the crops do not return with the coming of summer, we shall die: we have no reason to believe that causality serves nature. Culture, myths, help us cope with the fear of brusque transition, especially the fear that the food supply will suddenly stop. Esquirol discovers a similar abruptness in childbirth and tries to modify it. Myth-making asserts the value of recurrence, re-birth, timelessness, even of the neurotic state of suspended animation.

Sequestered

> Within his palace the king of Persia walked on carpets on which no one else might tread.[3]

Semi-divine figures carry the life process and, with it, the threat that the life process will stop if they are endangered. In Esquirol's argument, mothers in labour carry the life process. The future of the species depends on them: they carry life on a thin thread. If they die, we shall all die as species. We are unavoidably mixed up with the foetus-potentiality within them. The mother-to-be is besieged by all the threats of violation that the life process engenders.

Frazer does not directly relate the fate of his king-deities – scapegoats like Oedipus – to women in childbirth. He relates them to a cognate figure, the predecessor of the woman in childbirth, generative receptivity at its most concentrated: the girl in puberty, at the time she first menstruates. The parallel he draws is powerful.

Both the girl in puberty and the king-deity are liable to take nature into their own hands. They embody a dangerous potentiality. Nothing, it seems, can stop the girl in puberty from becoming pregnant. She is so fertile that even the wind or the sun might ravish her. She is all waiting for the stray seed and for the generation of the new. She is a threat to any culture which believes in the regulation of nature. If nature is uncontrolled, then nature might ramify unpredictably – or disappear. Potentiality is feared, by the fact that our imagination cannot control it. Girls in puberty must be hidden from the fertilising sun: their feet must not touch the earth. Frazer finds an analogy for the charisma of mothers, emperors and girls in puberty in electrical theory. He compares them to the Leyden jar, a precursor of the battery, whose electrical powers are discharged if it is brought into contact with a conductor – such as earth.

In some cultures, girls are for months suspended in cages (like ferocious zoological specimens) and starved to the point of

[3] Frazer, p.210

looking cadaverous. Girls who hunger to produce babies are obliged to act out some rite (analogous to the murder of a Messiah, crucified, his feet raised off the ground) in which they are identified with a foetus. In ceremony at least, they must be aborted.

Soft and hard

> Were she to eat fresh salmon she would lose her senses, or her mouth would be changed into a long beak.[4]

Her eating is hedged in by taboos of an anorexic ingenuity, and associated with sensations of softness and hardness. The sensations are often eroticised. She devours salmon – beautiful in their penile leaping and fecundity. In her eating (and sexual craving) she loses her senses and dissolves into incoherence. She appropriates penile strength, a sense of structure – of vertebrate hardness, by robbing the feeder. Feeding strengthens her. The acquired strength concentrates into her long beak.

The beak will help her to eat: it will keep her at some distance from her food. It is no longer penile: it has become an implement, a means by which she can reach food which she had formerly been unable to do. She might have become a long-beaked bird, that can probe into crevices that other birds cannot reach. The implement puts a distance between her and the exigencies of nature, it is a cultural object, a precursor of artifical non-organic alternatives to the natural breast, which in time must die: the dummy, the bottle, and their later derivatives – knife, fork and spoon.

Many of the examples Frazer reports are of girls brought into contact with hard objects, like bracelets, belts – or bones. There is constant anxiety (and some allowance made for the fact) that the girls will use the bones to scratch themselves with.

However, they also use the bones as polite eating implements, possibly as a preliminary training in sexual etiquette. The practice of table manners promotes the cultural (i.e. primitive) belief that natural desires, either oral or sexual, must be chastened by ritual.

[4] Ibid, p.212

Blood and stones

Girls in puberty and king-deities are sequestered and tabooed beings. They are related in another way, unmentioned by Frazer – they are aspects of each other. The girl in puberty and the king-deity, if imaginatively joined together, make up the figure of a pregnant mother, or a mother shortly after childbirth.

To envious eyes, the new-born infant is like a pampered and secluded Mikado, Kafka's emperor perhaps. Separate the couple by journeying back in time, and the mother becomes the girl in puberty once more, the epitome of unfulfilled desire and unlimited promise. The idea of her baby is constantly present in her flow of blood, one of the primary energies in the world, powerful, dangerous. On the slightest pretext, it becomes transformed into a flood of infants that threatens the species by their uncontrollability. (They eat all the food.)

A woman's fertility is thought of as a magical power; and the magical power is thought to be at its most intense in the pre-formed state of blood. Legend has it that at the time of her periods, a woman can bring down the walls of a hostile city. If a man sleeps in a place where she has been, his legs will swell up (as though in phantom pregnancy.) Her fertility arouses terror. She is presumed to use it rivalrously to undermine the lesser creativity of others. 'According to Pliny, the touch of a menstruous woman turned wine to vinegar, blighted crops, killed seedlings, blasted gardens, brought down the fruit from trees, dimmed mirrors, blunted razors, rusted iron and brass (especially at the waning of the moon), killed bees...and caused mares to miscarry. In various parts of Europe, it is still believed that if a woman in her courses enters a brewery the beer will turn sour; if she touches beer, wine, vinegar, or milk it will go bad; if she makes jam, it will not keep; if she touches buds, they will wither; if she climbs a cherry tree, it will die.'[5]

At times, Frazer had the glimpse of a more true and more private picture of the young girl. Rather infatuated by her, he saw her in his mind's eye as entering into a reverie about motherhood. Unsure whether her babies would be good or bad, 'she carried four stones in her bosom to a spring, where she spat upon the stones and threw them one after the other into the water, praying that all disease might leave her as these stones

[5] Ibid, p.232

did. Also she ran four times in the early morning with two small stones in her bosom; and as she ran the stones slipped down between her bare body and her clothes and fell to the ground. She prayed to the Dawn that when she should be with child, she might be delivered as easily as she was delivered of these stones. Her seclusion lasted four months.'[6]

Pinel

Esquirol acknowledged his mentor, Philippe Pinel, as the founder of modern psychiatry: he realised that Pinel had improved the treatment of the insane by changing the intention of confinement. A more rational system of therapeutics directed the treatment. Pinel believed in living with the patients and based his therapy on close observation. Hegel put it somewhat differently in his *The Philosophy of Mind*. Before Pinel, doctors had categorised the insane as those who had *lost* their minds and therefore had become inaccessible to reasoning. But insanity did not presume a loss; it was a derangement inviting re-arrangement; and Pinel had shown how it could be done. In Pinel's own words, insanity was curable by 'mildness of treatment and attention to states of mind exclusively.'[7]

Pinel was appointed to be director of the Bicêtre (a mental hospital for males) at the time of the French Revolution. He was a supporter of the Enlightenment, a keen student of Locke's theories on mind, a friend of D'Alembert. One of his first acts on taking up his appointment at the Bicêtre was to sever the chains on the inmates, an act (even then) thought symbolic of the progressive trends of the age. The gesture was Rousseau-esque; it was compared to the act of liberating the Bastille.

Pinel's feelings about the Revolution were complicated. He witnessed the execution of the king – was appalled; and wrote a moving description of the event in a letter to his son (like the king, named Louis). The Revolutionary Committee gave no support to his intended reforms of psychiatric treatment. On one occasion, the 'citoyens' broke into the Bicêtre. They terrorised the patients and smashed up religious statuary in the chapel. Pinel thought the greater madness lay with the intruders.

[6] Ibid, p.213
[7] Pinel, p.108

Asylums keep out some kinds of madmen, not all. Dr Guillotin first tested out his invention in the grounds of the Bicêtre, using corpses from its mortuary.

Sanctuary

Esquirol, director of the Salpêtrière, the mental hospital for women, was as sensitive as Pinel had been to the fact that asylums do not exist in isolation. He was curious about the kind of person who used its facilities and (following Pinel's pioneering techniques) applied statistical analysis to the theme of society and its confinements.

Of the 1119 admissions to the Salpêtrière during 1811 and 1814 (during which time Esquirol kept notes), 92 were puerperal or lactational breakdowns. Sixty of the 92 breakdowns occurred during 1812 and 1813 – when there were 600 admissions. A third of the women admitted during 1811 and 1812 were over fifty years old and so unaffected by the puerperal issue.

Esquirol shrewdly guesses that more breakdowns occur at times of childbirth than his statistics allow for. He estimates that about a seventh of all breakdowns occur after birth among the non-labouring classes. Among the poor, the incident of post-partum breakdown is higher (he argues, controversially, and yet very interestingly), because poor people often have to wean their babies abruptly in order to return to work.

He believes that observation in a clinical setting should exclude many factors. He excludes so many factors that he tends to render his observations unreal. His approach is Hippocratic. He thinks in terms of the theory of residues and of sympathetic influences. He conceives of the mother in breakdown as a type – statistically related to other members of the type. He depersonalises the community of relationships. He does not see his mothers as drawing on meaning from within the context of their families – or from an absence of a family. He does not observe their relationships with doctors, midwives or priests. Few of his observations touch on their interactions with their babies. He does not include cases of breakdown that belong more to the law or popular journalism. The meaning of breakdown is often revealed through a choice of setting. Our illnesses need to speak out – to find a language which allows them to be articulate. You are unlikely to find that language in the setting of a mental hospital.

You might find it, though, in the personal climate created by the individual psychiatrist. Esquirol warms to women. He is open to feeling. Pinel had liked people and begun to understand them through the stories they told; he realised the importance of story-telling as a motive in therapy. Esquirol, inspired by Pinel, feels able to write case notes that are not too constrained. Post-Revolutionary literature is a literature of sentiment: Esquirol's notes bear some trace of its largeness of spirit. He observes that his patients have swollen legs – but he also realises that they fall in love. A woman has gone mad because her lover has been guillotined. Another woman looks after her infant 'avec une exaltation de tendresse infinie'.[8]

Hallucination

I could not know from whence the form came or whither it went.[9]

Esquirol is among the first to to utilise the concept of hallucination. He understands that our perception of nature and our wish for it to be a seamless fabric do not correspond with each other. We see gaps in the continuities, and objects in the gaps, that are without a natural source.

'She hears cries. She catches sight of a surgeon. He is conducting an examination on a woman. He lifts up a hand covered with blood. She believes that she sees steaming blood and intestines floating everywhere.'[10] She (Madame L., that is) takes in an image of the raised, blood-covered hand and finds herself afloat on an image of floating blood and entrails. It is as though she had found the floating image in herself – as a shocked response, perhaps, to the blood-raised hand. Feeling the floating image intolerable, she puts it out into the world.

Esquirol cannot keep the resonances of culture out of his sanctuary. The raised, bloody hand is a neo-classical gesture, typical of the painting and sculpture of his age. We are not too far in iconography and feeling from Jacques Louis David's *Marat Assassinated* of 1793. There is a rumour of murder: of the death (and birth) of parents and of the death (and birth) of infants.

[8] Esquirol, p.132
[9] Descartes (1641), p.199
[10] Esquirol, p.128

The floating entrails are like the flag of liberation stretched out on the revolutionary breeze.

Greek art – lapidary and frigid as interpreted by the neo-classicists, consorts oddly with revolutionary fervour. Esquirol's sense of rationalism, tradition and continuity is also oddly (and fruitfully) brought into conflict with the discrepancies of hallucination. His interest in narrative coherence heightens awareness of the moments when narrative breaks down. The world and nature no longer obligingly fit the pattern. A Cartesian to the extent of being concerned with the clear and the distinct, he is troubled – as Descartes had been – by the fact that the clear and the distinct can be an effective vehicle for delusion.

Kierkegaard

A comparable theory of anxiety dates from six years after the publication of Esquirol's *Des maladies mentales*. Goodness (according to Kierkegaard) depends on continuity and regularity. The principal threat to it is the sudden. The sudden, or demonic, derives from Original Sin, which brought about the Fall from grace and brusquely weaned mankind from the Good. Original Sin is founded in discontinuity. The nature of goodness presumes a capacity for expectation, and expectation comes into being through a belief in continuity. Good people believe that space and time will not collapse on us: there will be no abrupt fall from the paradisal garden.

Kierkegaard makes discontinuity sound attractive, in spite of what he might have intended. He describes mutative states of many kinds sudden shifts into silence or immobility as well as the shock of abrupt change. He recalls the vivid, attractive moment in which he first became aware of the sudden as the demonic. He was watching a performance of the ballet *Faust*. The dancer Bourneville, appearing as Mephistopheles, made his first entrance in a leap that seemed to freeze in mid-air, chilling the spectator's blood. Bourneville conveyed an impression that belied the laws of nature; it seemed to exist outside any expectation of space and time, and to resemble a mental image whose actions can be taken out of nature – and played back and forth under scrutiny. The notion of sustainable styles, of successionism, of deportment, was breaking down: interruption, hiatus, disintegration had become themes for investigation.

Kierkegaard is interested in the same kind of phenomena as Esquirol. His approach is different. He sees the hallucinatory as demonic, as pointing to a certain kind of non-naturalistic reality, an aspect of the spiritual he would prefer to avoid, amazing, an anticipation of the newborn. He cannot withhold his admiration. It requires a great interpreter, Bourneville, to enact their non-representational meaning: the birth of the new and the breakdown of continuity. An artist of Romantic persuasion will argue that hallucinatory images are not errors in perception. They are forms of energy, as informing of truth as treachery itself. The devil, and his art of pleasing, is as real as any other conception of reality. The demonic (or something like it) is no figment of the imagination. It is part of a spiritual order that the naturalistic psychologist in us would deny. A Pakistani mother murders her newborn because she thinks he is the devil.

The sudden is the miraculous, and miracles are the work indifferently of good or bad authorities. For instance, Isaac Babel, working from within a cultural tradition quite different from Kierkegaard's, arrives at the same image of supernatural embodiment – in his story *Di Grasso*. A troupe of Sicilian actors arrive in Odessa. They arouse no interest until a certain moment near the end of their first performance. 'The shepherd – the part was played by Di Grasso himself – stood there lost in thought; then he gave a smile, soared into the air, sailed across the stage, plunged down on Giovanni's shoulders, and having bitten through the latter's throat, began, growling and squinting, to suck blood from the wound.'[11] How shall we understand this violence? A beast is unchained: and the people of the town, overjoyed, acknowledge the representation of the non-representational – by an actor of exceptional being.

Babel's narrator claims that there is more justice in outbursts of savagery than in all the joyless rules of the world. At the end of the story, he is given back his father's watch; he looks out on the moonlit boulevards of Pushkin Street and for the first time sees things as they really are – 'frozen in silence and ineffably beautiful'.

[11] Babel, 'Di Grasso' pp.378-9

Madame L

> She (Mme. L.) hears cries. She catches sight of a surgeon. He is carrying out an examination on a woman. He lifts up a hand covered in blood. She believes that she sees steaming blood and intestines floating everywhere. Intense terror seizes her. She is unable to free herself from phantoms. She realizes she is deceiving herself. She is given foot-baths. One of her arms is bled. Her symptoms grow worse. Delirium overwhelms her understanding. She loses her powers of intelligence. She is no longer aware of being mad.[12]

Esquirol thinks of hallucinations as being meaningful. He sees some point in recording them. The meaning to be perceived is not clear. Mme. L. gesticulates. She is in the throes of a shadowy suffering. Aware of deceiving herself, she is unable to communicate the nature of the deception. It is not certain whether self-deception, or her treatment by the doctors (foot-baths, bleedings), lead to her deterioration.

Esquirol is impressed by the pathos of the situation. He conceives of it as a staging in her mind. The hospital, as setting, becomes a slaughterhouse and a place of sacrifice – a Greek temple perhaps. He and the surgeon conduct an examination on separate women. One looks; the other enters into. Esquirol allows himself to split into a feeling self, identified with the patient, and a more detached self, identified with the surgeon in his executive capacity. He seems to enter into his subject, losing all sense of inside and out, losing the mental space to think. Entrails and steaming blood float everywhere. (The moment of birth is like an act of butchery.) The surgeon in him is filled with distrust at the nature of the experience.

(As the years passed, Descartes became increasingly drawn to anatomy. Possibly, he found the act of dissection preferable to the act of introspection – and possibly, he saw the act of dissection as an image for the introspective process. In the Cartesian view, mind can mislead. In mind we witness spectres and phantoms and forms whose origins are mysterious. Body is more sure. It can be compared, in its precision, to the continuous mechanism of a watch. But its sureness is deceptive. Acts of dissection are not straightforward. Bodies, as well as minds, delude us. A sufferer from dropsy will feel impelled to drink

[12] Esquirol, p.128

liquids; a natural craving; and therefore, supposedly, a healthy one. In fact, the dropsy sufferer is mortally threatened by any desire to drink: drinking will kill him. Descartes concludes: we have as much reason to distrust body information as we have to distrust our thoughts.)

We can read Mme. L's phantoms non-functionally, as we might a poem. Two images come together. One is of floating blood and intestines. The other is of a surgeon examining a body and lifting up a hand covered in blood. Mme. L. takes in through her eyes the sight of a man examining a woman's body. (Esquirol's French text of 1838 does not indicate the part of her body. The 1845 Philadelphia edition, translated into English by E.K.Hunt, gives 'a vaginal examination'.)

We do not know whether Mme. L. took in an image or (deriving a theory of mental function from a theory of body function) believed herself to have ingested an actual bit of the world – as though the world were a solid bit of food, out of which her eyes ate bits, leaving holes. The uses of hands and the uses of eyes tend to be interchanged through the uses of mind. We begin to see that the Cartesian assumption that mind and body can be differentiated from each other, clearly and distinctly, is of limited application, at least on this level of mind.

Her eye movements become lost in the movement of the surgeon's hand. She enters the patient's body. When the hand is removed, her sight is released also and brings with it a conjecture about the inside of the woman's body: not real knowledge – but a kind of stereotype that results from intrusion. Her eyes enter the body as though in travesty of male potency; and re-emerge with what appears to be a bloody vision of some slaughtered child. From Esquirol's neo-classical position, the slaughtered child might be Iphigenia sacrificed by her father.

He examined her for the first time, at the Salpêtrière, on 25 March, 1812, two months after the incident with the surgeon. She was aged sixty. (She is one of a series of extended observations of puerperal breakdown – fifteen in all – that he reports in *Des maladies mentales*.) His notes take the following form.

She was born of a mad mother. Her daughter was mad. Her daughter-in-law died in a state of insanity. Her periods began late. When she was fifteen, they stopped for a year. She fell ill. 'At 16, return of menstruation. Since then Mme. L. has given birth to 13 children.'[13] He does not pause over the issue of insanity in her family or the fact of her having had so many children. His attention is focussed on the nature of her periods. She had breakdowns after most of the births: but she did not stop having children. He does not find this worth further comment. His tone changes when he states that her fourth child died in infancy. She went insane from grief – and had to be admitted to the Hôtel-Dieu hospital for the first time. She was aged twenty-nine.

He associates breakdown with failures in biochemistry – his association of breakdown with grief sounds like a felicitous lapse. Within a sentence, he has switched back to an impersonal Hippocratic mode. Automatic body functions invite an automatic response in the psychiatrist. Suppress the lochia, and blood will rise to the brain, inducing delirium. 'After each consequent birth, shortly after the milk has risen to her breasts, Mme. L. is seized by mania, sometimes with a suppression of the lochia and the menses, sometimes not. The attack usually lasts a year.'[14] He comes close to the belief that bodies may articulate thoughts. He implies, by metaphor, that her stomach pains relate to her feelings. She has the sensation of 'an alien body lying on her rectum.' (The alien body could be a phantom pregnancy, a fear of constipation, a diffuse anxiety concerning some attack by the alien.)

He and she share the assumption that her suffering is inevitable – that she must suffer a breakdown with every child. She would seem to be living out the life of someone else, someone hated – her own mother perhaps. She has no inkling of pregnancy as a valued natural experience.

Each attack is preceded by stomach pains that extend the uterus. She feels an alien body lying on her rectum. The attack erupts with cries and convulsions. Her fear of going insane brings on delirium. She becomes agitated. She is unable to talk or to walk. A thousand hallucinations exasperate her. She hears people speaking whom she cannot see – and she sees strange objects that fill her with terror. She is unable to sleep and she has palpitations. She becomes constipated. During her attack, her leucorrhoea stops and her ozena (a fetid, muco-purulent discharge from the nose) is not noticeable.[15]

Attacks of this type, lasting a year, occur at each birth. She has

[13] Ibid, p.127
[14] Ibid.
[15] Ibid.

the most violent attack at the time of the final birth. She is aged forty-five. Four years later, she suffers from a painful flatulence which distends her stomach and makes it hard for her to breathe, especially after she has eaten. She goes through the menopause without incident when she is aged fifty. Three years later, she breaks down – at the time that her husband leaves for the army. She feels stifled by winds that rise to her head. She loses her reason.

Hallucinations, visual and auditory, afflict her. She has convulsions. Paroxysms build up to a climax every two days – a condition lasting for six months. She is brought to the Hôtel-Dieu hospital for a second time – and from there she is taken to the Salpêtrière, where she comes to Esquirol's attention. He is not able to do much for her. She recovers from her breakdown. Some time later, she lapses into an incurable dementia.

Our bodies speak always

Her breakdowns usually persisted for about a year: in adolescence, Esquirol observes, her periods stopped for the same length of time. Being unable to menstruate – and having to experience the possibility of babies denied – merge together in the state of breakdown. She is no longer able to think or feel sanely. The death of her fourth child and the departure of her husband affect her in the same way. Emptied of goodness, she fills with badness: painful flatulence, alien bodies in her rectum. She gives birth not to life, or death, but to anti-life. Her hallucinations and deliria are like bad conceptions, bad pregnancies, bad births.

Her body convulses into thought. 'We have no conception of the body as thinking,' asserts Descartes in *The Passions of the Soul*. Esquirol inclines to agree. Bodies are automatic: they either function correctly or incorrectly. The spasms and contractions, aspirations and intensities of Mme. L.'s body are disposed of as incorrect. He allows them no other meaning.

The spasms and contractions of a mother in labour are invested with meaning by the fact that a child is born. The present is made meaningful by anticipation or by hindsight. Our bodies speak always, as though in a dance of parturition or decease. Esquirol does not see it so. He has a little Hans kind of blankness. He practises detachment. As a nineteenth-century scientist, he considers detachment a scientific virtue. Detachment distances him from the often painful meaning of actions. He cannot account for Mme. L. Reason makes no sense of her. It reduces her fate to an accumulation of opaque happenings. It diminishes her suffering to states of organic deterioration, fragments of a lost totality – bits: such as you might find listed in an autopsy report. Perhaps our craving for some shared element in all experience stems from a fear that continuities have broken down. We build churches of the mind to hide discontinuity. Institutions and traditions protect us (in part) from abrupt change and loss. A hospital is such an institution.

He sees Mme. L. as a *patient*: as someone who must passively endure the actions of others, even when the actor in question is her own body. He sees her as a *woman*, as someone who frightens him – and arouses his pity. He never quite sees her as a human being. He would seem to doubt that he, too, was born of woman.

He is a pioneer for all that. He explores areas of difference between the sexes. Some of his observations allow for a more felt and extended study; his prose is less given over to taking note of physiological eruption. He writes about women in distress – so long as they are sensitive – with a genuine, if awkward concern. It is as though he believed women to be objects of passion, and compassion, in a way no man can be.

He reports the incident of a woman who, shortly after giving birth to a child, murdered it in a latrine. Reporting it at some length, he then dismisses it, as having no bearing on his concerns. It belongs, as a case, more to the law than to psychiatry. It occurs outside the province of the hospital: it is not available to his kind of investigation. A few years later, in a monograph on puerperal breakdown, L.V. Marcé refers to the same incident. He thinks it helpful to psychiatric understanding. Styles change. Marcé does not see the women he describes purely within a clinical setting or as figures in some frigid neo-classical staging. He sees them within a teemingly Balzacian urban scene. The definition of puerperal breakdown has begun to widen. It has begun to include a familial and social context.

Marcé

J.A. Hamilton – who has extensively reviewed the literature on puerperal breakdown in *Post-partum Psychiatric Problems* –

claims that there is only 'one comprehensive book on the subject': Marcé's monograph. It contains 'the most accurate description of cases'.[16]

Traité de la folie des femmes enceintes, des nouvelles accouchées et des nourrices was published in Paris in 1858. Marcé was aged thirty: he had only six more years to live. He worked for most of his career at a mental hospital, founded by Esquirol, at Ivry-sur-Seine. Its director was J. Baillarger – who had studied with Esquirol. Baillarger encouraged Marcé to take up the type of observation that Esquirol had practised. (Esquirol had died in 1840.)

The incident that Esquirol thought outside his terms of reference goes as follows:

> She does not try to conceal her pregnancy. She openly prepares for the birth (*elle fait faire une layette*). On the day of the birth, she appears everywhere in public. During the night she goes into labour. The next morning, she is in bed – and her child is in the latrine, slashed twenty-one times, probably with a pair of scissors. She is arrested shortly afterwards and carried away from her home on a stretcher. She protests at being put on display before the people in the street. With difficulty she sits up. She keeps saying to those about her: 'They aren't going to harm me, are they? They aren't going to harm me. I've done no wrong. They can't do anything to me.' A few days later, she is questioned. She admits to everything. She doesn't try to justify herself. She doesn't have the slightest qualms. She refuses to eat anything.[17]

No issue of biochemical transformation in this report; no hospital setting. Instead, the contrast of outside and inside, public and private. Public: she feels obliged to bear witness to her actions, to the people in the street and to the police. Private: her behaviour overnight is more inferred than stated, obscure in motivation, possibly horrific, mysterious. Her openness before the birth arouses suspicion by its very ordinariness. It appears both natural and (with hindsight) intended to deceive – candour as the most effective form of duplicity perhaps.

We cannot be sure whether she did the murder. The account of the incident leaves us in doubt. It might be a fable about the nature of a lying-in; the murdered infant being an image in the

[16] Hamilton, p.14
[17] Esquirol, pp. 115-16

mind of the woman resting after labour; a violent speculation, aroused by physical pain, that requires to be defused. A mother might feel slashed twenty-one times in the agony of an unsedated birth. She might wish to blame the baby for her suffering.

Lying-in is like the spilling out of energies from the Leyden jar – the draining away of an intolerable charisma, a freeing of the self from the state of taboo. Confinement, by its exclusion, is a public statement: the mark on the door that warns the passer-by not to intrude. The private enters the public domain – it becomes political, as a kind of impassioned theatricality. The gesturing of the woman from her stretcher is the kind of detail that Esquirol would have been drawn to: its flowing, stylised pathos is characteristic of his conception of femininity.

Pregnancy and the creative temperament

'It is another order of ideas that we must recover,' argues Marcé. He takes seriously the myth of the wandering uterus and modifies it, by relating it to a modern-sounding theory of infection. The uterus precipitates breakdown during the thirty or forty days – when it 'finds itself in the condition of a suppurating organ'.

The Platonists had believed that the womb exerted a sympathy over any organ which it gravitated towards. Marcé emends the theory: he thinks organic explanation marginal to breakdown. He supposes the uterus at most exerts 'an imperfect sympathy'. Its movements and powers do not cause illness; they offer a disposition to illness. He describes pregnancy as an 'intermediate moral state'. It is neither madness exactly, nor a condition of 'perfect intellectual equilibrium' (whatever that may mean – 'equilibrium' is surely a term more appropriate to the movement of a pendulum on a Cartesian clock than to the workings of mind.) The mental states associated with pregnancy are unusual, a cluster of feelings, as powerful, in their influence, as gravity. Many of his (male) predecessors had said that women's bodies, the uterus, femininity itself, defied the laws of nature – as magical and dangerous phenomena. He puts it differently, and with a softer tone. It becomes possible to see the myth of the wandering uterus as a myth about the nature of feeling.

Pregnancy has an emotionality peculiar to itself. All pregnant women have something in common with each other, apart from their physical condition. Their constellation of feeling, and its powerful, barrier-breaking influence on others, set them apart from other human beings. At the same time, the *idea* of the pregnant condition, the phenomena of an unusual emotionality sometimes confused with madness – the creative temperament itself – is a potential that exists in all of us.

What is the *idea*? Esquirol and Marcé attempt to describe it in their case notes. Intermittency is one of its characteristics. Esquirol sees it as a species of madness: Marcé, as an intermediate moral condition. In a sense, they accuse. They make a scapegoat of the pregnant woman, as others had made a scapegoat of king-deities and girls in puberty – or infanticides. The woman accused of slashing her infant to death is not an 'isolated' case. She is exemplary of the extraordinary rite of passage known as childbirth. We can generalise from her condition.

Consider, in the first instance, her seeming openness about her pregnancy. Nothing is concealed: and yet, as Bosola and Hamlet showed us, everything is concealed by swelling flesh and must be exposed by some cunning act: Bosola's 'abricocks,' the Mousetrap play. A pregnant woman is candour itself. Her beauty lies in outwardness, a filling out of natural space (proclaiming inwardness and compactness). She openly communicates with some secret, unseen presence – within herself. She arouses torment. We are tempted to sniff out a rat and to insist that her openness is a duplicity. Occasionally, a pregnancy is concealed from the mother herself, even until term. Esquirol points out cases of this kind. We stand amazed: we sense psychosis. We argue that such cases test any generalisation about some 'intermediate moral state'.

Pregnancy is unusual in its sudden accesses of intense exhaustions and strengths. We doubt whether these changes are purely physical. Many seemingly physical states in pregnancy and post partum probably derive from states of mind. In Marcé's murder case, we are lead to believe that a woman who has just undergone labour is able to inflict twenty-one scissor wounds on her infant. The violence of the attack seems disconnected from our image of her, as lying on her bed in a state of exhaustion.

Her exhaustion mysteriously returns after the murder – to such an extent that she has to be carried by stretcher to the magistrates' office. She is convinced that someone else has done the crime and (probably) has now poisoned her food. The murderous element appears to be split off from her.

Pain

An insight that Marcé finds impressive throws light on the woman's need to exculpate herself. Mothers in childbirth frequently identify their labour pains with the emerging infant. It is thought that the infant does not produce the pain – it *is* the pain. The pain it embodies is life and death. The infant becomes murderer and victim in one – and, also, an anguished source of psychic development. Within such pain, to kill or to be killed become indistinguishable events. The infant is both murderer of its mother and a victim of her violence. Pain of such an intensity seems to exist without motive or cause, in a realm of its own making, innately. It has the status of a Platonic idea: or, rather, to follow closely Plato's myth of the Cave, an intensity of pain opens us to a vision of truth, goodness and beauty – the vision of birth itself.

To make such an assertion is, perhaps, to enter into a *post hoc* idealisation of the pain. Marcé informs us that mothers in labour can find the pain so intolerable that they rip the infant out of themselves with knives. The reality is sordid. Corday slashes at Marat, a mother takes a pair of scissors to her infant in the latrine.

(At about this time, the case of Constance Kent stirs puerperal anxieties in England. An infant is found murdered in a lavatory; its governess is accused of having murdered it – inexplicably. The case has the effect of stirring public interest in the problems of the infanticide.)

A pain at the core of our being, whose existence we may spend a lifetime in denying, releases superhuman energies and lassitudes. A mother who has slashed her infant twenty-one times as a means of relegating her pain to someone else, becomes herself (as she lies on a stretcher) a helpless infant, terrified by the accusing – perhaps slashing looks of those around her.

At some primordial level in thought, the meaning of the baby, as a precious unique object that feeds meaning into us, is identified with the meaning of the feeding breast. It is the idea of the breast that is scissor-attacked. As a ripped-up haunting object, it returns to haunt its attacker – in the form of the enraged compatriots and judges, who accuse her. Ghosts – a murdered infant, a mutilated breast – can stretch out and terrorise a community. They are no different from witches in their immense psychic power. The oscillations in pain during the birth act, the contractions that bind mother and foetus in contract, anticipate the oscillations in feeling that can occur between an individual psychopathology and the frenzies of a community.

A characteristic of the 'intermediate moral state' is the volatility of the pregnant woman's sense of self. Under pressure, she shifts, at mysteriously great speeds, from being identified with an often damaged representation of her own mother in pregnancy – perennial target of infantile jealousy – to being the infant within. She feels locked into a state of extreme helplessness. At the same time, baby-ish, she may become the state itself of inordinate appetite, all mouth and intestinal tract – oral cravings and revulsions of a peculiar nature and intensity.

Eating and phantom pregnancy

A patient ten weeks pregnant is troubled by memories of a recent miscarriage. She keeps thinking of a younger brother who has died from dehydration. She cannot separate thoughts about her present pregnancy from thoughts about her mother's pregnancies of long ago, and from thoughts about her miscarriage.

She remembers a dream. She is chivying people to go to her brother's funeral. She tells them they must not hang about a garden, asking the gardener idle questions like, 'How are the roses?' She visited her brother's grave the other day. It is springtime, and hyacinths and primroses grew on his grave in a way that she thinks he would have liked.

Looking at various aspects of the dream, we came to the issue of some rose beds near the consulting room – did she think there might be dead babies buried in them? She answered, in an indirect fashion, that something had happened to her last night that she had found quite startling. She had been seized by the desire to eat a tin of gooseberries. She had had in mind the thought that babies are supposed to be found beneath gooseberry bushes. She ate the gooseberries – and almost at once her face had swollen up – she described it as an allergic reaction. She was barely able to crawl upstairs to her bed. She lay there in a state she thought akin to coma, from about 7.30 in the evening until about 11.00 p.m. She had felt dehydrated.

She had described the rose beds, which were unwatered, as dehydrated. Her brother had died from dehydration. Had the flowers grown at the expense of the dead baby? If you take the flowers, or eat the fruit, you steal a baby from your mother that turns out to be dead. Superstition claims that girl-foetuses magically steal the looks of their mothers: why then shouldn't a daughter be able to steal a baby from its mother? She had taken the loveliness of her mother – over which no one was allowed to linger (the flowers by the grave, the gooseberries) – and in taking the loveliness had stolen the baby at its source.

In eating the gooseberry baby, she had swollen up, as though pregnant through the appropriation, and then (to avoid retaliation) had entered into a state of deep sleep – in identification with the dead child, perhaps, or with her own mother's heavy sleep after the brusque weaning of labour. The movement from being a daughter, who hates her mother's next child, to being in a state of confusion, both with the attacked mother and the foetus, was exceptionally rapid.

A folklore of the digestive

Marcé was fascinated by the relationship between pregnancy and the extravagant gastronomic desires ('pica')[18] that – at least since the days of the ancient Greeks – have been ascribed to pregnant women. Animals in childbirth sometimes eat their young. Marcé believes that they do so because the young inflict intolerable pain. The foetus is all mouth. It threatens to gnaw away its mother. The mother, identified with the foetus in its universal orality, becomes – like it – a helpless yet all-destroying infant: eat or be eaten. You eat your lunch; and then the lunch in your abdomen, as though personalised, begins to eat you. Wives will devour their husbands, or take a mouthful out of them – in a manner that strains any definition of the love bite. Marcé tells of a pregnant woman who killed her husband in order to feast on his flesh.

[18] 'Harduin concludes, from Pliny's account of it, that it [pica] was a magpie. But we are rather inclined to follow Schneider in referring it to the jay, or *corvus glandarius*' (Adams's commentary on Paulus Aeginata, p.3).

Another story, which he reports as though newly-coined, is part of the folklore of pregnancy. A pregnant woman yearned to bite the shoulder of a certain barber. The husband paid the barber some money, and it was agreed that the wife should be allowed some bites. After the second bite, the agonised barber insisted that she should stop. She gave birth to triplets: the last infant was stillborn.[19]

The wife confuses a desire to bite the breast sadistically with the act of procreation: oral sadism being identified with genital potency. Each bite of the shoulder is presumed to conceive a child (by superfoetation). Marcé thinks of confusions in the same way as the ancient Greeks did. He places all eating disorders under the heading of hysteria: as difficulties related, in some way, to malfunctions of the uterus. He does not tell us what meaning he ascribes to the uterus – we assume he sees it as the site of an immense creative turbulence that can go wrong.

He reports a case from the *Gazette des Tribunaux* of November 1857 concerning a thief who bore the nickname of 'the pregnant woman'.[20] Every time she was caught *en flagrant délit* (as he puts it), she claimed to be innocent. She said she was impelled to steal by the fact that she was pregnant. The tribunal judges found her plea unconvincing – Marcé dissents from their view. He thinks of pregnancy as a kind of madness and liable to heighten any tendency to kleptomania. Characteristically, he looks to the law reports, and not to a clinical setting for his information. The law report story is identical in narrative structure to the account of the woman thought to have murdered her infant in a latrine.

The thief's actions are mysterious. Her pregnancy is like a disguise; she puts it on, as she might a cloak, when visiting a lover clandestinely; she is caught *en flagrant délit*, as though in some act of adultery. She has to account for her actions to judges, not to psychiatrists. She is brought before the people and before the tribunals of commonsense. Her mysterious and private desires are brought into the open and implicitly related to violent sexuality: they are obliged to tally with social expectation.

Marcé uncovers an uncommon sympathy between certain peculiarities of pregnancy and the mythologies of metropolitan

[19] Marcé, p.122
[20] Ibid, p.126

life – both centre on the act of guzzling. He discovers a modern urban interpretation for the archaic conception of the uterus's influence over body organs remote from it. He thinks of the uterus in terms of consumer greed.

Cities are like gargantuan bellies, consuming and evacuating massively. Their inhabitants welcome a folklore of the digestive. Esquirol had isolated mothers as though they were the digestive tracts of corpses: to be investigated post mortem. He had seen them, in the wards, reduced by their isolation. He had seen them as remnants, records, the fragments of history. Marcé looks elsewhere for his evidence. He looks to ephemera: the snacks that pass through the city's gut – the content of newspapers, magazines, posters, law reports, café gossip. The city is all appetite – a ceaseless source of provision for the survivors. It is all biological process. He writes history, in part, by looking into the content of dustbins.

Something persists beyond the circulation of the feeding process: the rubbish keeps throwing up the same stories, the same yearnings, the same doubts. We forget our folkore, as we do our dreams. It keeps returning to us, from some level in consciousness that precedes oral awareness. The cases Marcé reports tend to be sensationalist. You need to shriek if you are to be heard over the city's roar. You need to be all mouth, if you are to eat in such a competitive company.

Vampire

Popular literature in the nineteenth century has a predilection for vampirism. The great repressed was not incest; it was cannibalism, a voluptuous gourmet cannibalism: the connoisseur's gusto with which people seemed to eat everything, including each other.

Marcé recalls a story he had read (in the writings of a certain Dr. Boivin) about a woman who had become an idiot in the sixth month of her pregnancy.[21] She had totally lost her voice. She became repulsive. Other patients in the ward called her the vampire. Whether she had suffered some biochemical failure or some hormonal change is not known. The important Marcé point is that she aroused a distinctive response in those around her –

[21] Ibid, p.50

disquieting feelings and images, confirmed by the prejudice of the community. She had been judged without trial. Her companions thought her a vampire and presumed she was involved – in thought at least – in vampire activities. In the same way as some people will habitually claim that a girl foetus robs its mother of her looks, so they presumed that some blood-sucking foetus inside her had converted her to its own kind. They probably feared her proximity because they feared her bites – they believed they would be transformed into vampires also.

Groups tend to recoil from the unpredictable nature of pregnancy. People in cities tend to be wary of group processes, fearing some sort of conversion to mass dementia. With reason, they retreat into states of isolated suspicion. All forms of change upset them. The group often senses pregnancy fables in stories about transformations. (As in those Hitchcock movies, in which women change their appearances through clothes or wigs; or forever are packing suitcases, a variant on the powerful act of becoming pregnant.)

Stewed prunes

A complicated case of transformation – which Marcé finds compelling enough to report at length, concerns Baudry, a worker who married an eighteen-year old girl shortly after his discharge from the army.[22] The girl was intelligent. Baudry was troubled by some of her remarks. Once – without prompting – she said to him, 'You will die this year, and so will I.'

Marcé writes: 'On 3 January, 1855 at six in the evening, Baudry was having some dinner after his day's work.' He went to the sideboard to get some stewed prunes. He had eaten prunes that morning and found their taste bitter. He was now convinced that something was wrong with them: either they had gone bad – or he had been poisoned. He got rid of them hurriedly. At the time, his wife was three months pregnant.

An hour after the meal, he began to feel seriously ill. He was convinced he had been poisoned. (But Baudry might have been suffering from an acute attack of indigestion; or from some delusion of being poisoned – or he might have projected his own

[22] Ibid, 28th Observation, p.129

killer feelings about pregnancy into his wife.) 'Some time during the next morning, pieces of blue vitriol were found in the pockets of a dress.' Marcé does not say who put the vitriol there, nor why it should be associated with poisoning. William Harvey informs us that he often prescribed Roman vitriol as a cure for hysteria.

The authorities questioned Baudry's wife. Dramatically – over-dramatically – she admitted to a wish to poison her husband. 'Kill me,' she exclaimed, 'I am guilty.' She repeated her confession to her neighbours and to the Police Commissioner, in an act of public contrition that, as always, holds an exceptional fascination for Marcé. The public confession tells us little. She admits to having mixed vitriol into her husband's tobacco and prunes. She cannot say why she did it. During her trial she is assessed as a difficult character, a melancholic and – in flat contradiction to Marcé's view of her – as someone stupid. She looks an idiot: so much so, that children run after her in the street calling her names. Baudry argues that his wife has been unsettled by the experience of pregnancy – he is willing to take her back. The Public Prosecutor is not impressed: he decides he will not drop the charge. Pregnancy, he claims, does not disturb judgment. The jury, after some deliberation, goes against him. It returns a verdict of not guilty.

She is intelligent and yet stupid, a cunning murderer and yet an idiot. We become so absorbed by the changing pictures of her that we lose sight of the fact that the story might have been told by a witness less suspect than her husband. Pregnancy is an experience whose intensities put most of us into the role of the treacherous spectator. Even the pregnant woman has difficulty in maintaining her reality as a possible mother. 'Kill me,' she exclaims, 'I am guilty.' Of what? Of wishing to destroy a husband, or a husband as substitute for an unwelcome baby – is she wishing to block any move towards becoming a mother?

The position of disinterested spectator crumbles easily. We project badness into the mother, or wish to steal goodness from her, like a kleptomaniac or vampire. We become bemused by images of swelling and collapse, by the notion of changing silhouettes. Intelligence deteriorates into idiocy. The spectator becomes immersed in the theme of insideness. Something would appear to be lost in something else – of a differing quality. We suck at the prune – or tobacco-breast – and taste the bitter reality of a rival within, the vitriol baby, snug within the pocket of its mother's dress. A goodness must be stolen from inside the hostile store. Or a poison removed from the friendly place.

The underlying configuration

Hallucinations imply an area of imaginary space in which they can unfold – Mme. L's steaming entrails entail such a space. Marcé provides an example that adds to Esquirol's observation. He considers a draper's assistant, aged twenty-two, whom he calls Ch.[23] She was hard-working and intelligent – and she had never given any sign of mental instability. She has a close relationship with a young man named Adolphe; a seduction, thinks Marcé. In time she tells her lover that she is pregnant. He loses his temper, strikes her and tells her to leave the house. He warns her that if she brings to baby to his house, he will throw it out of the window.

She becomes subject to nervous attacks (*des attaques de nerfs*), violent crises, states of delirium. She had been formerly prone to attacks of this kind – claims Marcé, contradicting a little his earlier assertion that she had always been sane. She goes to stay with a woman friend, refuses to eat anything and has trouble in sleeping. She keeps running away (as though she were identified with the rejected foetus?) She is brought to the hospital on 31 May 1857. Marcé meets her. She looks haggard, trembles violently, moves uneasily. She is cut off from her surroundings. Marcé takes notes.

> At moments, she spoke brokenly. 'Adolphe, Adolphe...He said he was coming...Don't throw the baby out of the window...He will come soon....Adolphe...Don't throw it out.'
>
> She stood up and went to the window and looked out. If you had seen the look of terror on her face – her fear, her gestures in supplication, you would not have doubted that she felt she was involved in some act of murder. The thought of murder, let alone the act, had brought about her loss of reason. She seemed to hear the voice of her former lover. She stepped towards him. Suddenly, she retreated, startled. She began to weep. In a sobbing voice, she said, 'Don't throw the baby out of the window, Adolphe...He has done me a lot of harm.' She pointed to the pit of her stomach. In vain, we tried to bring her back to herself by asking questions and by other means. She remained insensible. She was absorbed in

[23] Ibid, 2nd Observation, p.58

memories of an obsessive nature, in a terrible spectacle created for her by her imagination.

She confuses foetus and lover – as in the remarkable moment in which she asks the lover to be witness to the fact that the baby has harmed her. She points to the pit of her stomach, the place she hates, the uterus – not her own uterus, her mother's uterus. Her uterus, in fact, is the imaginary place in which she acts out hallucinations of her complicity in seduction.

Breuer's Anna had tried to free herself from the tyranny of hysterical symptoms by 'chimney-sweeping', by talking out her past. Ch.'s dramatisations are too voluptuous, too self-pitying, to conduct the work of mourning. Her poetic fails to be cathartic and it clings to inappropriate representations. Anna had insisted that she was living in a room that was the room she had lived in a year before. She was unable to acknowledge change because she had lost some underlying configuration: the core of her psychosomatic problem.

When a mother gives birth to a baby, it is as though everything has changed. The room we sleep in becomes unfamiliar. Our mother becomes the wicked step-mother and the familiar becomes possessed by the alien. Conversely, if you move house, you may feel unreasonably disturbed because the change puts you in mind of a far greater upheaval – the fact that a baby has been born. If your father remarries, you will tend to link your stepmother to your fears of innovation. Bedrooms will become unfamiliar. We are pushed out of some habitual place in world and mind, so that space might be made for the baby. Hallucinatory space is intended to block such space for the baby.

Rooms may stand in thought for a mental space out of which babies, or definitions, can emerge. We are thrown into disarray when we are ejected from an actual room; and into an even greater disarray when we are deposed from some mental configuration – some underlying uterine place in the mind that holds and nurtures images and cannot be approached other than by its representations. The loss of configuration entails that nothing stops the evacuatory slide of images from loved mother into hated stepmother. The slide is so complete that we fail to see that both definitions – of mother and stepmother – cover the same person.

Marcé has some feeling for the underlying configuration. 'She seemed to hear the voice of her former lover. She stepped toward him. Suddenly she retreated, startled. She began to weep.' Her movements imitate an incipiency in thought. Her attempts to think will come to nothing – unlike the germ of thought in Descartes's dream, his seemingly grotesque bowings and scrapings. The crucial event to be nurtured and cherished, the nub of thought itself, will be pushed out of a mental window.

Mime, the 'chimney-sweepings' of Anna O., the identification of the self with a creative mother, all are helpless strategies in the face of a lover who mobilises so overwhelmingly a destructive power. The Adolphe she meets in her hallucinations is a murderousness in her heart that she cannot manage; and she is forced to retreat. She is unable to suffer the experience. Her capacity for symbolisation remains within an emotional orbit that her former lover would appear to have seized as hostage. Little remains for her; and the little that remains is brittle – bad theatre, unyielding to innovation. Mme. L. and Ch. are both irremediably 'artistic' in their choice of imagery: incorrigible actresses, hopeless cases.

They appear to be locked into configurations that belong to someone long dead: it is as though they were inside a bubble that someone has labelled as 'the past'. Marcé looks to the stereotypes of public information for pictures of breakdown. Madness often thinks in terms of fashionable clichés – and fashionable clichés are the archaeological fragments of a civilisation which has never come into being.

Ch. makes some sort of recovery. She is willing to answer questions. She is able to work a little and to think about the past. Her attacks lessen. She is treated with ferrous iron and quinine cordial. She is given cold applications. By 16 June, she has recovered. A fortnight later, she is about to be discharged, and she goes for a walk around the hospital. She enters into a state of relapse. 'She would sit with a look of astonishment on her face that verged on a look of self-abandonment.' She would laugh to herself, without apparent reason. By 12 September (Marcé noted) hallucinations were tormenting her once more. She insisted that Adolphe had sent three men to kill her. One of them was armed with a dagger. (Would this belief throw light on the sexualised look of self-abandonment Marcé had seen on her face? And who had they come to kill – her, or the foetus?) She became restless, could not sleep, was troubled by frightening dreams.

Her illness continued until term. She gave birth to the child in hospital. It died shortly afterwards: Marcé makes no comment. The mother's health begins to improve – 'and by February, her recovery was considered complete.'

As so often in Marcé's view, the foetus is the motive force in the mother's illness. The foetus is like some stimulus to development in the self. Not everyone finds it inviting – some mothers find it a torment. If some mothers think the child *is* the pain in childbirth, other mothers (like Ch.) think the foetus *is*, quite concretely, the illness in pregnancy.

With its death, she is released. Her dialogue with Adolphe implies that she and he wished it destroyed because it threatened to undermine their sado-masochistic alliance. Like all forms of the good, it divides the immature self: shall we nurture or destroy it? She is not able (even to begin) to take on the conflict. The baby dies. It happens to have been more than an intolerable potential in the mind of its mother. It was unique; and it had the makings of a unique individual. It dies without having lived. And it dies unmourned.

An image moving from side to side

A Nigerian nurse tells me the story of her puerperal breakdown. Esquirol and Marcé would have taken note of some of its elements: a sudden access of strength, confusions about the meaning of space, a split-second state of disjunction. At one moment she feels fairly confident; a slight tip, and she knows she has entered into a waking nightmare.

The perceptions of Esquirol and Marcé were bound by the preconceptions of a certain age. They had a certain style: it is not ours. The experiences of the Nigerian nurse could not be securely placed – we cannot consciously know the style of our time. Her thought seemed forever on the verge of the a-temporal and the a-spatial: an aspect of the style of our time. It was like a Cartesian dream: 'I could not know from whence the form came or whither it went.'

A sense of disquiet could be played down during our meeting – on the grounds that one kind of disquiet was inevitable (if not another) since she and I came from different cultures. She was a Nigerian, a nurse and and a woman. In each of these spheres she could lay claim to a knowledge that I did not have. As a mother, she had undergone (or failed to undergo) experiences which were mine only in imagination. What we both sought to deny, I now think, is the meaning of the uterus in her experiences. She conceived of the uterus in terms of mirror images and of self-reflection. It could have been conceived of in a different way: as an otherness, as a spaceless and timeless source of creativity – as indicating the non-representational and the infinite.

It was the nurse in her that spoke when she said that she had been admitted to hospital the day before the birth of her daughter because of albumin in her urine, headaches and other pointers to toxaemia. Her cervix had hardly begun to dilate, before she had begun to experience severe contractions. There was concern about the position of the foetus; and it was decided that birth should be by Caesarian section. She had opposed the decision – in her country women are despised if they do not bear their own children. She believed that bearing a child meant having an experience of bearing it. Her husband had put pressure on her to have the Caesarian, and she was still angry with him.

Her distrust of section had probably been increased (illogically) by a fear of being sectioned in a mental hospital: she had a history of mental disturbance. She feared she would have her baby stolen from her during labour. In a sense, this had happened. She had not been robbed of the baby – she had been robbed of the experience. If some mothers ascribe the quality of their labour experiences (whether good or bad) to the baby, there is no reason why other mothers should not think of the loss of an experience in labour as like the loss of the baby itself.

The theme of something being stolen – or taken from her, kept recurring. Her mother, she claimed, had entered into a state of unconsciousness, shortly after giving birth to her. The mother's state of unconsciousness had lasted, almost incredibly, for a period of three months. 'She didn't breast-feed me. I took milk. And I was left at the mercy of the nurses.' Her mood of torpid (probably sedated) distrust deepened when she mentioned the nurses: after all, she was a nurse herself. Her mood dominated our conversation – except at moments when I showed interest in her medical condition.

She had long suffered from headaches. She was sure headaches had contributed to her breakdown. In Nigeria a native woman had tried to cure her by cutting into the back of one of her hands.

The native woman had 'removed something like a snail, a small snail, from the water, the water inside.' It – 'did not solve the problem.'

The removal of the snail anticipated a Caesarian birth. The quality of her describing the removal made me doubt whether the birth or the snail business had actually happened, at least as she reported it. Her description of having the snail removed was disturbing – the idea was of a small snail in water being brought out of a non-existent space between skin and bone, of a spatial existence coming out of a non-space, of a baby emerging from within a mother, not so much unconscious as lacking some inside.

She had been dogged by nightmares. She was unsure of their content; perhaps she claimed to be unsure because she was suspicious of me. She thought they had something to do with the stealing of children. She became more confiding later; and I began to wonder whether the nightmare did not begin with a baby snail caught up in an object that had no inner space.

'At times when I have nightmares, I feel that somebody is pressing me on the bed, pressing me hard not to move. I'm very heavy on the bed. I have to struggle to get up. I can't get up. I will be shouting, but I can't shout it out, so that another person will hear it. I feel that I was shouting, help, help.'

During the time of her pregnancy, she had dreamt of giving birth to two children – a grown-up boy and a small girl. She did not recognise the face of the girl. She recognised the boy as the son of her husband's brother. She later gave birth to a girl.

Our reluctance in allowing our mother uterine space stems from a reluctance to let her have babies. We prefer a universe of limited stuff – where each must steal from the other in order to survive. We do not want to think of a universe of unlimited resources: the uterus as infinite. The Nigerian nurse had been the first of nine children. She presumed a cruel restriction on resources.

Two of her siblings had died: the fourth had died at birth, the seventh as a toddler. She could remember the toddler. She had not seen the other one. 'I didn't see that one. There was something funny, you know – because before my mother had the baby, I had a dream. I had a dream that my mother was going to give birth to a boy, and that the boy would so resemble me that I would die. Immediately he was born, he is going to die again. It happened in that way. When I have dreams, it is always true. I don't know why.'

'The boy would so resemble me that I would die.' The universe must be shorn of its possible freedom. It must become a reflection of her: or she will become a reflection of it – and die.

We want other babies to be like the myriad reflections that we see when we look into a pair of facing mirrors. Reflections do what we want, slave-like – until we begin to feel that their imitating of us might be a mockery. If our reflections were to escape from us, as they do in fairy tales, we would be seized by dread. We would look into a mirror; recognise our absence; and know that we had died. Reflections delusionally reassure us that we control a universe (devoid of imagination). Our dying allows for the birth of the world.

Her brother's dying had vouchsafed her living – she had probably felt powerful, and frightened by her power, when he died. She must have felt that she had pushed him out. Now she felt pushed out of her own family.

'We had "O"levels. There was a leak. The students got the papers before the examination, and so they had seized our results. I dreamt that the result was seized and I could not go back to school again. It happened in that way.' She was excluded, in the same way as the girls Frazer writes about had been isolated at puberty. The 'leak' she alludes to carries a pun. It could be that she felt her monthly flow of blood to be like some failure in examination; it indicated that she was unable to have babies – that she had failed – because she had formerly stolen babies from others. ('The students got the papers before the examination.')

The initial exchanges of our once-off, openly tape-recorded conversation anticipate its later development.

– 'Tell me why you are here?'

– 'The day I was brought here, I wasn't myself, you know. What happened was, my husband wasn't in. He went to college to have his studies that morning. I was left in the house.'

He had delayed collecting her Largactil prescription from the chemist: she had felt worse.

Her husband is a lynch-pin. Once he has been removed, she begins to separate out – at first like a self and its reflection in a mirror ('I wasn't myself'); and then like an element of the self faced by some other, uncontrollable element. There is a conflict between the self left in charge of a baby and a self that steals babies.

She will shortly raise an important issue: her sense of being divided, and of feeling helpless, invoke the sensations of being in the birth labour. 'I had wanted to bath my baby – but at the time I felt that somebody was trying to move my baby. And I saw someone using a mirror outside, you know, trying to show the mirror with reflections. And so I was on my knees throughout...'

What has happened – although we have not realised it yet, is that she has entered into a state of breakdown, of mental and grammatical condensation, in some way related to the movement of the mirror.

'...I was on my knees throughout and I didn't sleep till at the stage when I had to lay down. I felt like that I am having another baby, so after that (you know) I was crying out, shouting for help, and there was nobody to help me, as I was left alone in the house: so at this stage, I broke out from the house and went running along the street, and I was wearing just a nightgown.'

Inside becomes outside. The sociological point – Marcé's type of interest – conceals a more intimate configuration: the necessarily public exposure of inwardness during the act of childbirth. Like any mother in labour, she has lost any hold she might have had over her sense of privacy.

The baby stealer

In childbirth, strangers focus on your private parts. You enter into an act of public recantation. Your privates open and expand to an extent that you had never imagined possible. You begin to extrude your innermost self, your most shameful secrets (epitomised by faeces, urine, unfruitful splashings of blood). Your insides yield up your most precious essences – the baby itself, hope, an unimaginable beauty. Inside spills out – not so much spills out as, (so often) is torn out. You become a public presence, inward turned outward, less person than staging on a sacrificial altar.

The Nigerian nurse did actually have to be cut open, as though on a sacrificial altar. She was not allowed consciously to be there, she was made absent through sedation (she had become the reflection in the mirror) – so that someone else, her daughter, might take on being in the world.

At some level in her thought, she must have believed she had been given an anaesthetic (and Caesarian section) because it was the only way someone else might be allowed to exist.

'And so at this stage I broke out from the house and went running along the street. And I was wearing just a nightgown. There were no pants on, nothing except a nightgown that I was wearing.' Intimacy – nightgowns, the sensuous delight of not having pants on, spreads through the streets into everyone's purview. Sensations of space and of time condense. Or they suddenly enclose her.

'...nothing except a nightgown that I was wearing. So I was running up and I held two policemen...' (A sudden access of strength) '...you know, one on each hand. I held them. The other man was white. One man resembles my father. I was calling him father. And so the policemen...And at this stage I ran into a very big trunk, and then the trunk was shut up after me...'

The power that allows her to lift up two policemen retaliates on her: it seems to enter the trunk that claps about her. Did she feel the inside of the trunk to be like a state of no space – like the non-existent space out of which the small snail had emerged? The collapsing of space and time, and of grammatical sequence, appears to reflect the swallowing up of a psychic universe – and of the uterus at its heart. Her superhuman strength, feverishly created, in a frenzy of hostility at the authentically creative, cannot be maintained for more than a moment. She would seem to dread some failure in the authentically creative – the coming into being of some mother without an internal space. At her birth, her mother was reputed to have been unconscious for three months. As an infant she might equate the absence of a mental space in her unconscious mother with the later absent uterine possibility.

It is as though the mirror could speak and said to the nurse: you do not see a three-dimensional image – you do not see three persons, yourself, your mother and her baby (the baby being the third dimension). All mirrors practise the trick of implying a space, or dimension, which does not exist. Everything is flat and two-dimensional. There is no space inside your mother, apart from the feverish hard-to-maintain space you project into her.

A mother who is unconscious is a mother whose mind – manically – we might hope (imaginatively) to regenerate to keep ourselves alive. Once we have convinced ourselves of our power, we will have no trouble in believing we can unmake mind as well as make it. We have the power to obliterate the existence of thought. In the same way, reflections in a mirror wipe out the baby inside a mother – by denying the baby any inner space. She desperately tries once more to create a uterine space, as though identified with her own daughter at birth (a daughter whose mother was unconscious). 'The trunk was shut up after me. I break out of the trunk and came out pushing one man. I'd used some of the tests inside the trunk and threw it at the man, you know. At this stage they held me so tightly.' She does not explain the nature of the tests. They might be pregnancy tests, a desperate assertion of the wish to have a baby – in spite of the pressures to deny her one. The grip on her is a grip on her potentiality.

'They put me in a van and drove me – I don't know the place. It seemed like the place where psychologists work, or a charge office. They interviewed me and put me into a cell. I was in the cell for three or four hours, crying for help, and nobody came for me. They brought a pamphlet to be signed by me, in favour of my baby to be kept by Social Welfare. I signed the document anyway. They put me into a van again, with one dirty blanket to cover me, and drove off until I came here.'

Her mentioning now of being put into a cell distils many unpleasant past sensations. It revives her anxieties about labour – her helplessness. She is unable to protect herself or her baby. Her fear of having her baby stolen from her is realised when Social Welfare (perhaps with the best of intentions) takes her baby from her. It revives the shock of being detained in a mental hospital without her baby. (The Unit where I met her had the unusual policy of bringing mothers in breakdown together with their babies.)

She became more restrained when we looked, for a second time, at the mysterious moment of breakdown. 'And I saw somebody using a mirror outside, you know, trying to show the mirror with reflections...'

– 'What I mean is, I saw somebody using a mirror, you know, shining it, and I saw the image moving from side to side.'

– 'Outside – what, moving against a wall, sunlight?'

– 'Yes, outside, sunlight, and I saw the lady doing it. She was having a mirror in her hands, doing it, but –'

– 'Why was she doing that?'

– 'I don't know, I don't know.'

– 'How young was she?'

– 'She was a young lady, she *is* a young lady. A fair complexion. And I believe she is living in the place where I live... She is living upstairs. Her name is Mavis.'

– 'You mean, she was down below?'

– 'Yes, down below, doing it.'

Mavis is the baby-stealer. She appears to be far away from us; then, suddenly, she is close, the neighbour upstairs, almost inside us, controlling. She is also the figure downstairs, moving a dash of sunlight back and forth across a wall in a morse code signalling absence. Witches are most frightening when they cast spells during the heat of the day. 'I don't feel well with it. It seems that with that, she's reflecting something to do with my baby, trying to remove my baby or something. I don't know.'

Mavis is a timeless, spaceless element in thought, the obverse of the creative uterus. She is the self that enters into masturbatory transactions to rob a mother of her babies. She stands in front of a mirror and insists that the three-dimensional is a delusion, and all that matters is the smile of complicity exchanged between the self and its reflection.

The infinite

The use of the concept of uterus in psychoanalytic thought is similar to the use of the concept in biology. But the uses of the concepts diverge after a certain point. The psychoanalytic concept becomes metaphysical, non-naturalistic and non-representational at the diverging point. It begins to indicate something which cannot be represented i.e. infinity.

One of the difficulties the ancient Greeks had in using the concept of infinity lay in their trying to account naturalistically for its non-naturalistic uses. We become sensitive to the divergence between the different meanings of the uterus when we consider another concept, one that was important to Breuer's understanding of Anna: the concept of interruption.

A woman listened on the phone to another woman who was weeping as she recalled memories of being separated from her baby. The listener found that her thoughts about the separation of mother and baby were being broken into by loud and absurd clicking and cluckings on the phone line. She thought these sounds were like a hen clucking over its newly-laid eggs. The mother hen had appeared in her mind as a mockery of the woman who had been separated from her baby. However, she herself cannot bear interruptions of any kind. She hates changes, discontinuities or indeed anything that appears alien.

She says that her husband came home late last night. She switches smoothly (if abruptly) to another incident to avoid the unpleasant feelings aroused by her husband's lateness of appearance. She contemplates instead the recollection of a visit by someone else, a young relative whom she dotes on. Together, they went for a walk and enjoyed the evening sky as the light faded. Her relative had mislaid his spectacles, so that he could not see (what she could see) an immense cloud of birds passing by. Through his presence, she was partially able to avoid a sense of interruption – nagging and unwelcome thoughts about her husband's absence – and to remain within a condition of some complacence. Her condition did not entirely obliterate insight. She saw the birds, even if he did not.

She now thought of a foreign teacher at the school she works at. She does not like him. He is so different from her. He is an outstandingly gifted mathematician, and he had said to her – perturbingly – that the points in space were greater than any system of numbers could allow for.

One of the strange properties of the uterus, which obliges us to think of it as a metaphysical, as well as a biological, concept is that its multiplicity is of a kind that cannot be comprehended by mathematical calculation. It is beyond our comprehension. There are birds in the sky, or points in space, which we cannot see because we have lost our spectacles. The uterine operates in dimensions unavailable to the systems available in mathematical thought. It becomes meaningful as a concept about thought when theories of succession collapse. It arises from a mutation in thought and relates to the fact that the idea of mutation is important in any understanding of mental development. Disquieting conjectures of this kind disturb that part of ourselves that distrusts interruption and would wish to suck complacently at a never-ending flow.

Chapter 6

THE MOTHERS AT THE UNIT

> It still strikes me as strange that the case histories I write should read like short stories...(There is) an intimate connection between the story and the symptoms.[1]

Mrs. R. has journeyed here from a remote country. She has moved through many rooms. She is petite and palely dark. She has delicate wrists. She is a mother any baby might be happy with. The story she tells is about pressures that have disabled her motherliness. 'From the time I was in this country, I was sick. Pains in my tummy and my back and my feet. I worked in a chocolate agency in Edmonton. I was in the export department. I had to lift heavy weights. I was sacked when I became pregnant... I didn't have my NIS card when I was sacked. I went to Archer Tower to get my card, went to the employment office, and I got my next job. I was working at a home in B – Lane, an old people's home.'

She holds onto the actual world. She sees herself as a victim of circumstance – she has been sacked for being pregnant. Her complaints do not really engage with the actual world, and the notion of redress has little meaning for her. The sources of her distress lie in her mind. The baby has pushed her out of her job. It has pushed her out of what she might have formerly expected. She had felt secure in the fact that an actual world exists – a world which provides jobs (sometimes) and is a rich mine for grievance. Now, no longer. She has little or nothing outside herself to concentrate on. She is divided. She has to move in many directions: to get her NIS card, to go to the employment agency, to go to her job. Something has disturbed her attention.

[1] Freud (1895), p.160.

She is weighed down by a quite concrete conception of infancy – the baby here, within her. It adds to the difficulties of having to seek out bits of a scattered object.

'I got on well with the old people. I started to work. I helped the matron. I used to clean the dining room...the bedrooms. I used to clean all the tables. I was sick all the time. I worked until the year's end. I was seven months pregnant – and I was sick.'

Pregnancy was all work to her – all labour, we might think. The baby makes her sick; it is an incontinent presence within her. It soils through her mouth. She cannot control it, in any direct fashion. At best she can clean up some of its mess. Cleaning rooms saves her from drowning. It keeps the pregnancy on an even keel. She can avoid aborting the baby – and she can avoid giving it her assent. Cleaning has the meaning of bringing alive – of making life, a misconception of the procreative function. It also has the meaning for her (as we shall see later) of murder. To clean is to kill.

She had had a breakdown when she was nineteen. She was then living in her native land. 'My mother died when I was only ten years old. I had to work – from scratch. I have a sister. I grew up at my mother's sister's. My father remarried. My aunt was poor. She couldn't afford to send me to school. My father lost interest in us.'

Bitterness and worldliness overlie her grief. Working from scratch implies basic scourings. She had her claws out for an exploitative sister – and for others of a similar kind: an aunt, the woman who dared marry her father, myself as the idle listener. Resentment at losing her father – and the interest he had once shown in her – deflects her from mourning the loss of a mother. She decides to become a nun. She reads, she studies. Her uncle arranges for her to marry a man twice her age – he happens to be the same age as the uncle.

The man has a wife by natural law and three children. Some time before, the man's mother-in-law had separated him from his family. She had thrown him out. Compliantly, he had emigrated to England. Mothers, and mothers-in-law, have that sort of power in the native land. Mrs. R. met the first wife and thought her kind. The first wife did not complain at the break-up of her marriage. She showed no hostility to Mrs. R.

– 'Your mother died when you were aged ten. What did she die from?'

– 'She had a gallstone. She was taking treatment. Before she was to undergo the operation, she did vomit. She vomited green. They say it is an appendix. It had already burst in her, and she was already gone. She died at twenty-eight years.'

– 'How old are you?'

– 'I am twenty-seven. My sister was twenty-eight last year.'

– 'What do you remember of your mother?'

– 'I remember everything about my mother – and my mother and my mother – so long ago. They used never to take photographs. So we have nothing to show. Whoever joined the family, would know only her name. Everybody who knows her, talk about her name, just her name and how she was good and kind.'

– 'What was her name?'

– 'Ramratine. They just called her Darling.'

The death of her mother has diminished every moment. The oceans and rooms and jobs she must cross are meaningless. Colour and personality are lost. Attempts to find someone to love – initially, to find her mother – are dissuaded.

When she was fifteen, she fell in love with a boy who worked as a film operator. He lived in the house opposite to the one she lived in. She was not allowed to talk to him. Her aunt said that boys who worked in cinemas were unreliable: they attracted too many girls. Aunts, like mothers, are powerful in the native land. 'I used to feel hot and always go and bathe and change my clothes. I never used to eat my meals on time. Sometimes I didn't eat. Just like that, I get a breakdown. I had to go to mental hospital. They gave me electric treatment.'

The swift slide into illness – the harshness of treatment, call for explanation. She does not give it. She is unwilling to remember. She goes so far – and then tactfully keeps me at a distance. Or perhaps she has lost the memory.

Her mother's presence suffuses places. 'When I was working in the old people's home, the first patient that died was in Room 11. Her name was Alice. Her husband had died. Her daughter was overseas. When I was cleaning her room – and the sister finished giving her an orange drink – she started to bring up. I take tissues from the box. I start to clean her mouth. She was thanking me all the time. Before I finished cleaning the room, she died. I think I had a lot of blessings from that lady since then. Plenty more people died in the hospital before I left.'

It sounds troubling. Cleaning, like feeding, keeps people alive. Implicitly, if you are the one who does the cleaning, and your sister the one who does the feeding, it kills.

Her mother spreads out and scatters in her mind. Distances in the city seem to extend as she approaches the time of her baby's birth. 'I was sick, really sick. Someone was straying me away. When I finished work, I didn't take the bus home. I walked. All over the place. I'd go to the court, the school, the cinema, all the big buildings. I didn't reach home until seven in the evening. My husband was worried. My uncle wanted to know where I am.'

The court, school, cinema, big buildings might be points of reference from the past – places where she looks for affection. Is it the baby that strays her into these reaches? Possibly, she confused an earlier breakdown with a later one: the electric shock treatment that occurred, not in her native land, but after the birth.

'I end up in Westminster – where I used to travel with the 210 bus. I took the 210 bus and I go until the end of the 210. All that day I didn't go to work. I find all sorts of nonsense. I find out that the church – the church of my religion – they burn it down. I get so angry. The same day my husband went to my uncle and told him I didn't arrive home until seven o'clock.'

She was admitted to mental hospital before the birth of her child. Shortly after its birth, she was separated from it. 'I wasn't happy. I feel like my baby was taken away from me.' – As her mother had been taken away from her? She was unable to say what had happened: why she had been admitted to mental hospital, or why it had been thought wise to separate her from her baby.

Her memory of the birth was confident. 'When my baby was born, I was proud of myself. I say, well, I am a mother. I phoned for the ambulance to take me to hospital on Monday night. My husband didn't go with me. They say he need not. The ambulance had two persons. My baby was born on Tuesday morning, seven twenty-five. My husband came to see me at eleven o'clock.'

Delivery was normal. 'And she was healthy...When I go into hospital, they strapped my tummy with a belt. They gave me two injections – and something in my mouth to inhale, like to push the baby forward to engage. They strapped the belt to give me pain.' (The belt, presumably, was used to monitor the baby's heartbeats.) 'I was getting pain only every ten minutes. The machine wasn't registering right. The nurses were worried. They carried me into the labour ward. As I go into the labour ward, the baby is born. The clock was opposite me. I had my watch in my hand.'

Black angels

Mrs. L. is pale and sweet-voiced. She is aged eighteen. 'I'm a very unconfident person. As child I went through many things. My mother had many mental illnesses. She was in hospital for so many... I broke down after the baby. I went completely mad. I didn't know what I was doing. I went into – (a mental hospital) for a rest. I did strange things. I was completely mad.'

'Unconfident.' But she speaks with assurance. She has a grasp on the fact that she has a life to live. The frontier crossed by Mrs. L. is signalled by the phrase 'after the baby'. It equals breakdown – the condition of not knowing what one is doing. She enters a state in which the self loses its centre. Some violent and supernatural agent acts for her. She seems mixed up with her mother. 'I knocked over the tea-trolley. I bit my husband's face. I became very religious. I believed in God so much. I believe in God anyway – but I kept saying the spirit of God had got into me. I kept seeing people as devils at first, you know. I could see horns on their heads. I was completely mad. I was really out of my mind.' Out of her mind and into her mother's mind, never mind (as she says), knocking over a tea trolley and biting somebody's husband's face.

Her parents are divorced. She talks of them as '*broken*...up', with that sort of emphasis, as though they were broken in spirit, her mother confined to a place for broken things. The actuality is pale compared to its enactment in her mind. She confuses a violent intimacy with attacks on a feeding object – and with religious aspiration. Biting a husband's face leads her into stating that she believes in God, as though in the act of biting she had ingested a divine spirit. Presumably she cannot be sure she has eaten something good. Hamlet thought the devil had power to assume a pleasing shape. Mrs. L. knows that you can recognise a devil because it has horns on its head. She sees angels. They are not radiant. They are dressed in black. They wear hats. They sound like witches – or midwives seen fearfully. Appearances, and the meaning of appearances, are dissociated.

In birth she becomes a mother, at least biologically, if not in mind. She crosses the line into danger, madness and death. In birth, she enters an after-life thronged with angels and devils.

– 'What happened when the spirit of God got into you?'

– 'I can't remember it very well. It was just a strange feeling. I had to give everything away. All the stuff I had in hospital. All the stuff people brought me. I had to give it away. I couldn't stop giving. Everytime I saw something on television that said send money, I sent money. In the end I became broke.'

Broke – or broken apart, like her parents. She has been generous, mindless ('I couldn't stop giving'), her insides turned out. The baby you give birth to is picked up by others. They take away your insides. Is the inside precious or rubbishy – a baby or a waste product? She talks about the things she got in hospital as though they were rubbish.

Breaking and becoming broke carries another allusion. 'They had to break my waters. I was two days overdue. I locked myself up in my room. I didn't want to have my waters broken. I just became strange. I used to have a bath. I'd rush myself... I fought the gas and I hallucinated. I saw angels. Three angels. In black. They had hats on. They told me they were there to help me. It was all in my imagination. But the mind (they say) does turn funny. After having the baby, all my hormones got jumbled up, mixed up inside. That's why I became unwell. My blood seems all right. I had a high blood pressure. Mum's got blood disorder – and every seven years another breakdown.'

For her, a key phrase is 'knowing what you are doing'. She has a dream in which her infant daughter has already learnt to walk and to talk. Not knowing what you are doing is like not being able to walk or talk: it is to be helpless.

'I have this fear of dying. I buy all this stuff to make myself look young. I'm frightened of growing old. I feel horrible every time I see someone old. I don't want to die. None of us want to die, do we? In mental hospital I saw an old woman turn young. She must have been aged ninety. You can't describe it properly. I think you've got to experience it to understand it. You know what I mean? Never mind. I've been through quite a lot for eighteen.'

Bugged

A careful monotonous voice, as though brought before an interrogator. 'When I get disturbed, my thinking goes. I can think all sorts. I can think this place is bugged and there are people listening to our conversation. Or there is someone from outer space controlling my heart... I'm diagnosed as an episodic schizophrenic. I hear voices. I cry a lot. I have bizarre reactions to anything going wrong. I was in my dressing gown and nightie. I'd been discharged three weeks from maternity. I couldn't even wash or dress myself. My parents were there. I was watching a programme, the two Ronnies, still in my nightie and dressing gown. I just burst out giggling. I said, I'm sorry. I can't watch this programme. I was tingling all over. I've never felt so fragile emotionally before, without being on medication. I've had medication for years. Because of the breast-feeding, I couldn't have medication.'

Some time before her marriage, she had been through an abortion. 'I wasn't married. The father was a married man, a coloured married man. I had a termination. I had to sign that if they couldn't get the baby out through the vagina, they would have to cut my tummy to get it out. I was eleven weeks pregnant. Fortunately, they didn't have to cut my tummy. The irony is I didn't have an actual birth this time' (although she gave birth to an actual baby). 'They had to cut my tummy. I couldn't get it into my head that it was my baby. Every time I went to the toilet, I used to look at the scar. I used to say, that's where my baby came from. He must be my baby – that's where he came from. The first baby was a skeleton in the cupboard. They didn't cut my tummy then; but this time they did. The two ideas are linked up emotionally.'

In the psychiatric hospital she would wake up screaming. 'I remember one night I said – execute the baby. Can you imagine a mother saying that? They gave me two sleeping pills. I used to go running out of the ward into the corridor shouting, execute the baby. But I don't want to execute the baby. It's our most precious thing.'

Her history is one of reaching out for something she desires and of its being denied to her. The something is cut off, intruded into, taken away. She joined the Royal Navy as a secretary and found herself posted to the office of the Admiral of the Fleet. She was overwhelmed – and dangerously excited. 'I worked for six months and then broke down. I began to notice things were sticking up on the carpet. It was a patterned carpet – and the pattern was raised. I thought I was having hallucinations.' She becomes infatuated with an ADC in the office. She finds herself giggling and losing control. 'I came from a humble home and working for such a top office without any growth emotionally – I couldn't cope.' She left the office and entered a psychiatric hospital. Her employer gave her a reference bearing his full title. 'I daren't show that reference, because I can't come up to what that reference signifies.'

Her troubles began in puberty. She was late in beginning her periods. She did not understand why other girls were excused showers at school. She thinks she got suspicious in breakdown because she had got suspicious then about what was going on. 'I didn't know what it was. Also, how do you lose blood? I used to think you lost blood under your arms as well. It's so obscure for a developing child, isn't it? Looking at the other side of things, I used to study so hard for my Latin and French. I had a religious background. Everything was in apple-pie order, so far as upbringing, home and education were concerned. And yet, emotionally, I was so incomplete.'

Night bird

Many of the mothers I met at the Unit had been previously confined at the same psychiatric hospital. All of them, without exception, praised the Unit. Some of them found the manner of nursing helpful. Others emphasised the value of being able to talk to other mothers who had been through breakdown – thinking you are unique in your madness has the power of intensifying madness. None of them dissented from the view that the Unit was valuable because it allowed you, under the closest supervision, to be with your baby. The Unit was a place where efforts were made to understand you.

Little could be said in favour of the psychiatric hospital. Its administrators tended to separate you from your baby – and to prescribe drugs and series of electro-convulsive treatment that left you feeling awful. Efforts seemed to be made to misunderstand you. The contrast of the two institutions sounds like the splitting of some nurturing object into good and bad aspects. But not entirely. There was probably justice in these assessments.

Mrs. G. was no exception to the other mothers in her feelings about these two places. She had been given eight ECT's which had appalled her and she had been distressed by the effect of drugs. She was delighted by the Unit because she was able to be with her baby. At the psychiatric hospital she had been separated from her son for a period of three months. At the moment of separation, he had been aged three months.

In the psychiatric hospital she had been surrounded by drug addicts.

'I remember getting up in the middle of night, wandering about and pestering the night nurses. I was very much a night bird. I would be awake at night and sleep by day...I had to go round in my dressing gown. They feared I'd run away again...A girl who was here before me had wandered out in her nightdress with two umbrellas and stopped the traffic. That made me giggle. I did the same myself. I ran out into the traffic myself. Another girl, the first night she came into the Unit – we didn't know why she had been admitted. She seemed perfectly normal. In the middle of the night, she was screaming on the landing – I want my baby, you can't take my baby. There was so much noise: we thought there was a fire. The night after that, she was trying to get to the phone all the time. She wanted to phone her husband. She nearly broke her neck trying to get down the stairs. One girl thought she had died. She didn't move. And then she got up as if nothing had happened.'

She went through two miscarriages, one at eleven weeks, the other at sixteen weeks. 'I used to be a quiet person. I bottled up depression inside me. I didn't cry a lot.' Her husband works for the military police. During the breakdown she locked herself in the bathroom and screamed out of the window, then 'barged' into the house next door with a belligerence that was out of character. She began to make huge noises, screaming out of windows, revving up the car, turning on the television sound at full blast. 'I thought the house bugged. I thought people were watching us all the time. I tested the different channels on the radio to see that they didn't change channel.'

All had gone well for the first three months after birth. Then she and her husband and the baby were returning from a motoring holiday in Scotland. 'Coming back from Scotland, the car started – not to break down, but to lose power. I had the baby with me in the back seat in a carry-cot. My husband said I began to say silly things.'

He told her later that she had talked about her parents and about their dying some day. She had talked about last wills and testaments and about who would inherit what. Thoughts of death, and of someone gaining at someone else's expense, coincided remarkably with the condition of a car that was petering out and the deterioration in thought that was alleged of her. They reached home. She continued to talk 'nonsense.' She could not sleep. She kept her husband awake all night. He took her to the doctor. Pills proved ineffective. She was bundled off to the psychiatric hospital.

As a child, she would dream of 'things getting bigger, coming closer and closer and crowding in on me, and then going away again'. It was 'like a television on a televison on a television, going on forever. Things would get bigger and smaller.' She tends to blank out. 'I see things in space, a vast space, as if there is nothing in my head. And then things close in on me.'

Bad sister

Her first words are startling. They take us too close. 'My father was a drunk, and he used to come home at night and threaten to kill my mother, and this made me very frightened as a child, and I grew up afraid of men, and then I had a complex about wearing glasses. I thought I looked awful in them. And I think this all built up in me, and then I went out with a fellow, and he was going out with other women behind my back, and this upset me very much, and I had my first nervous breakdown, which was a mental breakdown, where I heard voices and imagined all sorts of things. And I was in here six months. I also had epileptic fits through the tablets that the doctor gave me being too strong for me, and after that I had shock treatment.'

She speaks in a flat, washed-out voice, slurred a little, from drugs probably, yet not inappropriate, as a mode of communication, to her opening – 'My father was a drunk.' She at once links her opening train of thought, with its succession of shocks, to the birth of her baby. The flatness in her voice would seem to melt and to swoon into a space ample in perspective, as she talks of this infant. He is, she says, 'God-given'.

'When I was fifteen I wanted to join the Salvation Army. I was quite religious at one time. I doubt God at times because of the pain you suffer and the pain that animals also suffer, who've done no wrong.' She had wanted to reject her baby at first. He had caused her so much pain – in pregnancy, in labour, and afterwards. 'I thought I might die, you know. I wanted my husband with me, and he was with me through the birth. When you suffer so much pain, it makes you doubt God.'

The pain she had felt during the 22-hour labour, the fear of dying, the sense of physical weakness and the confusion increased by what she felt to be contradictory advice from the nurses, is there in her startling opening words. It is as though some underlying shared thought existed beneath both the shock of giving birth to her son and the undigested, and possibly indigestible, impressions of her father having drunkenly and sexually attacked her mother. She has frequently tried to commit suicide by taking an overdose of the tablets her doctor gives her: 'I wouldn't like to slice my wrists – too much of a coward for that... I had a lot of pain feeding him. I was breast-feeding him, and the nipples got cracked and sore. I used to get all tensed up before I started feeding him. I couldn't relax, and he used to suck very hard, and so I decided to come off breast-feeding, and while I came off I had to express milk, and I went through a lot of pain with that as well.'

Her sister is six years older than she is and lives in a spotless house. Her sister has given up men. She has a fourteen-year-old daughter, whom she cannot stand and some time back put into care. 'She's got a cat and her flat. And she's got her job.' The job, it turns out, is to work as a cleaner in a day nursery. She is surrounded by children. The sister doesn't mind. They are not her own children.

The fourteen-year-old daughter, Dinah, is alleged to be on intimate terms with a sixty-year-old man – 'people imagine the worst.' Dinah's father is a cripple. She may go and live with him. 'I don't know whether that's a good thing or not, really. He's a bit old to take on a girl like that, you know. She's a handful... We can't have her. She wouldn't do any housework or help in the house. You can't trust her either, because she tells lies.'

Her sister is like her mother in thinking of sexuality as disgusting – the assaults of a drunken father. Mrs. H. adores her little boy. Any hostility to babies is channelled into her sister. Scrupulous cleanliness and the rejection of children is bound up with fears at loving an incontinent father or baby.

'I got on well with him. When my sister was born, he was away for six years. When he came back, she never talked to him. But he was there when I was born. I grew up and I knew him. He wasn't always bad. We played draughts. He used to buy me sweets and give me pocket money. The trouble was he drank too much. He died of thrombosis. They said that he rotted his body through drinking and smoking too much. He died at fifty-five. He was ill for five years and in those five years he was a different person because he couldn't drink. I loved him and my sister hated him. When I saw him in hospital, I felt I didn't want him to go on living and suffering as he was suffering, because he did suffer a lot, a very lot.'

Burnt eggs

Mrs. T. wants to forget whatever it was that happened to her. She is willing to speak to me – because she is conciliatory and because she thinks it is good to talk things over. I have the feeling that she wants to establish a new and agreeable orthodoxy about what happened in the past.

She gives no more than a hint as to the nature of her breakdown. 'I'm more concerned now about the baby than I was. At the beginning (when she first got home), I couldn't cope. I've got over that stage now and I can cope very well. I'm very proud to be a mother today. My husband is very proud too.'

Many mothers after breakdown want to forget. Events are so abrupt and unusual, so outside the norms of most lives, that forgetting them is not too difficult. The upsetting can be left to fairy tales. Babies most thrive in settings where shock, abruptness and violence are excluded; and yet shock, abruptness and violence are intrinsic to the moment of birth and to the definition of their humanity.

'I remember a coloured nurse telling me to hurry up and push because she wanted the baby to be born before she went off duty.' Mrs. T. thinks she was being rebuked for being slow; she weeps at the thought of this. 'She just said, hurry up. You've got a little – (term of racial abuse) there. The baby wasn't born until she went off. Much kinder nurses were working then.'

Mrs. T. usually gets on well with black people, even the black nurses at the Unit. She is a former nurse herself, a psychiatric nurse, who has worked with chronic schizophrenics. Whether she felt the nurse in the labour room was giving her a bit of her own medicine was not disclosed.

She conveys the resonance of an illness, not its story. 'When the baby was born in the – hospital, when I came home that night, it was like getting out of prison, the car went all shakey all over the road.' She adds nothing to her remark about the car going all shakey all over the road; and perhaps she has no need to. The image, and the atmosphere she puts over with it, arouse intense disquiet; but about what exactly is hard to say – the terror, perhaps, of being inside some object that lurches and squidges about and, by the nature of its being uncontrolled, opens you up to lethal impact from some force outside.

Another resonant image. 'I was quite upset really, and I went to bed with my husband. And then the next thing I realised, my husband got very upset about me, because I was boiling six eggs that morning when I was making the breakfast. I felt so full of energy, and then (it) just ended up that I came in here to hospital.'

Burning the eggs (for this is how she later describes it – 'I fried them and the pan was black'), hardly warrants the fact that her husband, a Health Worker, her GP and a doctor from the Unit should have hastened to bring her to the hospital in an ambulance. We can speculate on what the destroying of eggs meant for her. At the same time, she wishes us to respect her reticence and her need to conciliate. 'I am more careful now. I can cook very well now. I am very good cook. Even my husband can tell you that.'

Spooks

She tells me that her husband doesn't like children. 'I think it's because of his background. I don't know much about him. He doesn't talk about his childhood...' The Nazis exterminated all his relatives.

Her mother-in-law is a trouble-maker. On hearing of the pregnancy, she phoned her son and told him to arrange an abortion. 'He looks to me for guidance. But often I don't know what to do. If I had parents I would ask them what to do. I have tried going to marriage guidance, but it doesn't help.'

She is congenitally deaf: her father was deaf also. Her husband can read one sign. He knows when she is having her periods. At the time of her periods, she becomes unbearable. 'I remember when I first came to have my periods, I went with my father to a stadium to see greyhound racing and I remember feeling I've got a pain and I've got this colour (you know), and it looks like blood. I don't know what to say to my father because he is deaf. He was deaf anyway, and I never talked to him very much. But I think he realised that I'd had a period.'

Her father became totally deaf during the war. 'The house collapsed – bombed; and when they got him out, he'd lost all his hearing. He'd always been partially deaf, like me. It just made him worse. We had to start using sign language. The only time he ever knew that I was angry was if I'd bang the door. I loved my father, even though I was frightened of him.'

Since the baby's birth, she has become worried by the neighbours, Iranians on one side, Trinidadians on the other. In a dream, she found herself in one of the neighbours' houses. She and one of the neighbours were in a state of undress. 'I think I'm living with spooks. I hear only loud noises. One of my neighbours sleeps on the ground floor – he has his bedroom there. I put my baby down; and he kept listening. He was talking or whispering through the walls. I got frightened. I thought I was going off my head again...I don't want what's happening to affect my baby. I don't know what he hears. If people whisper, I get paranoid. I'm frightened that when he gets older, I'll be shouting all the time.'

She has been through about five breakdowns in ten years. During one of them, she followed car signs and imagined people to leave their houses and jump around. 'They were like puppets, you know.' Sometimes 'they would just burn away'.

She had worried whether she would give birth to a cat or to Kermit the frog. The epidural took away all sensation. 'They couldn't do anything with forceps, and they said to my husband they would have to do a Caesarian. I remember they gave me something to drink, a mask went over my face, and I didn't know anything else until I woke up and saw a baby on my pillow. I remember seeing dark brown eyes in a little bundle. It was odd, when they next brought him to me, he was fair and had blue eyes. He doesn't look like either of us. He's got beautiful blue eyes.'

Doodle bugs

'I stood in the front room and screamed. My husband and my mum didn't know what was wrong with me. I was shaking all over. I said, I don't know where to begin, I don't know where to begin.' Mrs. A. associates her screaming and shaking with some inability to begin. She does not know *where* to begin. 'I had a lot of trouble. I haemorrhaged. I had a normal birth. I haemorrhaged and had to be stitched up twice. I was left in the room on my own after the baby was born – with the baby. I didn't have a clue what to do with the baby.'

Her daughter was born at one-thirty in the morning. It was an easy and natural birth, barely no pain. The infant was a healthy seven-pounder. She had felt despondent after the labour. At about three in the morning she observed that her stomach was swollen. Her husband said that it looked as though she had a another baby in there. He went to inform the parents of the birth; she dozed off; and then awoke with a 'really fierce pain'. She cried out that she was haemorrhaging. A doctor came eventually. 'He pushed all the blood out with his hands, and then I had to be stitched up again. I was discharged from the hospital. Two days later I was back. They gave me a D & C and found afterbirth in me.'

She appears to have experienced the placental residue as another baby, a bad and intolerable presence, unexpected and unplanned. 'When I had the D & C, all I remember is saying I wish someone would kill me, because I was in so much pain. They laughed at me, the nurses. I remember coming round, and the doctor said "afterbirth", and I never queried it.'

'I've always been interested in the second world war. My mum used to tell me that when she was a little girl, she saved my aunt from one of those bouncing bombs. They were walking down the road and she saw one coming – doodlebugs, I think they're called – and she lay on top of my aunt and saved her. The bomb went off nearby.'

The fear of being blown up appears in a different guise during her breakdown. 'I remember I was lying on my mum's bed. My dad was sleeping on a camp bed; and I was sleeping with my mum. I kept saying, shh – you've got to be quiet, they're coming. I had to have dead silence. I was waiting all morning for it to be dead silent. At about two o'clock in the afternoon, I looked at the clock. It was dead quiet around my mum's estate. I heard a milk bottle. Someone broke a milk bottle. I thought: they're coming now. I thought: we're going to die any minute. I thought they were going to drop the atom bomb.'

Once, after she had taken an overdose, she had a vision of dead film stars – Marilyn Monroe in particular – beckoning her into the after-life. Her mother said that she had entered a dream world. She walked around the meadows in a nightdress. Her mother had to bathe her and dress her and feed her.

'After three days at my mum and dad's, I remember my mum was having a wash in the bathroom. I kissed the baby and said, "Bye Janie, I'm going now, I won't bother you any more", and I went into the kitchen and found some matches and set fire to my nightclothes. I think that death by fire is the worst thing that can happen to you. I've always been scared of fire. I don't know what made me do a thing like that. Luckily, my mum came out of the bathroom and saw me. She had some wet nappies in her hand and she put them over me. She called an ambulance. I felt nothing, no pain in my leg, nothing. I don't remember the flames. All I remember is seeing my mother's face. She was very calm. I remember finding the matches and seeing my mum's face coming out of the bathroom and the flames creeping up my legs.'

Stomach time bomb

'I was going on about a time bomb in my stomach. I don't remember this, but he had to ring the doctor. Apparently I screamed down the phone that we were going to explode, my stomach was going to explode.' She is under sedation. She speaks carefully, holding onto the words, a humming retardation of vowels in her throat. 'I kept thinking he did not understand the baby. I went round and tried to contact a friend. I couldn't phone from home because I thought my husband would be overhearing everything.'

Her son was born on Armistice day. 'It was easy. I hadn't thought about it the whole nine months – I hadn't been scared of it. My husband certainly helped at the last stage, holding me up. It was lovely the way this little creature came out of us. It was really good. My husband was holding the baby when his eyes opened for the first time.' She was still 'on a bounce'. But the baby was sleepy, worryingly so. 'I just had to prod at him. The nurses were tapping his feet to get him to wake up. I got a bit upset then.'

She was sure he was waiting for lactation to begin. Doubts about being an effective mother were increased when, shortly after the birth, 'they took him away from my breast just for a while and gave him oxygen.' She remained in hospital for eight days. She came out on Sunday. 'I thought on Thursday that we could get things back to okay. I spent most of the time in the bedroom – at least I remember that. I also charged up the attic staircase, barefoot. I didn't feel anything. Apparently, I lifted him up with one hand – he's six foot. I had super-power strength at the time. I went to jump out of the window.'

She tried to stave off catastrophe. 'I remember patting him all over. I thought that if I didn't go round patting everywhere – there was a certain set order of doing things – otherwise we were going to be lost for all eternity. The phone calls that happened all day, I kept thinking – well, obviously, they were about me. I thought if I could relax, I could bring it all back. I patted areas on the ground. Otherwise it would disappear and we would have nowhere to walk. I tried to get my husband to pat the bed, and I was patting him. I was making him do it. I kept thinking, well, how do we get back? We had to go backwards the whole time to what it was before. But before what I can never work out.'

The Unit was set up to cater for short-stay patients. Mrs. J.L. had spent an unusually long time there, over a year. A social worker told me: 'She's is one of the most disturbed young ladies we've had on the Unit. There is total disagreement throughout the team, as to what the difficulty is – whether she is psychotic, whether she has a personality disorder, whether she is a mixture of the two. I think the prognosis is very, very poor. You feel the baby is being used as a pawn in a game you don't understand. To a certain extent, her actions are deliberate. But she does drift in and out of psychosis. She tends to flip over very quickly. I feel very much for the safety of the child. Nothing has been done overtly to harm him. Something far more worrying is going on: which is a prolonged emotional rejection.'

Bigamist

She looks out of a window. She sees a mist. She thinks it a big mist. She comes to the conclusion that her husband must be committing adultery, since a big mist suggests to her a-big-mist or bigamist. She passes two churches. Two churches – ah, she is convinced her husband will remarry.

She admits to her jealousy quite late on in our conversation. Her jealousy is veiled. She is depressed, sensitive, anxious at the thought of hurting anything. When she was brought to the Unit, she yelled 'piss off' at the nurses. She thinks her behaviour 'unlady-like'. Unconvincingly (as though speaking by rote) she says: 'It wasn't at all nice, because they were only trying to help me.'

She is full of thoughts of dying things. She is sure the dying things are out there, in the actual world. At the same time, she talks about them as though they were remote aquatic objects deep inside her. 'I keep praying to God that things will be all right, you know, and that the sun and the moon and the stars will all come back. I haven't seen the sun – and yet it's summer. It's all light and dark, isn't it? There's no sun and there's no moon and there's no stars. I think I've done this to the world, and do you agree with me?'

For the first eight weeks of pregnancy, her baby was in breech. She felt identified with it, thinking of herself as 'on my head instead of my heels and I feel frightened.' Its breeched state frightened her. 'It frightened me and I shook. It was the day before Good Friday. I had a bit of back trouble, so I was sleeping by myself, in my little girl's room.'

She believes that anything she does is dangerous. Her breakdown began on the third day after birth. 'On the third day, he had a motion that was black, like tar. I thought I might have damaged him by smoking when I was pregnant. He's got cradle cap. I keep thinking that when the snow falls, he's going to die.' She enjoyed breast-feeding, but her husband stopped her. He gives her little or no support. He is hostile to her relationship with the baby. 'One night at the hospital, I said to him. Do you want me home? He said, no, not really. It was that night that did it.'

Marplan

A disquieting sense of being outside herself, of watching herself, of managing somehow, yet feeling faint, giddy and depressed. 'On the sixth day after the birth, I had a panic attack in the evening. I was terrified. I'd had a nervous breakdown about five or six years before – with a similar sort of feeling. I had felt I was trying to run away from myself.' Dissociation has been familiar from childhood. It occurs when she considers the 'incredible miracle' of having given birth to her son – or at moments of terror. 'I never seemed to take part in my dreams. I seemed to be outside, like a third party, watching all the time, things going on, usually of some violent nature.'

When she broke down, she would lie on a sofa all day, sucking a thumb, calling her husband Daddy and her mother, who was helping out, Mummy. 'I was resorting to my childhood.' She is put on Marplan. 'It had the most alarming side effects. Fainting and giddiness – I wasn't warned of them. I was pushing my baby across a zebra crossing. I went flying. My head was like a raging torrent. I had to be taken back to the hospital in the evening and calmed down. I knew I would have this electric current passed through my brain. I saw this chap wandering around with a black rubber thing. I assumed he would shove it into my mouth to stop me swallowing my tongue. There was a nurse at each corner of the bed. I imagined they would be holding my legs down, while I struggled with this electric performance. I went into this treatment fearfully and came out of it even more so. They decided to discontinue it.'

Thinking about her son, breast-feeding him, keeps her going. She fears the drugs she takes will contaminate the milk. 'There was a limit to the amount of drugs they could give me, in case it went through the milk. I started hallucinating, seeing all sorts of horrible things. I saw water coming through the window and land on my ankle. I went to touch it, a big droplet, to wipe it away. There was nothing. It was just dry. I threw a polythene bag into the rubbish bin. It felt as though it were full of water. My hands were dripping. I kept rubbing my hands: there was nothing there. I saw insects crawling along the pelmet in the bedroom. I saw a man hanging from a tree. I'd watch television; I'd feel someone pulling at my clothes and at the chair. It was like dreaming you are falling. The doctor said the feelings would go.' The nightmare was receding now. 'It takes time to ease itself out of your body.'

Ventuse

She did not trust anyone at the hospital. 'I said to the nurses round the ward, I'm having terrible problems breast-feeding. I was making the baby chomp away at my breast all the time. Everytime she stopped sucking I made her suck more. She would scream when I picked her up. Suddenly another voice took over. I said, the horrible nursery assistants hadn't helped me. The little nurse said, I agree with you. I said, I want the whole world to know. They gave me an injection in the bottom and sent me off to sleep. I realised I'd had a nervous breakdown.

'When I got home I tried to explain to my husband what had happened. I gave him a terrible night. The following morning, my Health Visitor came to see me. She said, "How's everything?" I bit my lip and said, "Just fine." She left – and I went beserk. My husband phoned the GP. I was shouting, and my husband held me down. He gave me a drink. I spat it out all over the floor. Luckily, the GP. sent me here (to the Unit). I didn't know such a place existed.'

She had been taken into the maternity hospital at midnight. 'My waters burst at home. I knew I had to go in straight away. My husband got together my gear and off we went. Twenty hours later, the baby was born.

'I don't know if you have heard of the Ventuse method? They put a suction cap onto the head of the baby and actually pull the baby away. I don't know whether my pelvis was a bit small – they haven't made an investigation into that, as yet. I said to the midwife, "How much longer will it be?" She said, "An hour." Five hours later, the baby was born.

'I didn't have any anaesthetic. The baby was suffering. It wasn't coming away as quickly as it should have been. She was born with the cord around her neck. The birth damaged my bladder. The morning after, I got out of bed and all the water came away from me. The consultant finally came to see me and said, we'll give you a catheter. The nurse who fixed it up didn't really tell me what to do with it. I said, what do I do with this? She said, I haven't got time to stop and tell you at this precise moment. She went off and left me with this bag. By the fourth night, I found I had so worried about my problem with the water that I hadn't really concerned myself with the baby. I tried to get up to the baby and to cope with the catheter as well. I found the baby was having green stools, a sign of underfeeding. I took her along to the nursery, and they told me, green stools are quite normal.'

Plasma

'When I'm washing her clothes and squeezing them out, I think I'm wringing her neck.' She sits on the sofa looking into the middle distance, speaking softly, fragile, snub-nosed. She appears to be speaking into some object in front of her; I have little or no place. 'I think that everybody's had the symptoms I've had: bedwetting, diarrhoea, piles. My slippers say they come from piles. St Michael's, Marks and Spencers. The lining is wool. The different colours of the eyes, when I flushed the toilet. My eyes went down the toilet.' At moments, she is clear. She describes powerful feelings (in a dissociated way). She gives us something to latch onto. Her husband loves her – for her looks. She feels she is going round and round (in a state of sexual excitement – or is it a state of jealousy?); she finds that she has complicated feelings, loving yet rivalrous, about her baby daughter.

It makes sense of a kind. Anyone might wish to wring the neck of their baby daughter. But she tried to do it and (I am told) almost brought it off. She refers to people and things that I know nothing of. The way she refers to them conveys an atmosphere of portent: how she manages it, I do not know.

'He was always going to get himself a pair of glasses. We'd collected money for him to get a pair of glasses. It's my eyes, though. I think I'm colour blind. (Long pause.) I feel I've committed adultery: which Brigid knows about. I think I shouldn't be here, should be dead. I've got a fear of God. I saw Brigid as God when she was dressed up in a white-blue nightgown. I'm a Roman Catholic. I fear I changed my religion because I died of a heart attack. I'm sure I did – with Piggy.'

'With Piggy?'

'I feel as if I'm still in the middle of an arena. I can't get out of it. I'm stuck. There's something to do with telescopic and purple and the presents I got at Christmas time – off him. I pulled down the decorations. The black people have been good to me – like Mavis and her husband.

'I've got all the gold and the money. But I've got some disease called plasma. When I have my slippers on, they are all colourful. I've given chicken pox to Stella. I don't know if you have seen her, one of our nurses. She was off with chicken pox.

My sister Eileen and me had chicken pox together. I was the one that was immune. It was my family that always got something, German measles or chicken pox. I was immune. In other words, I'm still sitting on my pot for Doris, who is a coloured nurse and pregnant.'

She talks in a way that impels us to decode her. Does she recognise herself as cryptic? It is not enough to say that she is in an opaque condition – the familiar condition known as madness. The explanation in no way accounts for the pressure in us to reach out and understand her, or the wish to protect her and her baby.

Psychic

'I felt my dream period, which should happen during the night, was being pushed into the early hours of the waking part of the day. The thoughts I had were always coming out of memories. By mid-day I was able to operate in the present. But with this mixture of the past. Actually, the mixture of reality and fantasy was all fact: things that had happened.

'I've got two sons, six and three, and this third one wasn't planned. Throughout the pregnancy my husband James referred to it as Mary. And I thought of it as a boy because I've got two sons and I didn't want to be disappointed. It was a short labour, only two and a half hours. My husband was with me. The lights were low. I saw the baby come out. We both thought it was a boy, at least in the first flash. The midwife said, it's a girl.

'On Monday morning, I woke to feed Mary, early about three or four o'clock, and I didn't go back to sleep. In my mind all things like windows left open by my husband, front door left open – all these things suggested that my husband was jealous of my relationship with the children and was trying to do them away. I thought he had laced the Phenergan with something to murder them. In the morning, I couldn't wake them and their eyes were dilated.'

A portrait hangs in her mother's house of a great-great-great-grandmother. 'Seven steps back from Mary. Exactly the same look, dreamy sort of eyes, beautiful actually but she's just the same.' She meets a therapist. He 'talked for an hour about the relationship of mother to baby – and things in my childhood seemed to come up. At the end of it, I felt that he had helped me.

In fact, I think he hypnotised me. One of his eyes went big and black behind his glasses. I couldn't move or think. I just listened to his voice. He was saying: when you want to change her nappy, do you feel you want to change your own? A strange sensation, literally of filling a nappy happened. That carried on for about the next three and a half days.'

'When I was about ten, I had a dream of my bed floating off into space and I couldn't get back. I was travelling around the world. I remember I wanted to talk about the dream the next day. My mother shut me up and wouldn't let me talk about it.' She thinks of herself as psychic. She is descended from the last woman to be burnt as a witch in England.

Curling up

'I desperately wanted a baby. I had lost one and I wanted to replace it as quickly as I could with another one. I became pregnant again – the first month. I was under strain. I had severe sickness all the way through. When it was born, it was a marvellous thing – all her fingers and toes were there, and there was nothing wrong with her.'

Mrs. F.'s own mother had been through a breakdown at the time of Mrs. F.'s birth. She had been brought to the Unit shortly after it had first opened. When Mrs. F. was seven months old, her mother had to be operated on for a hole in the heart; had broken down once more; and returned to the Unit. Mrs. F. went to stay with an uncle and aunt. 'That was the first time they took me in. I was about eighteen months old before I went back to my mother. In the back of my mind, I've thought that since it happened to my mother, it's going to happen to me. She just couldn't cope with normal everyday things. I wonder if I'm going to be the same as her. She still gets depression. She still needs tablets.'

She looks to her baby for support: she does not get it. 'She just screamed and screamed when I tried to feed her. I thought, it's my own child and she doesn't want me. In the end, I didn't want to get up in the morning. I felt so guilty. I didn't feel capable of looking after her. My neighbour fed her, and I sat there and cried. Putting a spoon to her mouth, or making up a bottle, was beyond me. I couldn't cook a meal. I couldn't think straight. I didn't want to go on any more. I wanted to curl up in bed and to be left on my own.'

Knives

The pregnancy had gone well. 'I was really over the moon. I used to go to the shops on my own and put my hand on my tummy and talk to the baby and say things like – what will we have for dinner tonight? Maybe I was a bit too happy. He was born: a gorgeous little boy. Everything was perfect for the first four days in hospital. All of a sudden I burst into tears.'

A doctor thinks that the crying will end in two or three days. 'It got much worse. That night I lay and shook inside and I shivered all night long.' Normally she is a great talker: the words spill out. Now she could not talk to anyone. She started to have dreams about knives.

'I've never ever dreamt about knives or harming anyone before. It really scared me.' Her husband did not understand what she was talking about. He thought everything would get better. She continued to shake violently.

She did not want to touch the baby. 'I made myself go and change him. I was breast-feeding him – crying, and I remember he looked up at me (he was only a few days old) and it was as if he was saying, "I know that there's something wrong with you." Every time I looked at him, he seemed to look at me, as if saying, "What are you thinking about knives for?"'

'I used to see the knife in the kitchen and turn and run. I would think, I can't make tea, I can't, the knife is in there. I used to see knives on television. I used to look at my husband and say, did you see that man with a knife? He would say, yes, but it's only a film, do you want me to turn it off? I'd say no, don't, it's only a knife – and inside I was so scared. I would turn over to the other channel, and there was a knife on it. I used to think, they're doing that just for me.

'One day a friend of ours came. I told her all about it. She says she remembers when she was a child, nipping at a little baby so as to get it to cry. She said, where is the knife? I said, in the kitchen. She said, do you want to throw it out? I said, yes, I do. We took the knife and threw it out on the rubbish. (Laughs.) I had to go and buy another one. I needed a knife to cut the bread with.'

A dream kept recurring. 'It was the fourth night in hospital. I was shivering inside. It was about eleven o'clock at night. I remember closing my eyes – and I could see a knife sticking into a baby. I could see someone swinging the baby in our hall at home, swinging the baby round and round in the hall. I remember screaming. I don't think anyone heard me. I'm not sure whether I actually screamed, or whether it was a scream in a dream, but I can remember the knife. It's a particular knife I have at home, a bread knife, a funny-shaped knife that I've had for a long time. I've never thought about knives before. I don't like them. They scare me.'

Chapter 7

CROSSING THE BORDER

A recently pregnant woman described the foetus within herself as 'a blob that clings on tenaciously'. She wished, in part, to get rid of the pregnancy. She called the foetus 'a blob'. She felt blank, and wished to feel blank, about its nature. But she could not resist giving it some inkling of personality – and some notion of personality managed to slip through, when she described it as 'clinging on tenaciously'. An unknown and possibly unknowable object threatened her. The unknowable object has an uncertain status.

For some (Locke), the unknowable object is characterised by blankness. It acquires selfhood, and distinction, as it enters into some conception of space and time. It establishes its being empirically by its testings out and by its having attributes that can be tested. For others (Augustine, Leibnitz), the unknowable object contains the entire cosmos. Its significance is pre-experiential. Everything that matters happened before its coming into being. Everything that matters denies the reality of space and time as containments of thought.

The different regulations of mind and body

A woman tells me about a much-loved family piano in inlaid wood. She had moved house. The removal-men complained about having to move the piano. It was too heavy. She arranged to have it broken up. She had been unsure about its value, anyway. It was old; and it was strangely untunable. It could be tuned in relation to itself: it could not be tuned in relation to other instruments. It could not be given a middle C. For years she had enjoyed playing it and thought it was in tune. One day someone had played the recorder with her. At first she had thought the recorder dissonant. She had been dismayed when she had learnt what she believed to have been the truth.

Her feelings about the piano were relatable to her feelings about her therapist. He was about to go away on holiday. A time for moving was a time for removal. The therapist had become a burden to her. She required to have the object broken up. She had enjoyed the uniqueness of the relationship – so long as it was an ongoing relationship. Its being interrupted forced her out of the delusion that she and the therapist could collude in eccentricity. More positively, she had become aware, through a steady exposure to introspection, that the inner world is regulated by laws of a different kind from the laws of the natural world.

A Pythagorean insists that our capacity to tune musical instruments depends on the presence of some universal regularity. A Pythagorean looks for some norm in nature (the harmony and regularity of planet movements, for instance) to underwrite the meaning of the music. In terms of mind, the Pythagorean theory does not apply. When I listen to music, I am uninterested in its possible universality. Music speaks to us uniquely – whether as a group or as individuals. It sounds like a unique message that has always existed, outside space and time, as a kind of innate recall.

Music is similar to the language we speak: it depends for its nature on the type of (internal) feeding object into which we tune. If the object becomes incoherent, we become incoherent. We lose the music – in the same way as we can lose our powers of speech.

The argument has an unpleasing twist to it. We may think to control the music by controlling the feeding object. It still manages to escape us and to transform itself – in an unpredictable fashion. We cannot stop its being associated to some wild uterine lake. Or to its becoming identified with a foetus-monster, that would wish to oust us. We begin to fear the idea of inspiration. We abandon any conception we might have of some inner world that differs from the actual world. We seek out norms, guidestones, something to hold onto.

One language does not supply a norm of verbalisation for another. There is no absolute language against which we measure all speech. We learn languages by moving from one base in experience to another, the act of moving being like a leap into the dark. We are dependent on an unknowable and uncontrollable object. At such moments we no longer wish to be inner-directed. We desire that the music given to us by the feeding object should be compatible with other people's music and tempered by some absolute tuning-fork. We insist on an universal regularity. We may even insist that space and time should be a condition for all experience.

Torch

The woman who had told me about the wayward piano then described an incident whose likeness in structure to the piano incident drew a beautiful parallel to it. She had been thinking about the theory that private languages might be an impossibility. She thought that the logic of 'know' did not allow any of us to say that we 'know' somebody else's pain. She moved onto a seemingly different subject. She had heard of a relief doctor who had turned up drunk on duty. He was supposed to examine the sore throat of a little girl. He had taken out a torch and directed it into his own throat, and not into the throat of his patient. She thought the doctor had taken leave of his senses. She disapproved of anyone taking leave of their senses. You are probably misguided if you take leave of your senses in medicine. In terms of the mind, it was a different matter. The senses, as impressions, do not take us far enough. To make full use of the senses we have to see them as a tentative shorthand for spiritual meanings.

It seemed possible to relate the drunken doctor, through the therapist, to the piano that is only in tune with itself. The doctor's behaviour was meaningful in the following way. His turning of the torch into his own throat represented a kind of introspection which allows us to understand pain in others. Having the light of insight turned into oneself adds a dimension to the idea of 'knowing'; it may even make meaningful the idea of 'knowing pain.' The light of insight is like the nurturings of milk. If I allow myself to be fed, I may be able to feed others. If I allow myself to be understood, I may be able to understand others.

The torch casting light into the doctor's throat has other meanings. It underlines the patient's irritation with what she feels to be the therapist's self-absorption. He does not rate her more highly than his other interests; he is about to leave her, at least temporarily. The torch in the throat becomes an emblem for coupling. Its light represents a semen that eases aches – not her aches, the aches of someone other. At this point in her life, she cannot see why somebody else's relief should be meaningful to her.

The town

Theories which necessarily locate mind in space and time put an inordinate emphasis on memory as the faculty which relates an idea of the self in the past to selfhood in the present. Charcot writes of a man who returned to his native city and failed to recognise it. He looked into a mirror and saw no one he knew. What is it that we look for, identify with, recognise?

A man tells me of how he went back to the small seaside town where he had spend a part of his childhood during the years of the second world war. He had not been back to the place in thirty years. He recognised nothing about it. He felt in pain. He was conscious of strangeness. He had driven confidently through the town to the house where he had lived with his parents and brothers. He had no idea of the direction, nor how he had been accurately guided. He had often thought about the place, usually at moments when he was falling asleep. He had strong visual memories of it.

He could not discover his memories in the present place. Houses had been built on cherished fields; and stone walls demolished, on which he and his brother had contemplated the movement of snails. The brickwork on the pub at the corner had deteriorated. He had to look twice at the building to locate it.

Every look intensified poignancy. The man thought of his dead father – of his dead father's modesty and wish to enable his children. The dead father was invisibly everywhere. The place slowly began to yield up the past. At first, it yielded up the past quite abstractly. Spaces were tormentingly familiar. The width of a pavement, the dimension of a shop's interior, conveyed a repository of experiences accumulated. None of the experiences were individually available. It was possible that the child he had lost touch with had bought sweet rations here.

Widths evoked a generalised impression of treks. The man knew that children had sexual thoughts. He had somewhat disconnected this belief from himself. He was amazed now by an intensity of erotic recollection – as in his recall of sleuthing for couples on the sand dunes – amazed and somewhat self-congratulatory.

The poignancy of the place was like a music he could not tolerate. He and his family had been left tired by a long car journey, and they knew that they soon had to find lodgings elsewhere. The place was too good to be true and too substantial to digest. He knew he would have needed a considerable amount of time (which he did not have) to take it in. He realised that it was not he who had left the town formerly; it was the town which had left him – the real place, that is, not the repertoire of memories with which he had consoled himself over the years. The real place had left him with so an unpleasing an effect (in its sweet truthfulness) that he had lost all recollection of it.

A tongue you do not know

The self that does not recognise its native place meets its little Hans likeness in the self (perhaps you) that wakes on morning and finds that it speaks a tongue which it does not know.

After a moment or so, the case modifies itself – and not knowing turns out to be a partial deception. As the day proceeds, you realise that you have been taken over by more than a tongue that is alien to you. You have been taken over by something total. You no longer think of space and time as conditions of being. You wonder whether you are discovering something new – or something that you have always known. All you can be sure of is that these walls, these bricks, these fields, this sky about you no longer belong to you, nor you to them.

Appendix

FREUD AND THE KANTIAN MODEL

In the Clark University lectures of 1910, Freud claimed Josef Breuer to be the discoverer of psychoanalysis – during the two years in which he worked with Anna O.(1880-82). Freud was so disconcerted by Breuer's account of this case that it took him years to see how it might become the mainspring of his own work. Much later, in his last survey of the psychoanalytic field,[1] Freud broached the theme of psychic incoherence. He indicated the seeming illogicality of that 'part of the personality' known as the Id. He was astonished by its nature. He could only describe it by analogy. There was nothing in it that could be 'compared with negation... We perceive with surprise an exception to the philosophical theorem that space and time are necessary forms of mental acts.' The editors of the Freud Standard Edition inform us that the 'philosophical theories' referred to derive from the writings of Immanuel Kant.

A mental event by its nature cannot exist outside space and time. Or can it? In certain forms of projective identification we put ourselves into an object that (once we have entered it) obliges us to exist outside space and time – in a condition of here and now, dissociated from a spatial and temporal context. Our ideas of the eternal and the infinite are imbued with this sort of quality: as in the story of the old man who returns to the glacier where his friends died half a century before and sees them through ice suspended in the first shock of youth.

A baby has all the time in the world

A patient tells me just before a Christmas holiday of two women who had a striking characteristic in common. They both had a

[1] Freud, Standard Ed., 22, pp.73-4

talent for arousing fury in the people they met. The first woman had gone through a pregnancy without realising she was pregnant. Not everyone presumed she was psychotic. Some held to the view that she had not known she was pregnant because she happened to be so stout. At the time of the birth, no one had known what was happening and she had been taken to the casualty ward of a large hospital. As usual, she managed to stir fury (and confusion) in those about her. A fostering unit took the baby from her, three days after the birth, on the grounds that she had neglected a previous child.

The second woman who aroused irritation tended to overwhelm the patient with her gushing. She talked unceasingly; she gummed herself to him. She worked in a nursery and seemed unable to extricate herself from her work. She was so eager to become a mother that in a most casual way she arranged to get herself pregnant by a stranger. She appeared quite cut off from the act of conception.

All this took on a certain clarity in relation to the Christmas holidays. The patient felt the holiday was a time when some baby would be born, some psychoanalytic Jesus. He felt his wish to be party to the birth, as father or spiritual adviser, had been snubbed. Like the pregnancy of the second woman, the birth had a touch of an immaculate conception about it.

The patient felt identified with the first birth. He was a first child. He was convinced in a self-pitying way that he had emerged unnoticed from his mother. She had not even known she had been pregnant by him. He was sure he had never been really fed or loved by his mother. He did not feel he had ever existed in space or time. He now said something that put a different complexion on the spaceless and the timeless. He said, wistfully: 'A baby has all the time in the world.' (Meaning not him, but the baby about to be born.) In states of deep intimacy with its mother, a baby may be thought to exist outside space and time. In adult life we recapture such moments when we listen intently to music.

The experience is precarious. The patient related it to fears of self-destruction. He associated thoughts of a baby having all the time in the world to a dream, in which he was driving with a woman friend (whose name resembled mine) through paths and thickets near Greenwich – long before Greenwich *Mean* Time had been established. He had reason to believe that the drive through the thickets signified timelessness, by way of a genital relationship – and also a violent road accident, in which you entered the timeless by dying.

Objective and non-objective

De Quincey claimed (in an essay on the last days of Immanuel Kant) that every morning, at five to five, Kant's footman, Lange, would come into the philosopher's bedroom and bark out the summons, 'Herr Professor, the time has come.' The professor would rise from his bed automatically and move through the day's routines without the slightest deviation in schedule. De Quincey believed that the stability of routine contributed to the great length of Kant's life.

More than once, Freud refers to Kant's finding a likeness between the workings of conscience and the regular movement of the planets, a harmony between inner and outer that (Freud thinks) is not quite true. 'The stars are indeed magnificent, but as regards conscience God has done an uneven and careless piece of work, for a large majority of men have brought along with them only a modest amount of it...'[2] Just before his death, Freud wrote a mysterious note. 'Instead of Kant's a priori determinants of our psychical apparatus. Psyche is extended; knows nothing about it.'[3]

Kant's a priori determinants give us fixed points. They reclaim the importance of Aristotelian placeness. They invite us to accept a definition of sanity – in my view, as misleading as the definition implied by the theory of the discontented womb. The Kantian assumes that nature has unity. It is governed by regularities. Thoughts are either real or unreal, and the real ones have their 'objectivity' guaranteed by a built-in order of succession – which identifies them with the unifying attributes in nature.

A sceptic will point out that the unity of nature cannot be demonstrated: nor indeed can the Pythagorean assumption that mental states have a likeness in cosmic occurrence. Concepts of pattern, similarity and unity assert impressive conventions. They stir the imagination, much as Aristotle's concept of Form

[2] Ibid, p.61
[3] Freud, Standard Ed., 23, p.300

stirs our imagination when we relate it to his concept of Matter. Taken as facts, though, they hamper introspection. They impose on us a picture of mind and its uses which disables research; and they do so, I would suggest, to have us avoid some reverie (derived from infancy) of the universe as a mother that might disintegrate.

In the Second Analogy to the *Critique of Pure Reason*, Kant places two powerful images in contrast – to describe how mind fails, or succeeds, in acquiring 'objective' knowledge. His two images articulate a body of shared assumptions about the nature of 'reality' that governed much thought from the time of Newton (at least) to Einstein.

First, the non-objective image – to be related to the inconsequential imagery of what Kant calls 'mere dreams'. In no praiseworthy sense, he calls the non-objective image imaginative. Take a house in actuality (or imagination) and allow yourself to move from attic to basement, basement to attic – or to walk outside the building from left to right or right to left. Kant sees no inevitability in these relationships of self to the parts of the house. The image does not fit his definition of 'experience' as a representation of preceptions *necessarily* connected (by the determinants of space and time). He does not raise the issue of how far inevitability might lie in our feelings about the house: how our feelings impel us in this or that direction.

In the second objective image, he considers a spectator observing a boat move down a river. The spectator observes that the boat at one moment fills one space, at the next moment fills another space. The image takes on meaning because it occurs in space and time. Remove the idea of inevitable succession (in space and time) and the image falls apart.

The objective image is given status over the non-objective one. Kant sees it as true. (He relegates the non-objective one to the limbo of delusional states and 'mere dreams'.) He underpins the authority of the objective image with ideas that derive their appeal from Newtonian geometry – such as measurement and succession (especially the potent idea of 'nextness'). The spectator is able to control the object of his preceptions by imposing on it an invisible grid, multi-dimensional in space and time. If the boat does not move in this manner, if it jumped back into the previous second and previous space (as it were), we would know we were dreaming or had gone crazy.

Controlling the creative otherness

One of the consolations of the Kantian grid is that it shows us where we are. It gives the spectator, as well as the boat and the river, a (summary) kind of identity. It is not unlike Aristotle's attempt to define place in terms of a boat on a river, or the preformationist model of reality as a box within a box within a box. Interestingly enough, Newton uses the same illustration of placeness, as Aristotle does, of a boat on a river.

We gain the same consolations from the uses of perspective. In a perspective drawing, everything takes on a place accessible to mathematical reasoning. The spectator's eye (and ego) control the perceptible universe. The spectator's consciousness is the necessary determinant of experience. This is a bachelor's conception of the universe: how a Kantian Robinson Crusoe or little Hans might view things. In perspective, people or things that are distant become small. In terms of our feelings, this is wishful thinking. In feeling, beloved figures and things loom large when they are absent.

Discard the consolations of perspective: what then? Imagine an apple in space – in some context where measurement cannot define place. The apple grows smaller. The lines of perspective would re-assure us now. We would think of the apple as withdrawing into the distance.

Without perspective, we are faced by disquieting questions. The apple diminishes because someone is swallowing it – perhaps ourselves. Or: the apple seems to diminish because we have grown inordinately, like Alice, and wish to assert our superiority to it. Perspective deters us from making enquiries of this kind – enquiries that are threatening (we want to label them psychotic). They oblige us to realise how little we know. Perspective allays fear. It increases tendencies towards academicism and states of feeling isolated. We become the Kantian spectator, controlling and aloof from the object of contemplation.

Newton touched poetry when he saw a likeness in the fall of an apple and the movement of the planets. He did not extend the comparison to fluctuations in the psyche. Kant did. The order of the cosmos finds its counterpart in the moral order: specifically in the dictates of what Freud called the super-ego. Kant evolved a theory of perception, in which there was no place for dreams or discontinuity – the discontinuity Freud ascribed to the Id, as inferred from the study of dreams. In sharp reversal of the Kantian position, we ask whether the grammar of dreams can provide us with the basis for a theory of perception, in which the idea of discontinuity would be central to any meaning we might derive from the theory.

Kantian nature is thought to be known through and through, in spite of the fact that we can know only a bit of it. (To presume its unity is to claim a God-like knowledge of a totality unavailable to man, even if we presume it to exist.) Kant had to subscribe to fictions of this kind to maintain his perspective view of the world. He opposed Creationism: the belief that the world is re-created anew at every moment. He thought that appearances could not emerge ex nihilo. The 'mere possibility would destroy the unity of experience.'[4] A Kantian interrogates the facts, as though he were a magistrate. His neck is clamped by some myth of objectivity. How do we arrive at an idea of the unity of experience, if at all? Not through introspection, nor through the investigation of the ways other people think.

Letting go. Letting the creative form us

Kant's outlook on nature is very different from the turbulent process that Cézanne underwent when, say, painting an apple. At one stage in the successive acts of perception, Cézanne actively felt the universe to be in a state of disintegration. He had to face some extreme – the deathward visage of absolute cold, the absolute heat of the Platonic Sun – in order to reach some conception of otherness (as embodied in the painting), in which the perceiver and the object perceived are integrated together.

We may, or may not, feel that we have to face states of incoherence, as Cézanne did. We may think that having to face states of incoherence is irrelevant to the growth of mental co-ordination. Or we may think of it as crucial to emotional development. The question is: can we put up with them? Breuer was faced by this problem in his often tempestuous meetings with Anna O. He must have often thought she was driving him mad.

[4] Kant, p.230

Nature unchained and truly attended to, truly listened to, truly perceived, will always raise this sort of challenge. To open ourselves to experience is to risk disintegration. There is no guarantee that we will come together once more. Whatever the case, Kantian claims to an authority over nature do not stand up to such a challenge, if we take the challenge seriously.

Experience has other analogies, apart from the possible determinants of space and time. W.R. Bion has compared the elements of experience to the letters of the alphabet – which have the mysterious, and seemingly miraculous function, of being re-formable into words that we previously had known nothing of. The components come together in ways we cannot predict. In our reveries, as before sleep, Kant's house can yield a knowledge we had not realised was accessible to us.

Landscape and nude

A dreamer contemplates a boat on a river and arrives at some image of beauty through metaphor – not unlike the transaction that occurs in Giorgione's great painting of the reclining Venus in Dresden. (We may have approached the picture by way of studying the boats on the river outside the gallery.) The landscape and the nude transform back and forth, one into the other, in a metaphor unceasingly charged by the light of beauty – possibly, the brilliant a priori determinant of both. Metaphors of this sort plunge the spectator into a condition of unknowing that renders claims to objectivity improbable. The spectator forfeits delusional notions of status in order to open himself to awe.

Acknowledgments

My thanks to the following:

– The staff at the Unit (who prefer to remain anonymous) and the mothers who took part in the interviews; also Dr T. Bardon, Dr J. Bavvington, Dr L. Sohn.

– The librarians at the Middle Temple, the Royal College of Obstetricians, the Wellcome Institute for the History of Medicine, the London Library.

– Mrs Sheila Kitzinger, Mrs Joanna Donat, Professor John Weightman, Ms Pam Berse, Professor R.G. Proudfoot, Mr Alan Shuttleworth (for an anecdote), Mrs Miriam Gross, Professor Gabriel Pearson, Mrs Janet Richards, Ms Sue Weiss, Mrs Sue Bickerdike.

– The secretary and members of the New Imago Society.

– Mr Josef Herman and Professor Karl Miller, for generous encouragement.

– My former colleagues and friends at the Paddington Green Childrens Hospital and at the Children and Parents Department of the Tavistock Clinic: especial thanks to Mrs M. Harris, Mrs E. Bick, Mrs B. Copley, Mrs M. Rustin, Mr R.E. Money-Kyrle Dr W.R. Bion (for two intensive series of seminars), and – above all – Dr D. Meltzer for help in many ways.

– My wife.

References

Ausonius *Works* (London 1919) in two volumes
Babel, I. *The Collected Stories* (London 1957)
Blake, W. *Poems and Prophecies* (1927;1954)
Breuer, J. See Freud, S. (1895)
Burnet, J. *Early Greek Philosophy* (London 1892;1920)
Cassirer, E. *The Individual and the Cosmos in Renaissance Thought* (Oxford 1963)
Descartes, R. *Cogitationes Privatae*, in *Oeuvres Inedit* (Paris 1859)
(1628) *Rules for the Direction of the Mind*
(1637) *Discourse on the Method*
(1641) *Meditations on First Philosophy*
(1649) *Passions of the Soul*
(1701) *The Search After Truth* (Haldane & Ross translations, Cambridge 1911;1979)
Esquirol, E-D *Des maladies mentales* (Brussels 1838)
Frazer, J.G. *The Golden Bough*, 2nd ed., vol. 3, ch. 4, 'Between Heaven and Earth')
Freud, S. (1893) *Charcot* Standard Ed. 3
(1895) *Studies in Hysteria* Standard Ed. 2
(1909) *Analysis of a Phobia in a Five-Year-Old Boy* Standard Ed. 10
(1933) *New Introductory Lectures* Standard Ed. 22
(1938) *Shorter Writings* Standard Ed. 23
Gowers, W.R. *The Border-land of Epilepsy* (1907)
Hamilton, J.A. *Post-partum Psychiatric Problems* (St.Louis 1962)
Hippocrates *The Medical Works* tr. J. Chadwick and W.N. Mann (Oxford 1950)
Kenny, A. *Descartes. A study of his Philosophy* (1968)
Kant, I. *Critique of Pure Reason* (Riga 1787; London 1950)
Kirk, G.S., Raven, J.E. & Schofield, M. *The Presocratic Philosophers* (Cambridge 1957;1983)

Klein, M. (1940) *Mourning and its Relation to Manic-Depressive States* (*The Writings of Melanie Klein*, vol. 1. 1975)

Laycock, T. *A Treatise on the Nervous Diseases of Women* (London 1840)

Leibnitz *New Essays* (1704), tr. Remnant and Bennett (Cambridge 1981)

Theodicy (1710)

Marcé, L.V. *Traité de la folie des femmes enceintes, des nouvelles accouchées et des nourrices* (Paris 1858)

More, H. *An Antidote to Atheism* (London 1662)

Pinel, P. *Traité medico-philosophique sur l'aliénation mentale, ou la manie* (1801), tr. D.D. Davis (Sheffield 1806)

Plato *Charmides* and *Timaeus*, tr. Benjamin Jowett, 2nd ed., vols. 1 & 3

Paul of Aegina *The Seven Books of Paulus Aeginata*, tr. with a commentary by Francis Adams (London 1844)

Rohde, E. *Psyche* (London 1925)

Sacks, O. *Migraine: Evolution of a Common Disorder* (1971)

Shakespeare, W. (1605) *Hamlet* (Cambridge 1934;1980)

Sophocles *The Theban Plays*, tr. E.F. Watling (Penguin Classics 1947;1952)

Spinoza, B (1677) *Ethics* (London 1910. Andrew Boyle translation)

Tylor, E.B. *Primitive Culture* (London 1871;1891)

Webster, J. (1612) *The White Devil* (London 1948)

Williams, G. *The Sanctity of Life and the Criminal Law* (London 1958)

Zilboorg, G. (1929) 'The dynamics of schizophrenic reactions related to pregnancy and childbirth' *Amer. J. Psychiat.* 8

(1931) 'Depressive reactions to parenthood', *Amer. J. Psychiat.* 10

Index